# GARY PEARSON

## SHORT FICTIONS

black dog publishing
london uk

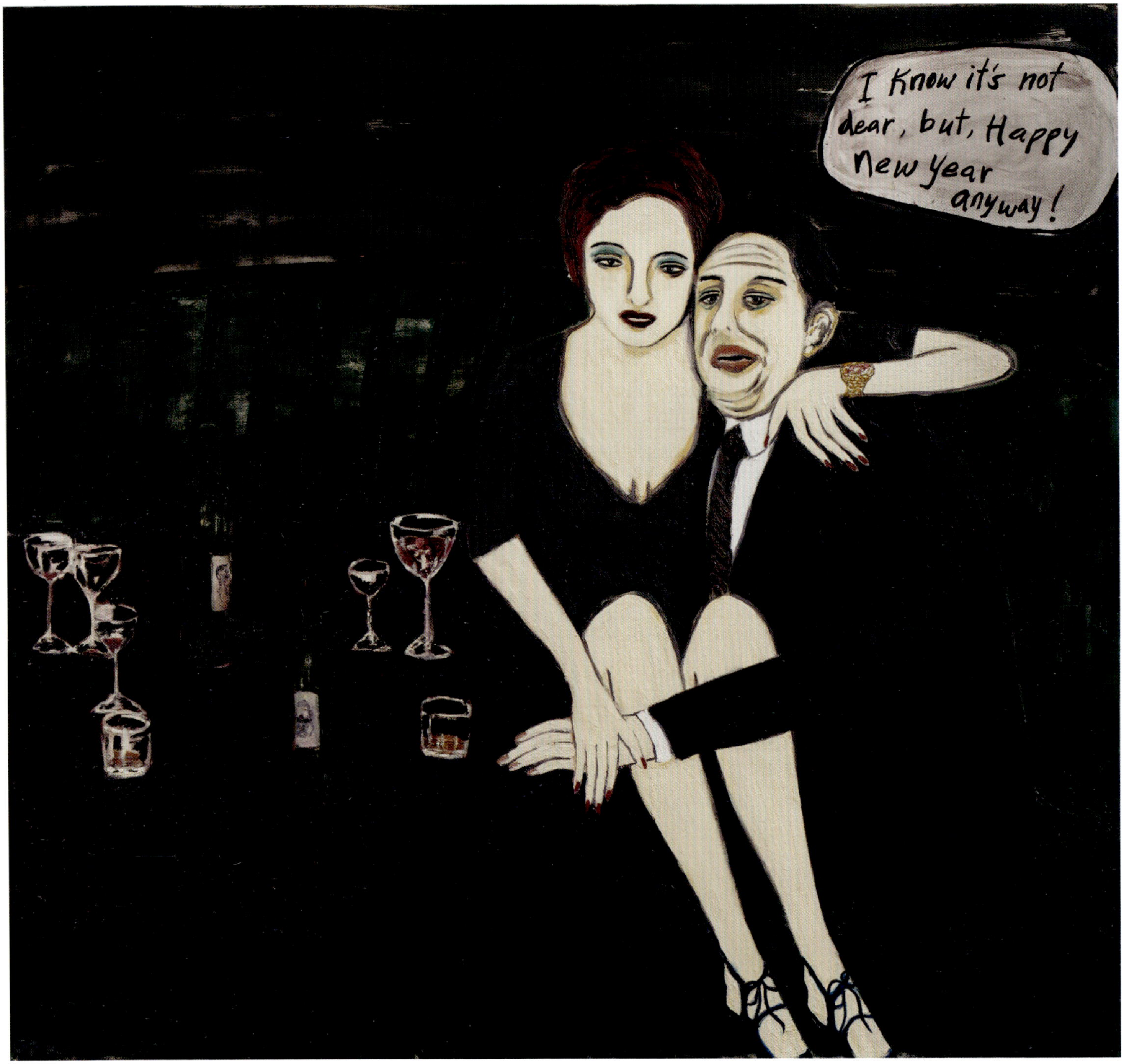


*Happy New Year*, 2016

*All captions read top to bottom, left to right

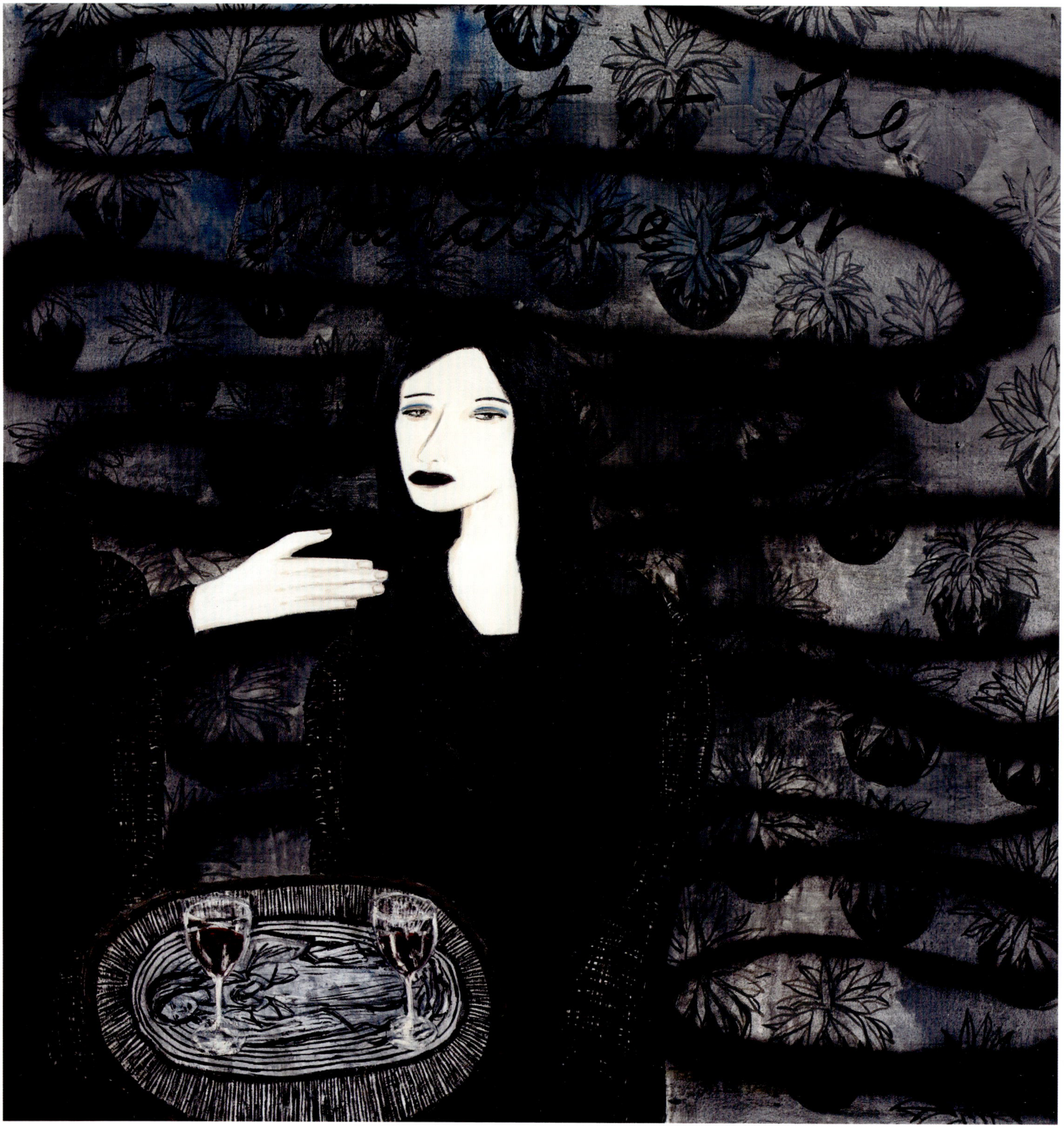

*The Incident at the Guadalupe Bar*, 2011

## Acknowledgements
Nataley Nagy
Executive Director

This book has been published on the occasion of a solo exhibition of paintings by Canadian artist Gary Pearson at the Kelowna Art Gallery, 13 January–18 March 2018.

On behalf of the Board of Directors and staff, I would like to thank Gary Pearson for his dedication and contribution to this project. Thanks to our former curator, Liz Wylie, for her enthusiasm and rigour realizing the exhibition, and for her essay "Lines Around Your Eyes". In addition, we are delighted and grateful to include texts by Aaron Peck and Michael Turner and an interview conducted with the artist by Ihor Holubizky.

We also extend our gratitude to the lenders of work to this exhibition, both institutional and private, without whom this exhibition would not be possible. The Kelowna Art Gallery appreciates the support of Opus Art Supplies, Kelowna, for generously providing framing for many of Gary Pearson's works on paper in the exhibition.

As always, thanks to all Kelowna Art Gallery staff, who work collaboratively to realize important projects such as this one.

Finally, we are deeply indebted to all our supporters, members, volunteers and sponsors for their continued support. The assistance of the City of Kelowna, the Canada Council for the Arts, the British Columbia Arts Council, the Province of British Columbia, Central Okanagan Public Schools and the Central Okanagan Foundation allows us to bring important exhibitions and publications such as *Gary Pearson: Short Fictions* to fruition.

KELOWNA Art GALLERY

OPUS
Opus Art Supplies
Resources for the Creative Individual

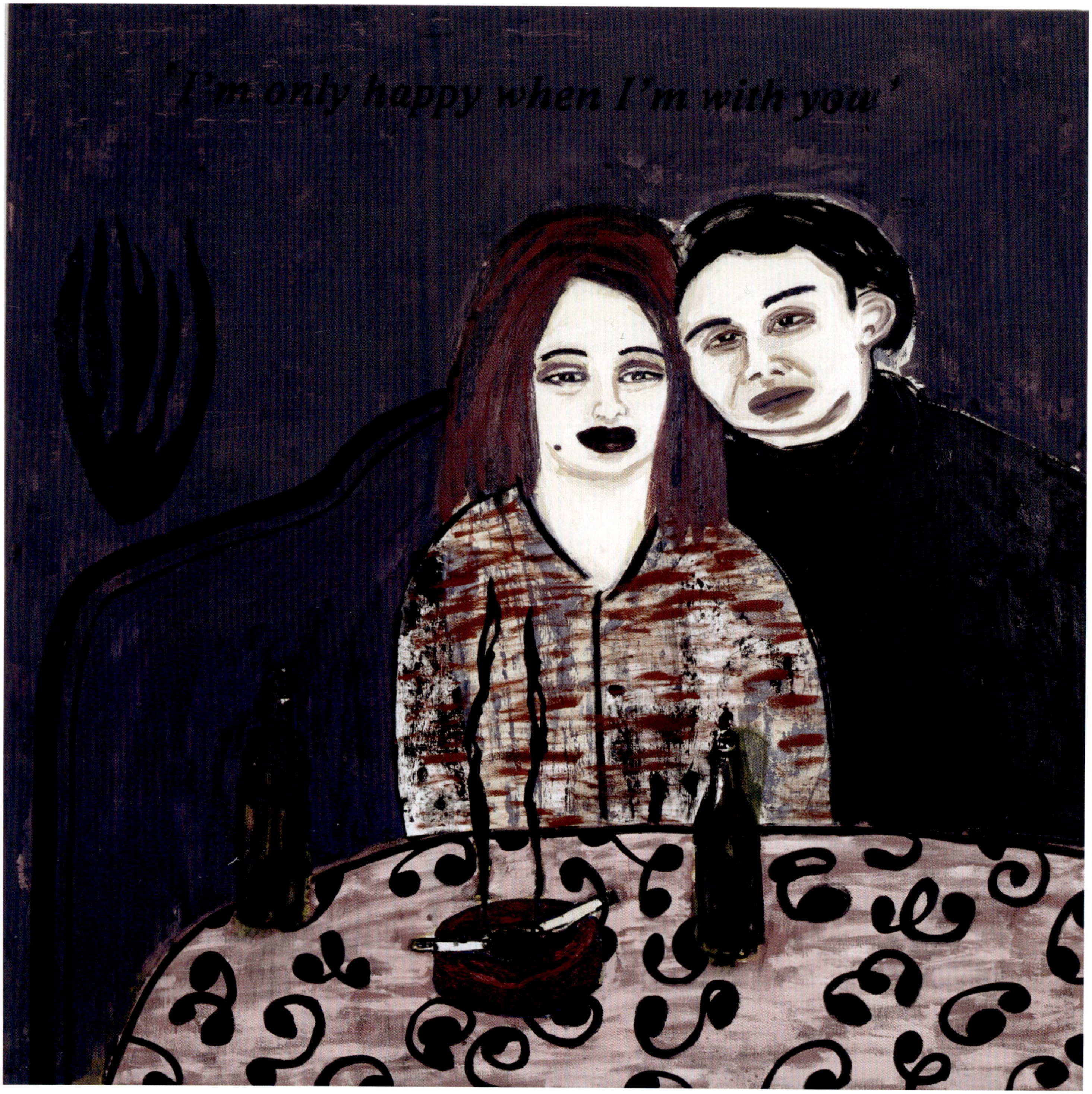




*I'm Only Happy When I'm With You*, 2000

## Foreword
Michael Turner

*One can always say that all paintings move at the same speed. Sometimes they pass on wings, as if guided. Sometimes it seems that the force leading them is shown like a wave that buries itself, with its black-blue colour.*

Marguerite Duras, "The Painting Exhibition"

I

Despite periodic spotlights on interdisciplinarity, sculptural assemblage, post-conceptual photography, installation and community-engaged social practice, the story of postwar BC art remains one of painting. Indeed, a closer look at these spotlit tendencies reveals artists whose primary training is in painting, who continue to paint or who use paint to make their work. Yet just when it seemed that painters and painting were absent from the burgeoning social and relational practices of the mid-2000s, a new and distinct group of painter-first artists emerged. This was a younger group, excited by teaching artists like Neil Campbell and Elizabeth McIntosh, who were less interested in the abstracted landscapes of earlier BC moderns Emily Carr, Jack Shadbolt, BC Binning and Toni Onley than in a geometric, affective or 'zombie' abstraction inspired in part by the work of American and European artists whose work was regularly featured in international art magazines—painters like Raoul De Keyser, Bernard Frize and Mary Heilmann, to name a few.

But there are, of course, other painting approaches that have come and gone in BC over the past half-century—paintings that continue to be made, exhibited and written about. In addition to landscapes, portraits and still lifes rendered in oils and acrylics and displayed in many of the province's commercial galleries are flourishes of hard-edge and 'neo-geo' abstraction, to say nothing of a long and resonant history of figurative painting, particularly in the mid-1960s with the work of Maxwell Bates, Claude Breeze and David Mayrs. These moves were followed by a West German-influenced 'neo-expressionist' revival in the early 1980s, as seen in the canvases of Allyson Clay and Attila Richard Lukacs and, shortly after that, Lawrence Paul Yuxweluptun's surrealist re-articulation of Northwest Coast ovoid motifs—a project that the artist describes as "history painting".

It is in this invariably reductive and unfashionable context that I would like to consider the work of Gary Pearson, an artist and educator known for his paintings, yet whose practice includes sculpture, video and text. Conversant in the Western art canon and its progressive modern rhetoric, but with expressive, graphic, figurative paintings that resemble at times the work of an intuitive 'outsider', Pearson's painted subjects have more in common with cosmopolitan art centres than with towns built on gold, fur and orchards. Whether this context is acceptable at a time when European art history is disappearing from art school curricula is beside the point, for Pearson's work is informed by—and emerges from—a conversation that, like painting itself, remains real as a perceptual force and, as such, real by its consequences.

II

In reading through Pearson's autochronology one senses an artist who, if he is not living a charmed life, has crafted one. It is no coincidence that this son of Swedish immigrant parents, who grew up in the pulp and paper town of Prince George in the 1950s and 1960s, was an "avid reader and drawer", and in his teenage years, "self-identified" as a writer. In his first year of post-secondary education he was introduced to the writings of Dylan Thomas, Ezra Pound, Charles Baudelaire, Sylvia Plath, Charles Bukowski and Robert Creeley, an intriguing range of poets, novelists and essayists who no doubt had a hand in honing Pearson's narrative and lyric skills and supplied him with an equally generative range of philosophical and psychosexual content. These lessons were likely enhanced by his ever-widening travels as a young man, as he was "almost always 'on the road', hitch-hiking to Vancouver, the Okanagan, the Kootenays, Washington, Oregon and California".

But it is later—in the mid-1970s, after Pearson returned from a grand tour of Europe's museums—when his focus shifted to visual art. In 1975 he enrolled at the Kootenay School of the Arts in Nelson, BC, where he took classes in foundation painting, drawing and anatomy. Excited by his studies, he transferred to the University of Victoria in 1977. Once there, his paintings were influenced by Expressionism and Pop, while an interest in sculpture was accelerated by artist-instructor Roland Brener, who introduced him to the newly published book by Rosalind E Krauss, *Passages in Modern Sculpture*, 1977, which "served to fill gaps" in his understanding of twentieth-century sculpture, particularly through the work of David Smith and Anthony Caro. It was only later in his degree program that Pearson became interested in the Volksempfänger works of American artist Edward Kienholz, whom he visited in Hope, Idaho, on a road trip after his graduation in 1980.

My introduction to Pearson's work came some 15 years later, when I saw a magazine reproduction of his painting *The Scream*, 1990.

Here, the square canvas is divided into two horizontal sections. The bottom plane is a dark brown rectangular monochrome, while the upper section is occupied by two gridded rectangular boxes—one discrete, the other only partially in view. Emanating from the near-centre of the discrete box is what appears to be an obtuse triangle that exits the frame in the same direction as the second box. If the triangle, 'filled' with a coil shape, is the scream, is the gridded box an audio speaker?

Pearson's *The Scream* can be read as a technologically-mediated update of Edvard's Munch's painted series of the same name. But it is more than that. The referent that came to mind upon first seeing it was Kienholz's *Volksempfänger Parade*, 1977, an installation that consists of a small pillar and a bench, atop which are placed a series of Volksempfängers—an inexpensive radio receiver issued by the Nazis in 1933 to connect the voice of the Führer with the German people. Kienholz came across these receivers at public markets and junk stores during a residency in West Germany in the 1970s and purchased a number of them to bring back with him to Idaho.

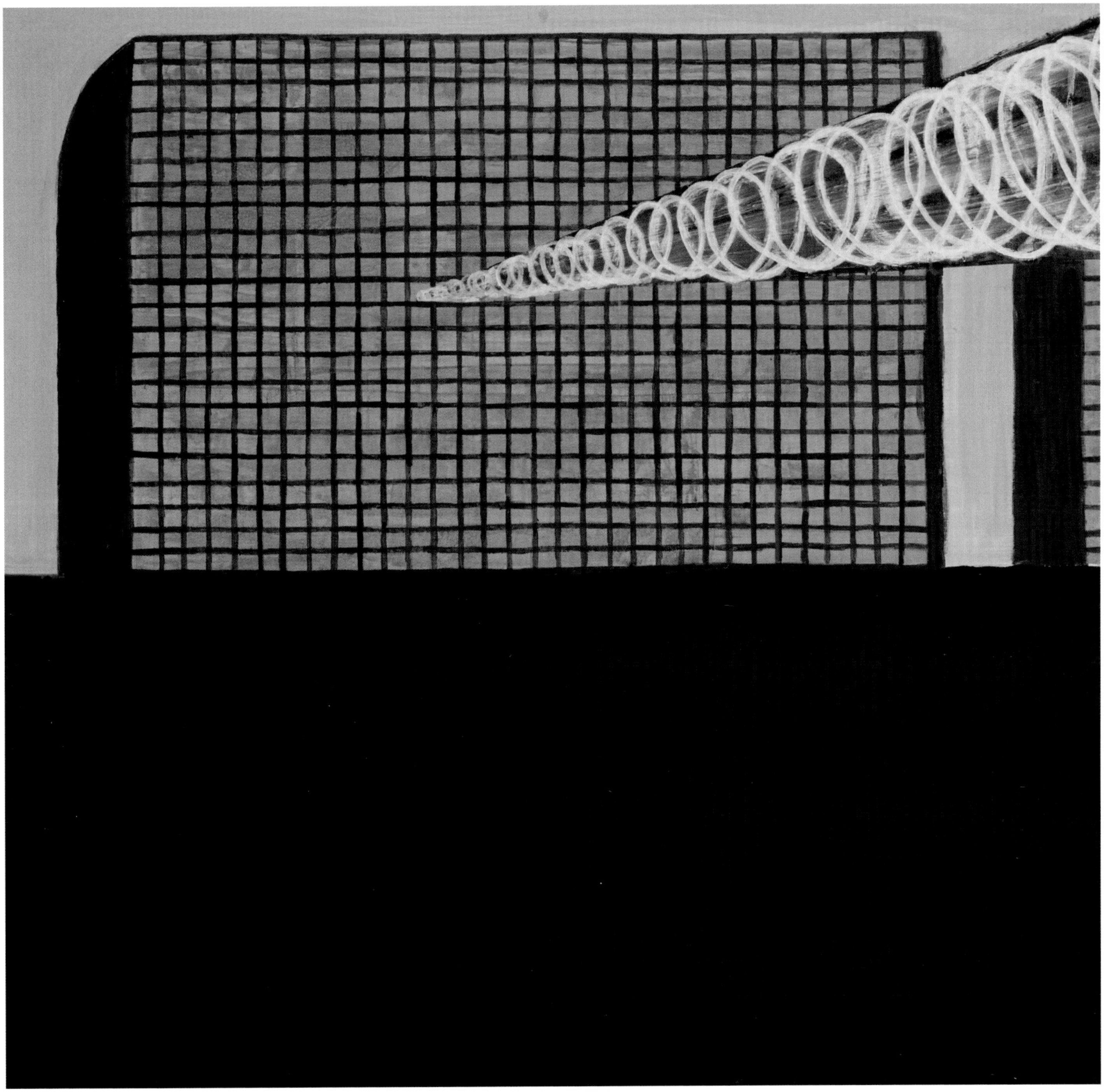

*The Scream*, 1990

I bring up Kienholz's *Volksempfänger Parade* in relation to Pearson's *The Scream* not only for the presence of Kienholz's work in Pearson's painting, but also because I see in this painting a portal to Pearson's transition from an abstract painter to the figurative painter we know today. Whether Pearson's shift was motivated by similar concerns as American painter Philip Guston's own shift to figuration in the 1960s (from modernist aesthetics to political ethics) is secondary to a more relevant proposition that has the totalitarian voice, whose content is represented through a triangular, coiling and/or conical form. This form approximates an interior condition that 'appears' to be at work in the figurative paintings that followed—none of which depict the agricultural arcadia that the Hitler administration heralded in its broadcasts, but a Marienbad of malaise-stricken, twentieth-century urbanites adrift in a world predicted for them by nineteenth-century Enlightenment critic Friedrich Nietzsche (and more recently by Fredric Jameson, who saw in late capitalism its own fresh hell).

III

It is hard to believe that over a quarter-century has passed since Pearson painted *The Scream*. In that time, we have seen not only the dismantling of what was once referred to as the Second World (Cuba and North Korea notwithstanding), but the emergence of a neo-liberalism that has transformed subjects into consumers, after which finance, not politics, brokers power. Indeed, this condition pervades many of the figurative paintings Pearson has painted over the past 27 years, some of which feature a revolving yet paradoxically recurrent cast of largely Euro-Western men and women in cocktail attire, hanging out in bars and cafes, somewhere between the punters in the 1876 *The Absinthe Drinker* by Edgar Degas and Pablo Picasso's own absinthe drinker—*Portrait of Angel Fernández de Soto*, 1903.

Whether Pearson's figurative paintings were made during his Berlin years in the late 1990s, as they once seemed exclusive to; or at other international residencies; or in his Kelowna home studio, is suddenly inconsequential to a new world order that has conflated *anywhere* with *everywhere*.

And this brings us to where Pearson is now, both in place and in time. As of this writing he is in his studio, recently retired from a teaching position at the University of British Columbia Okanagan, but still at work in a city whose downtown cafes and bars looks very much like those in Berlin, New York, Paris or Vancouver. For the Kelowna of today is no longer the rambunctious farming town that once scared its aspiring young writers and artists away to urban centres, but an international resort that has traded inner tubes for jet-skis, canneries for wineries, pick-up trucks of foul-mouthed teenage boys for SUVs of equally foul-mouthed cougars. Taken together, these are the behaviours that drive many of us indoors—to the cocktail bars, art galleries and repertory cinemas where sophistication is said to reside. But to what end? To take comfort in a milieu that is less where we are when we are inside these spaces than where we imagine them to be? The received and homogenizing world of global market forces?

In her story "The Painting Exhibition" Marguerite Duras visits the studio of a painter as he prepares for an upcoming exhibition. In a passage that directly precedes the epigraph above, Duras, like those adrift in the interior floating worlds of Pearson's paintings, shifts her focus from the studio and the painter to the paintings:

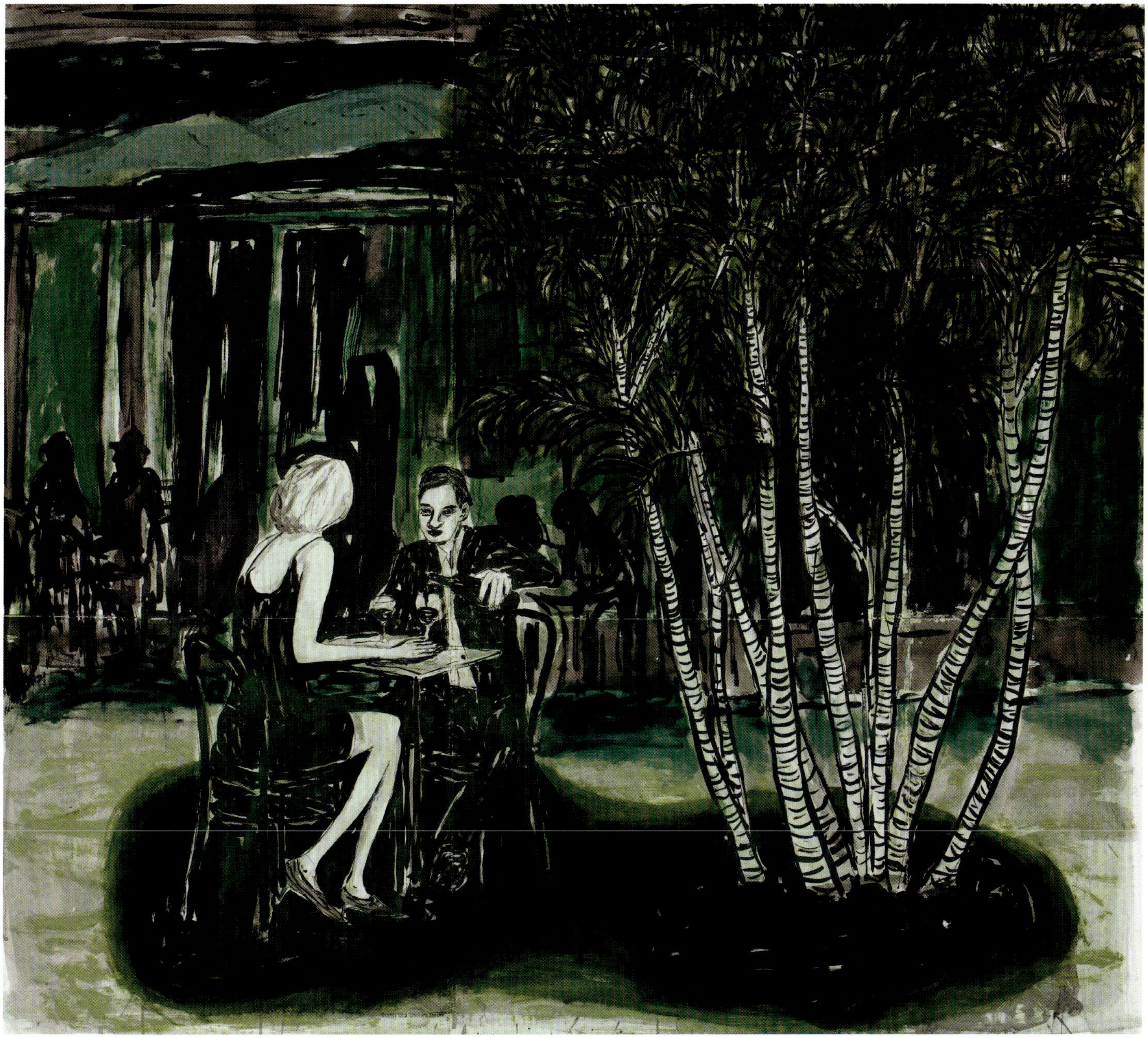

*Everything Comes and Goes*, 2011

> We look at them, at them alone. The man speaking is the one who made them without knowing what he was doing, outside of meaning, in a profound distraction.[1]

This assessment by Duras would never do as criticism because no painter *really* knows what he or she is doing. Nor is any painter entirely free from the tyranny of meaning, whether intended or imposed. As for distraction, this is, since the Nixon administration's 'constructive ambiguity' foreign policy of the early 1970s, the most operative form of social control—and yet paradoxically, in this era of Putin and Trump, our escape from it. Pearson's paintings do not come with what Duras describes as "wings" attached, nor are they "guided"; rather they are motivated by their own interior force; a coil that unwinds "like a wave that buries itself, with its black-blue colour".[2]

1 Duras, Marguerite, "The Painting Exhibition", *Writing*, Mark Polizzotti trans, Minneapolis, MN: University of Minnesota Press, 2011, p 113.

2 Duras, "The Painting Exhibition", p 113.

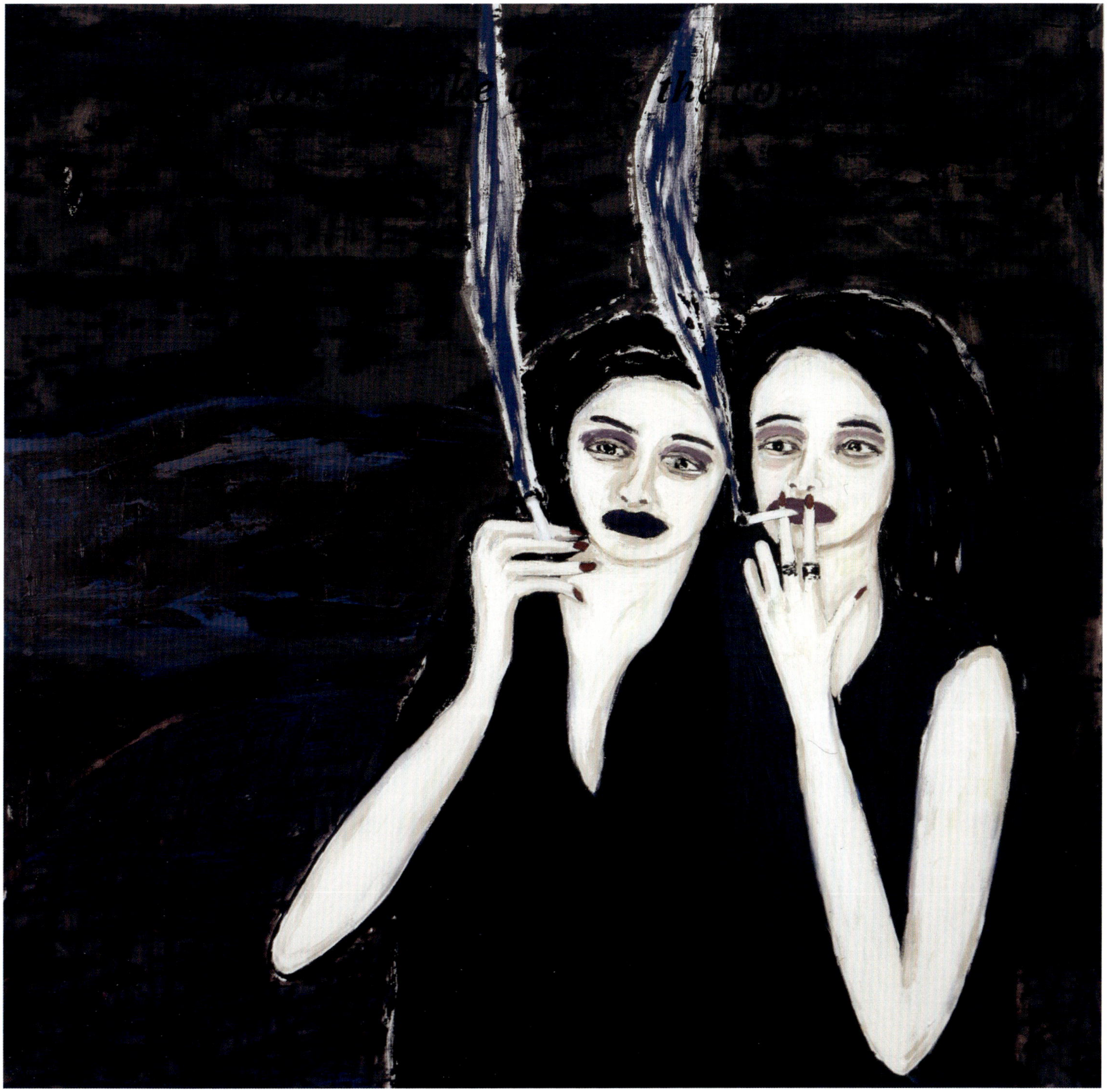

*Please Don't Smoke During the Concert*, 2000

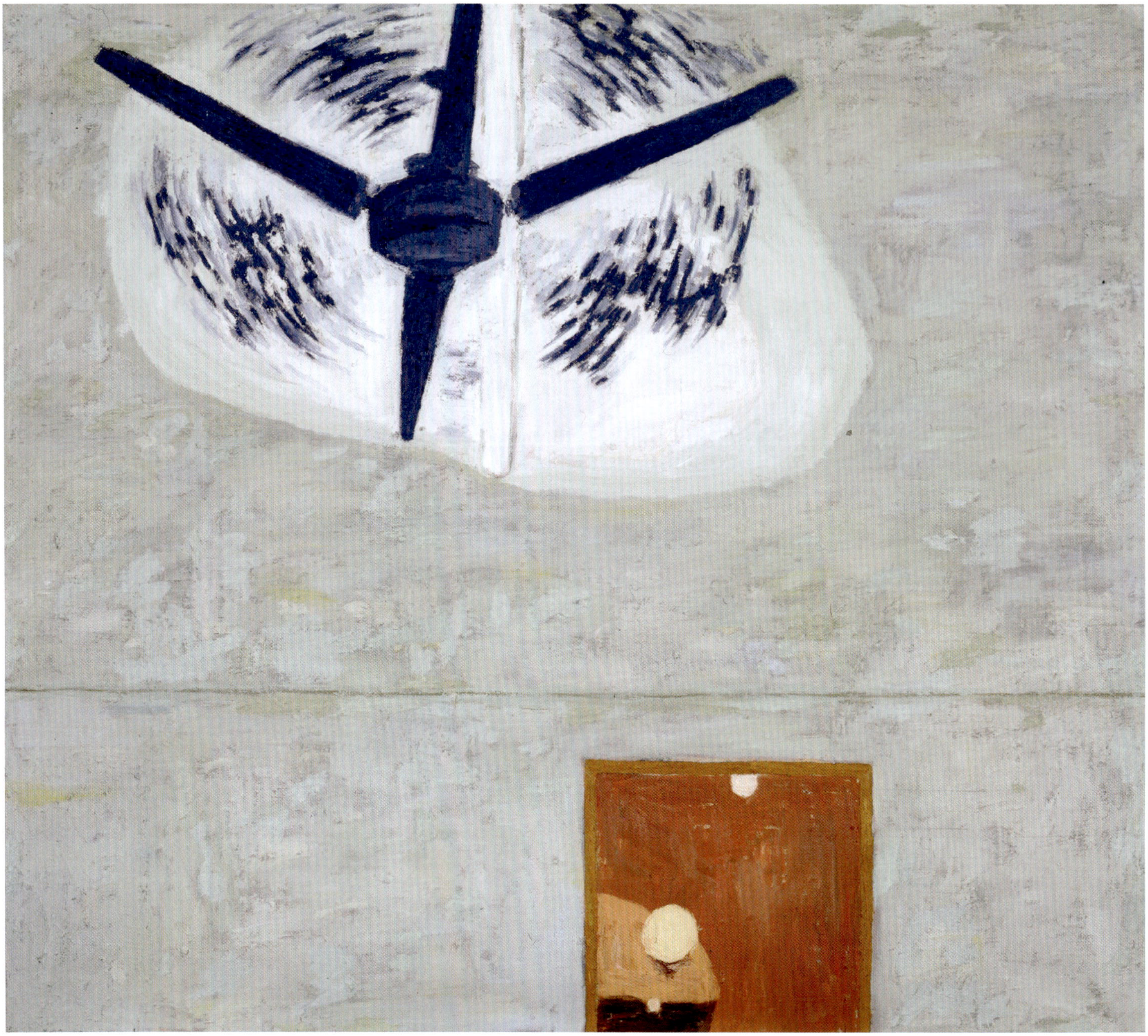



*Hotel Room*, 2002

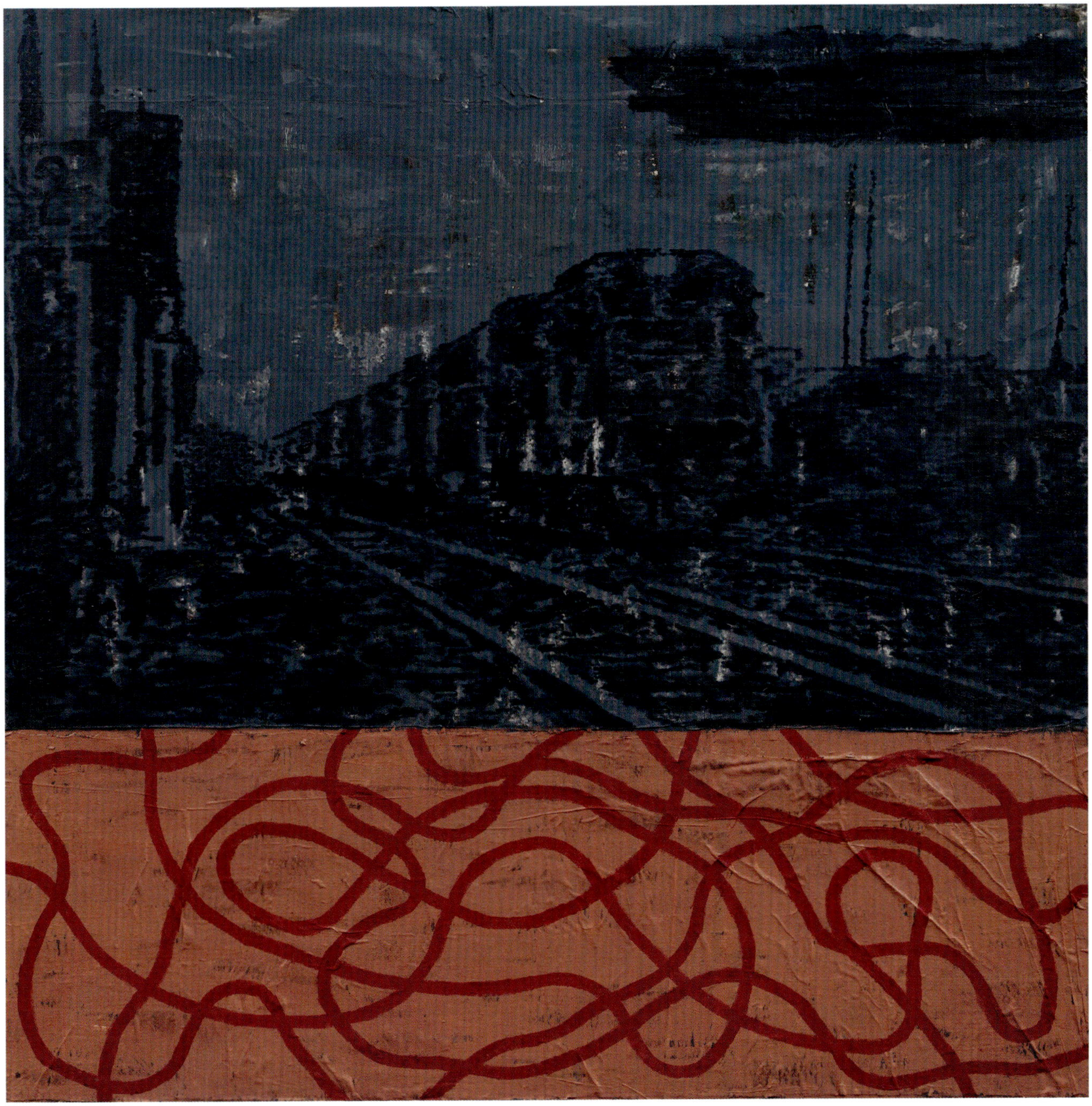



*One Way Ticket*, 2002

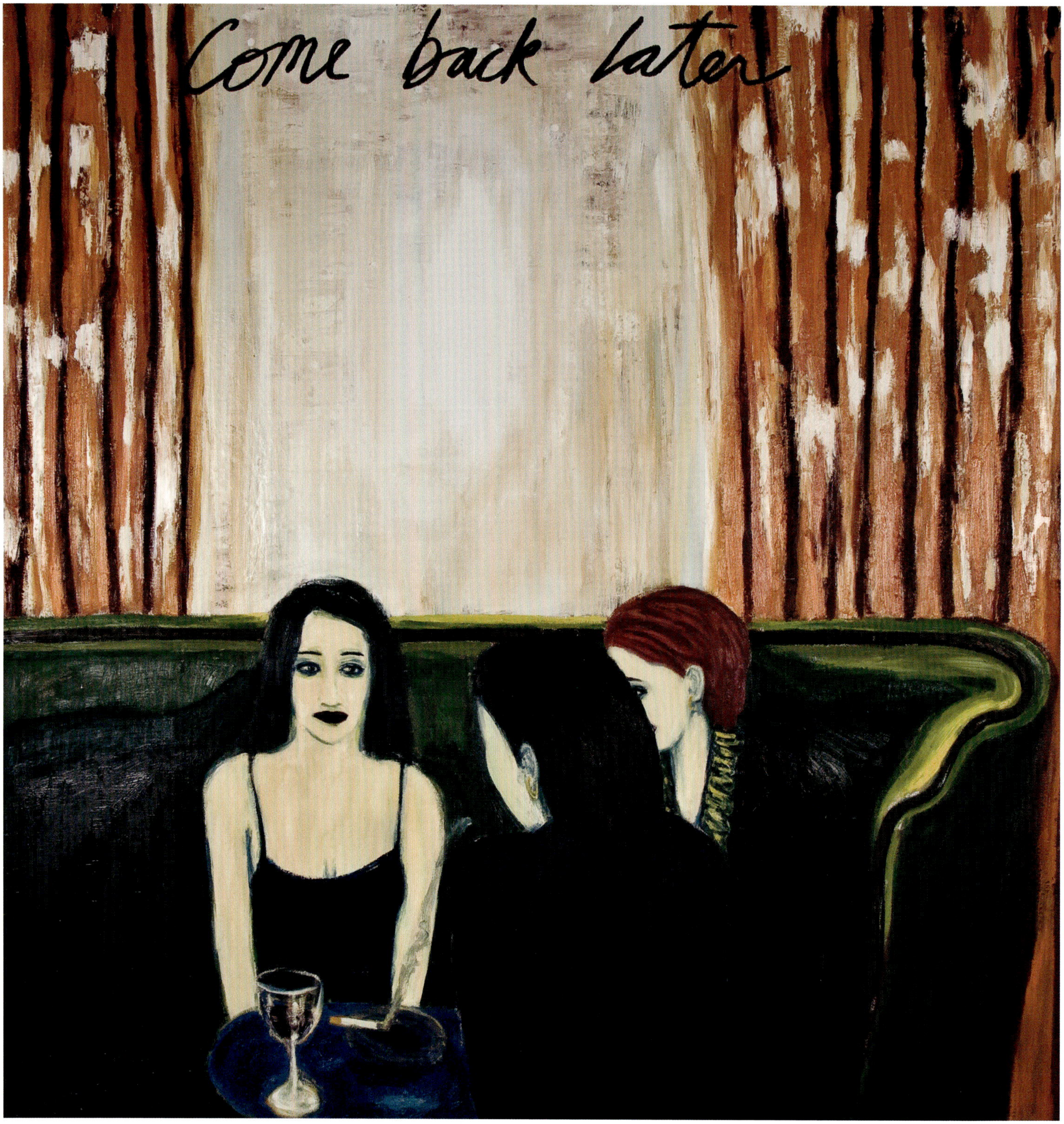




*Come Back Later*, 2007

# Lines Around Your Eyes
Liz Wylie

*Life is an intoxication. The only sober man is the melancholiac, who, disenchanted, looks at life, sees it as it really is, and cuts his throat. If this be so, I want to be very drunk. The great thing is to live, to clutch at our existence and race away with it in some great and enthralling pursuit.*

WNP Barbellion, *The Journal of a Disappointed Man*

Both the intensity of tone in the above epigram and its notion of a "great and enthralling pursuit" seem apt in relation to the work of Kelowna, BC-based artist Gary Pearson in several ways. In his paintings Pearson has never depicted the banalities of quotidian life. Instead, he creates charged, stage-set-like settings for his human figures or trees that are extrapolated from anything actually observed into a netherworld of his own invention. The mood of his work is generally dark and brooding—he is a true inheritor of the Northern Expressionist tradition. There is often the sense of some underlying narrative that is never actually revealed, as though his paintings are like paused films, arrested and full of tension, as we wait for the action to continue. There truly is something thrilling about this, as we feel that frisson perhaps known to the voyeur, or the visitor at a peep show.

The path of some artists' work over time is just a steady and gradual evolution of their thoughts and style, without dramatic incident, but with Pearson there was a marked turning point that occurred in his mid-career that radically altered the nature of his work. If you had been in Berlin in the spring of 1998, then on 19 April you might have attended the concert given by the Diana Krall Trio at the Quasimodo nightclub. It was apparently very crowded and extremely smoky inside from the customers' cigarettes. The Berlin Wall had come down nine years earlier, and the city was enjoying a new lease on life, becoming an important centre for contemporary art. So the overall mood was buoyant. Maybe you were seated at the back and didn't have a great view, but perhaps you were in a good spot, and happened to notice a slim-looking fellow with craggy features—this man being Gary Pearson, who was there that night. Apparently the concert was excellent, and would prove to be a watershed event for the artist, as his work would immediately undergo an irrevocable change. And if you look through the various works Pearson created as he continued to recall that night, maybe you will see a face that looks like yours, or that of another denizen or two of the Quasimodo.

Pearson had been staying in Berlin for an artist's residency at Künstlerhaus Bethanien from March to May of that year. He was 47 years old, and, since completing graduate school 15 years earlier, he had been working on paintings, works on paper and sculptures that were based in abstraction but not non-objective. He borrowed a term invented by the late Canadian artist Jack Shadbolt, "symbolic abstraction", to describe his work, and it fit: partially abstract works that included images of industrial buildings, stylized flame shapes, geometric figures and forms that read as visualizations of sound. These paintings and works on paper were generally created in earth colours with lots of greys and black. The shapes or images, floating in time and space, were not depicted in urban settings per se, nor in wilderness ones, but, as with dream images sometimes, appeared to be untethered from any context. With his works on canvas Pearson applied the paint thickly and displayed a graphic sensibility (as opposed to a painterly one), and these qualities both continued as hallmarks of his approach or style, remaining constant in his work to this day.

Pearson's earliest works, produced as an undergraduate at the University of Victoria, 1977–1980, and during his MA years at the University of Saskatchewan, 1981–1983, were imbued with a Northern melancholy and gloom. At least some of this was likely absorbed from looking at the work of the late Canadian artist Maxwell Bates, 1906–1980, with which Pearson became familiar when studying in Victoria. This mood and its attendant

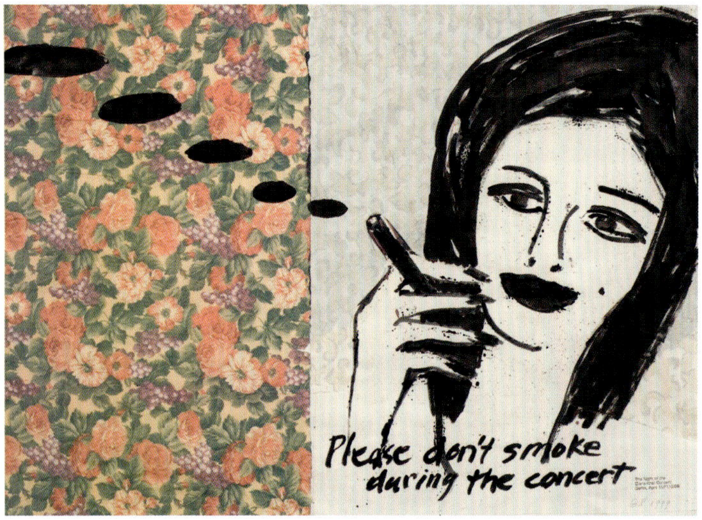


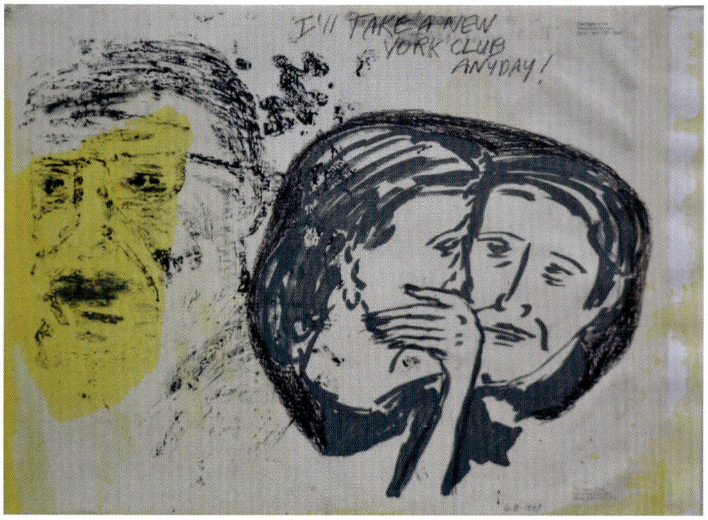


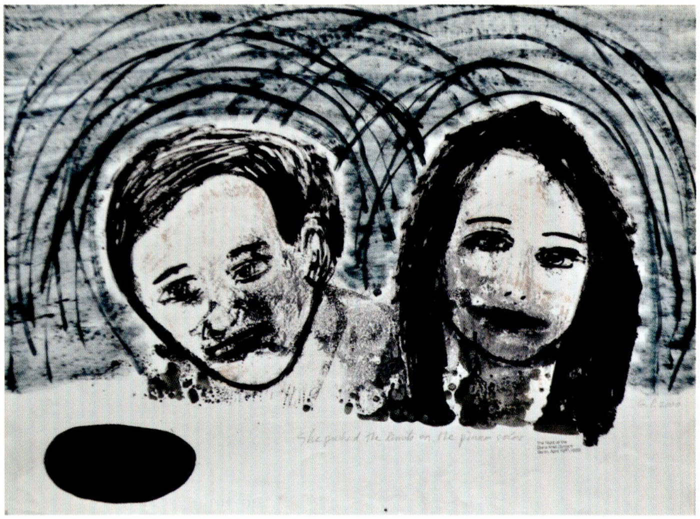

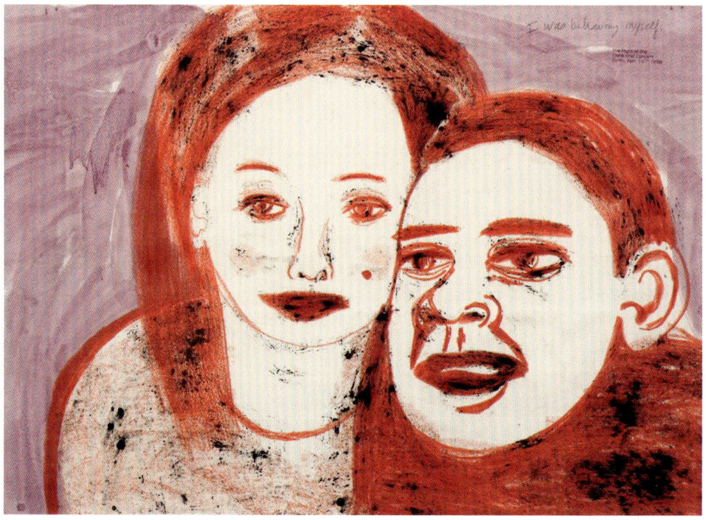

*Please Don't Smoke During The Concert*, 1999
*I'll Take a New York Club Any Day*, 1999
*She Pushed the Limits on the Piano Solos*, 2000
*I Was Behaving Myself*, 2001

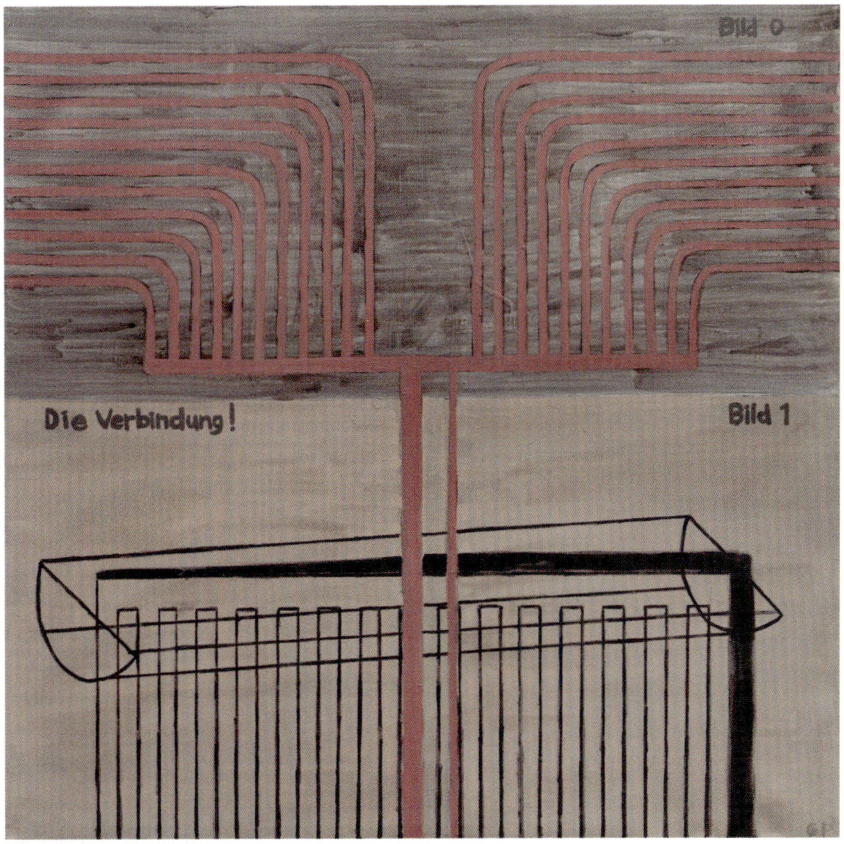


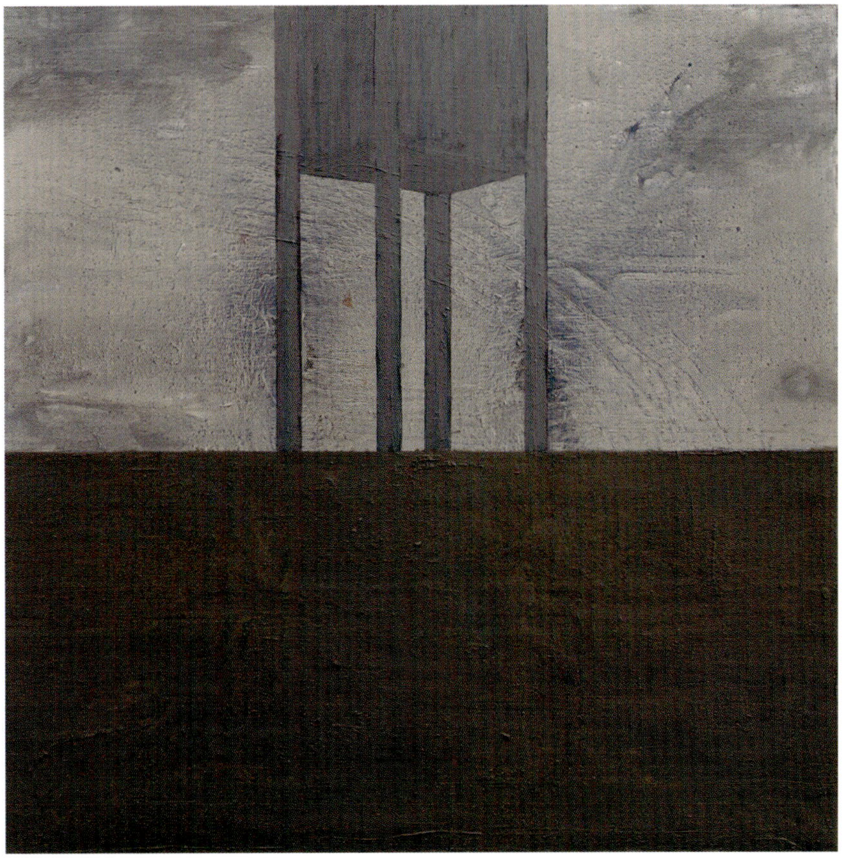

*Die Verbindung*, 1990
*Rainbow Effect*, 1990

stylistic choices were pressed into the service of a generalized anxious expressionism on Pearson's part.

From 1990–1991 Pearson had the opportunity to live and work in New York for a year when he was awarded the Canada Council's PS1 studio. This space was a former school, located in Long Island City (now run as a satellite space by the Museum of Modern Art). Flying under the radar, Pearson lived in his studio space. It was a year of intense and prolific work, stimulation and artistic growth for Pearson. He described this year-long residency in an unpublished statement:

> I had made annual trips to New York since 1982 so I was very familiar with Manhattan especially, and Brooklyn and Queens; however, to have the opportunity to live there, if only for a year, was another thing entirely. To put things into perspective David Dinkins was the Mayor of NYC, who is rightly credited with programs that lowered crime rates and poverty, and for kick-starting Manhattan's general clean-up; Soho was still the principle gallery district, and subways still took tokens. It was still a gritty city, however, and still relatively affordable. In my studio I was doing various experiments with abstraction and symbolism and was drawing a lot of inspiration from New York itself.
>
> I'd been interested in the 'silence' of painting for many years, and had often worked with sound-related projects in poetry and performance, so I was very alert to the sounds of NYC. When I read about the recording experiments that Laurie Anderson had undertaken in the Ellis Island Immigration Center in 1991 prior to its renovations I was inspired and intrigued to continue connecting my ideas, at least in part, to sound. (Laurie Anderson had spent a week at Ellis Island Terminal working with NASA sound-recording technology and had discovered that sounds and voices from decades past were still actively present in the main hall of the terminal.) So I spent some time in the New York Public Library reading about sound, particularly how it is measured, and as a result, I had the idea to use various linear diagrams in my work that were derived from textbook diagrams of sound, such as I used in the painting *Arthur Rimbaud in New York* from 1991.[1]

While in New York, Pearson developed the idea of making a painting about the French poet Arthur Rimbaud (1854–1891) from looking through an exhibition catalogue on the work of Enzo Cucchi, in which there was a reproduction in black and white of a 1985 painting by Cucchi called *Arthur Rimbaud in Harrar*. Pearson recalls: "I wanted to make a painting about the spirit of Arthur Rimbaud and of his poetry, which, especially when read aloud, is an expression of sound and the writer's spoken voice."[2]

In this work the figure of the poet is dressed in a white suit, just as in Cucchi's painting. Rather than being set in a landscape, however, Pearson's faceless Rimbaud floats on a scrubbed brown ground and has

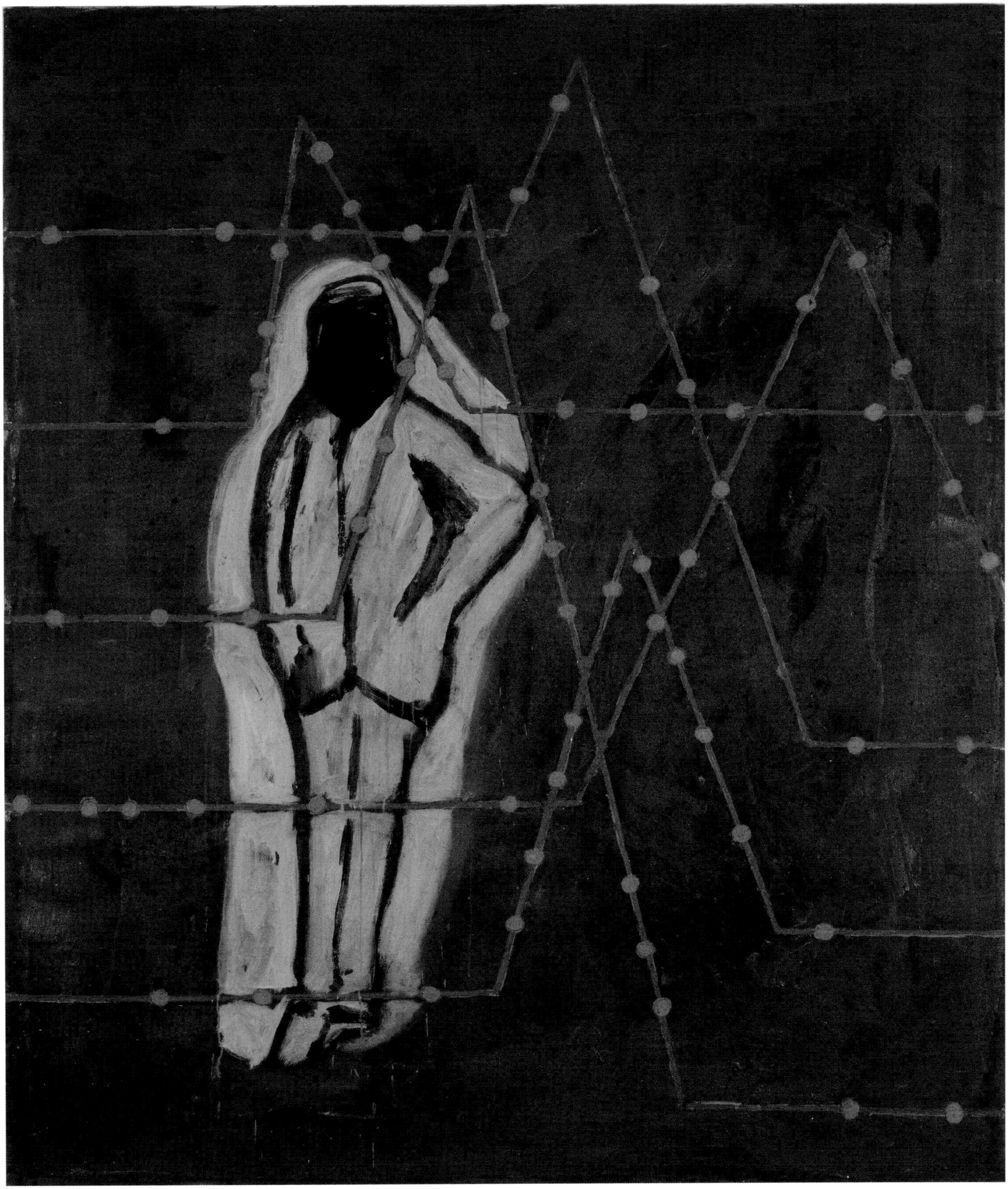



*Arthur Rimbaud in New York*, 1991

a white aura around his body. A set of the artist's sound-diagram lines travel in front of the figure, visually affirming the flat surface of the work.

Two fascinating works, one in drawing, the other in painting, both called *The Gates of Paradise*, also occupied Pearson for some weeks while working in PS1. The drawing is a rough, scratchy work with passages that look like frottage that define depictions of weeds, and with scratched lines and a darkened, amorphous, cloud-like form that enlivens the composition. In contrast, the painting is a work of symmetrical calm, with imagery that could be inspired by ancient sources, perhaps from the artist's New York museum visits.

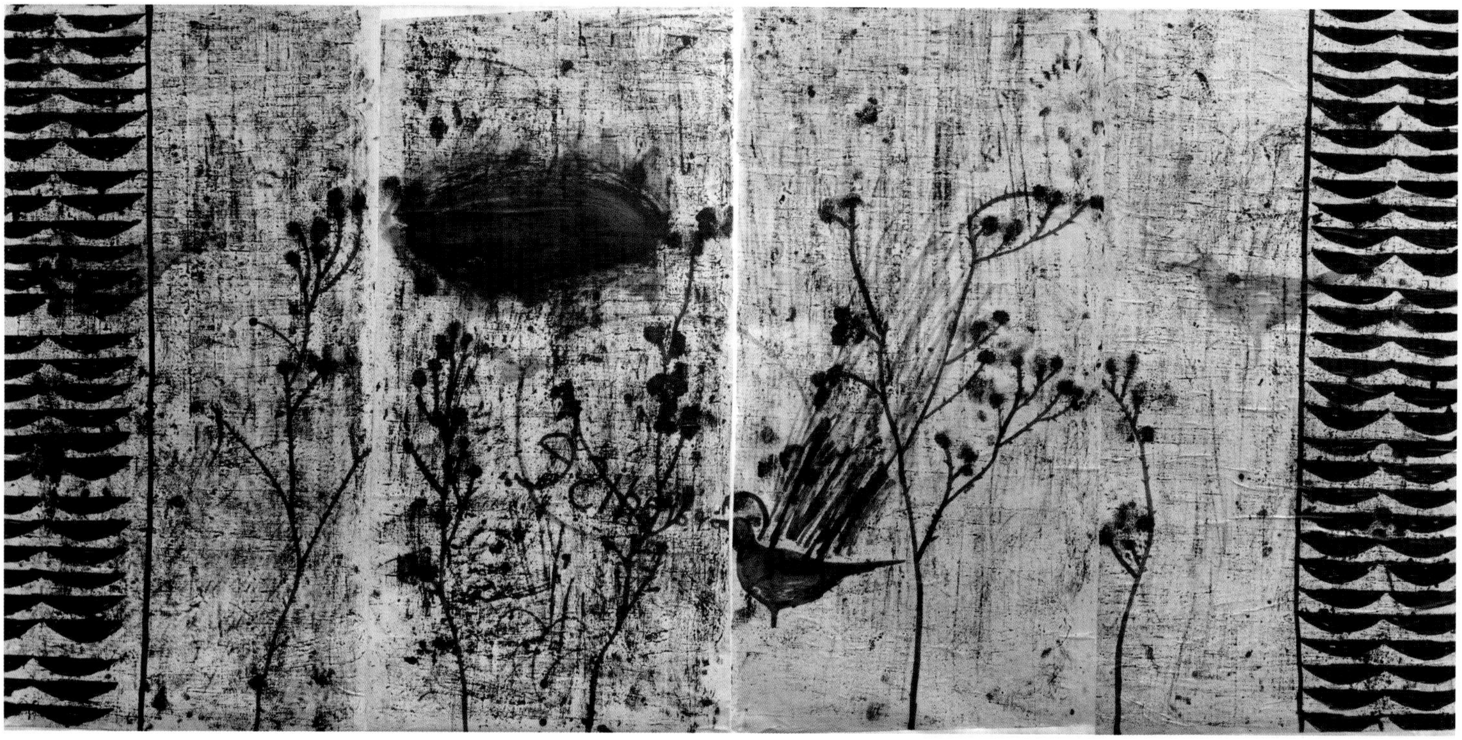

*The Gates of Paradise (Large Drawing)*, 1990

In February 1991, while Pearson was still in New York, he was given a solo exhibition at the Kelowna Art Gallery (then housed in a small room in the Kelowna Museum), titled *The Geometrics of Conjecture*, which was guest-curated by Vancouver-based Robin Laurence. In her catalogue text she wrote:

> Painting remains for Pearson a metaphysical enterprise, a way of grappling with relationships between humankind and the cosmos, between the artist and his world. Pearson's art proposes a confrontation with imagined horror, devastation or adversity, towards an ultimate state of creative or psychic realization.[3]

Once back in Canada, Pearson was hired to teach at Okanagan University College (the Fine Art program was later absorbed by the

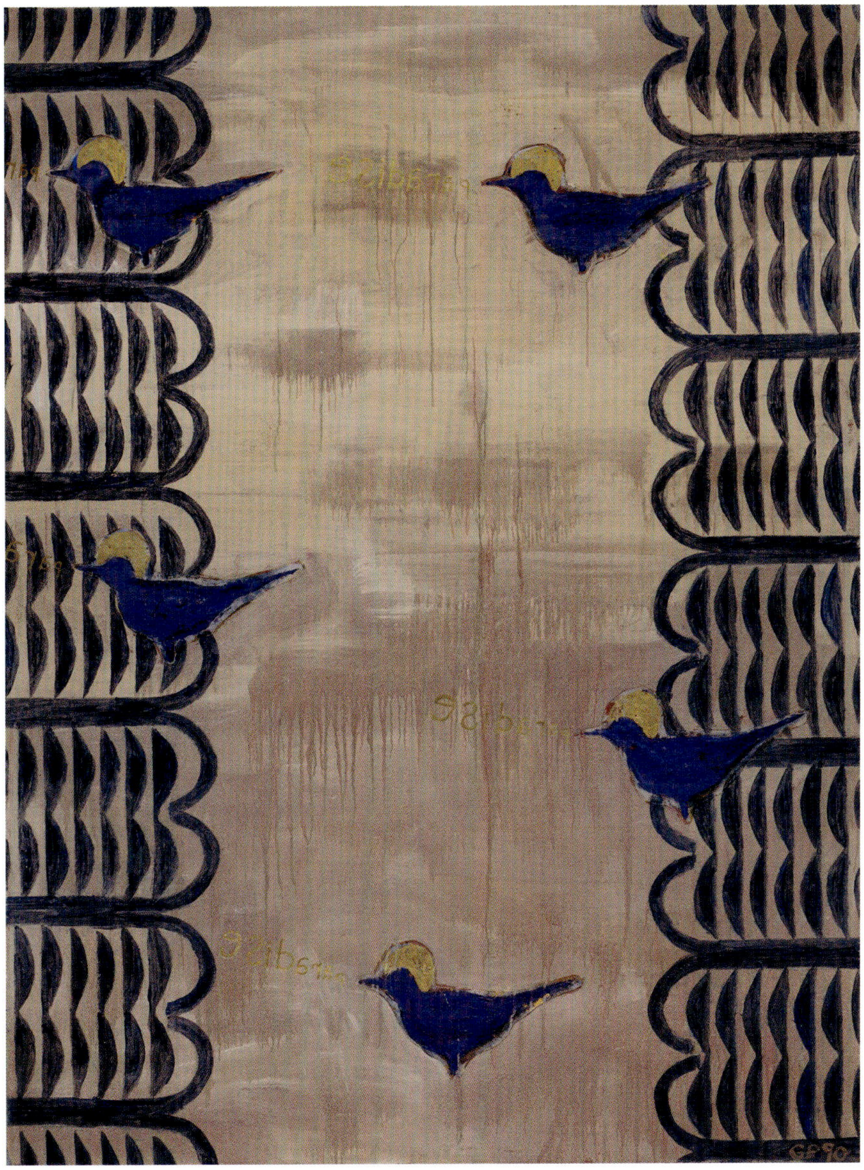

*The Gates of Paradise*, 1990

University of British Columbia Okanagan in 2005) in Kelowna, where he still lives. His work in the 1990s became more complex and multivalent in meaning, and the titles he gave each piece were important vectors toward the works' interpretation. He continued to work in the vein of 'symbolic abstraction' as the decade went on. A motif that he developed of twinned outlined human heads, one upside down, is particularly striking. While his works appear simple in terms of the small number of elements, they have been carefully considered and condensed, and unpack with a powerful kick generated by their graphic rendering.

In what might be considered an aside, Pearson produced a suite of 27 monoprints in 1997 called *Ashtray*, which depict a smoldering cigarette or cigar perched on an ashtray. These free-form, expressive and inventive works show Pearson at the top of his game. The variety among the works is astonishing, and one quickly forgets to pay attention to the subject and just focuses on the terrific variety of lines, shapes and areas of strong, bright colours.

In fact, the depiction of smoking would recur often in Pearson's works, both in his people-in-bars paintings and in his 2006 and 2008 video duo, *Soliloquy* and *Soliloquy2*. His recurring homage to smoking calls to mind passages from literature on the pleasures of cigarettes. We might recall, for example, Oscar Wilde's famous lines from his short story "The Picture of Dorian Gray": "You must have a cigarette. A cigarette is the perfect type of a perfect pleasure. It is exquisite, and it leaves one unsatisfied. What more can one want?"[4] Pearson embraced the subject of smoking, and titled his 2012 solo exhibition at Winsor Gallery (his Vancouver dealer) *Scenes for a 'Smoker's Theatre.'* This is a reference to the twentieth-century German dramatist Bertolt Brecht, who wanted to emancipate the observer of a play (or any art form). He wished to eliminate audience empathy for the characters on stage and instead foster a critical attitude among them. The ideal or fantasy theatre-goer would sit back dispassionately and smoke a cigar during the

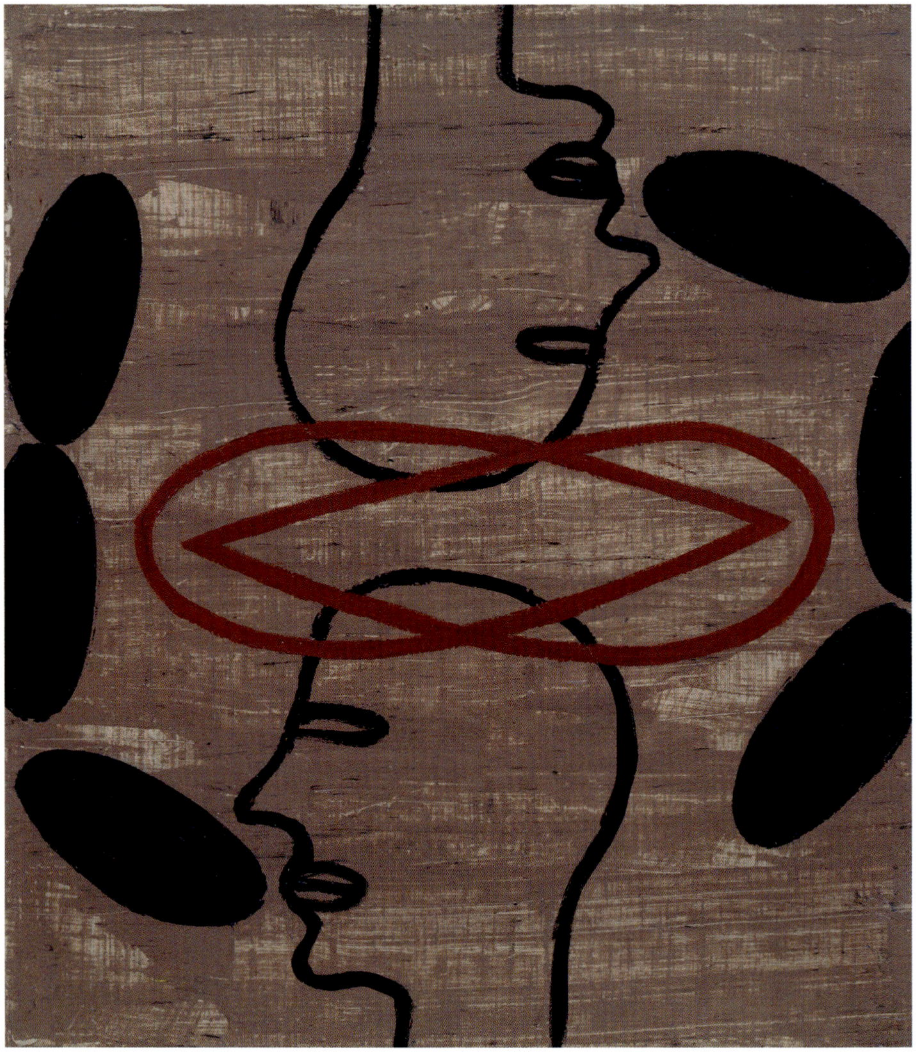

*Untitled*, 1996

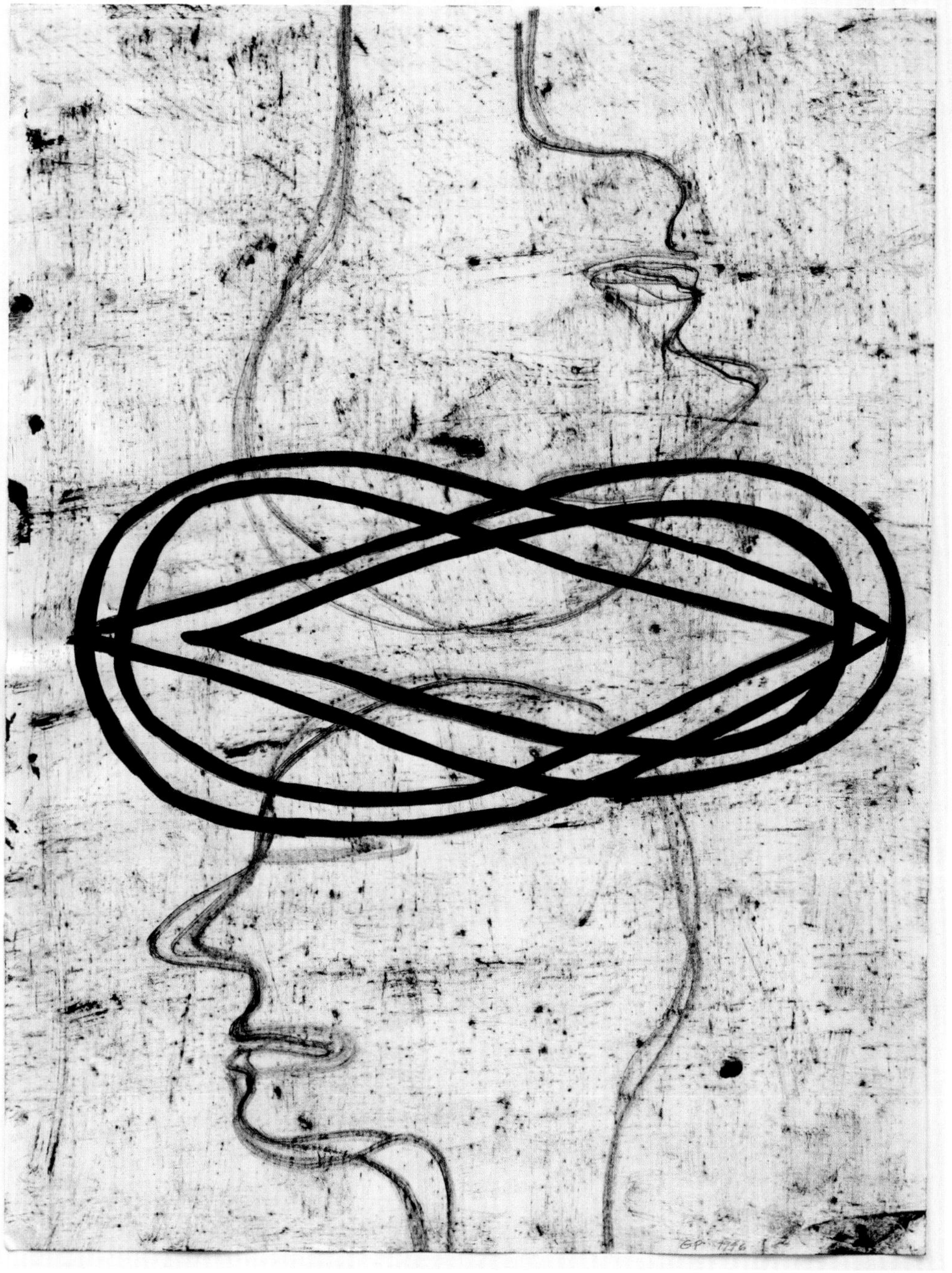

*Spectacle*, 1996

performance. Perhaps Pearson wishes for the same sort of response in viewers of his paintings: not to be swayed or seduced by anything pretty or naturalistic, but to look at his work from a place of critical remove.

If we consider Pearson's subjects to be actors on a stage or on screen, rather than portraits of real people, then it is only a small step to imagine Brecht's notion of the 'alienation effect' at play, whereby the set dressers, for example, might take a sip of the prop whiskey while getting things ready between acts of one of his plays, in order to remind the audience that the play is not real. Pearson seems to be after the same

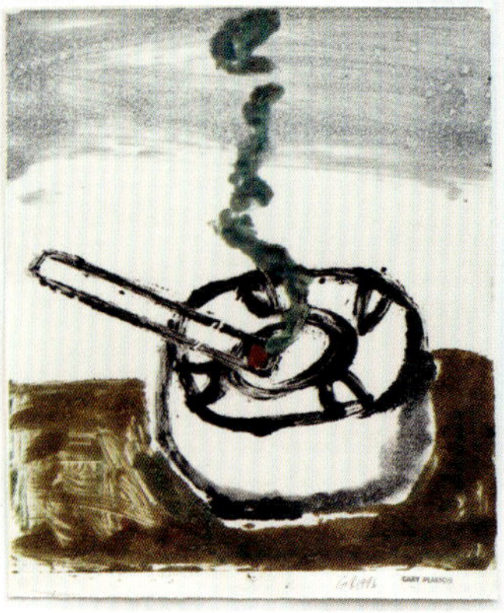
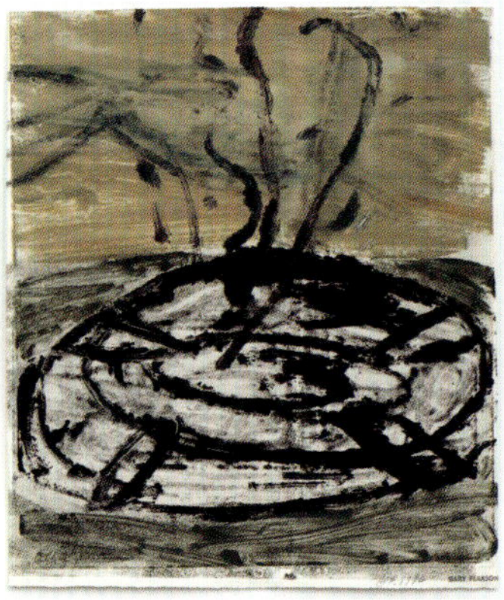
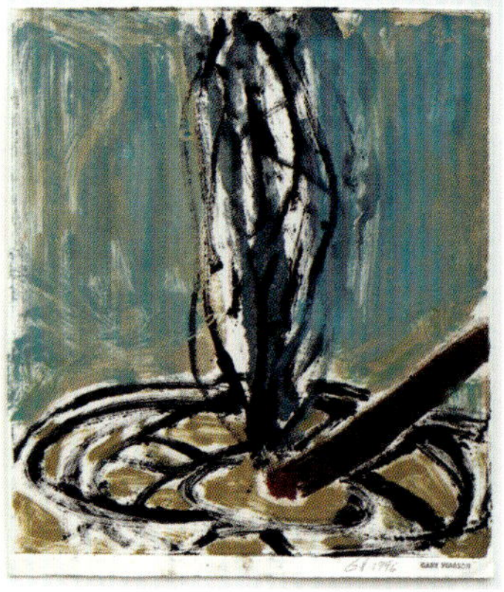
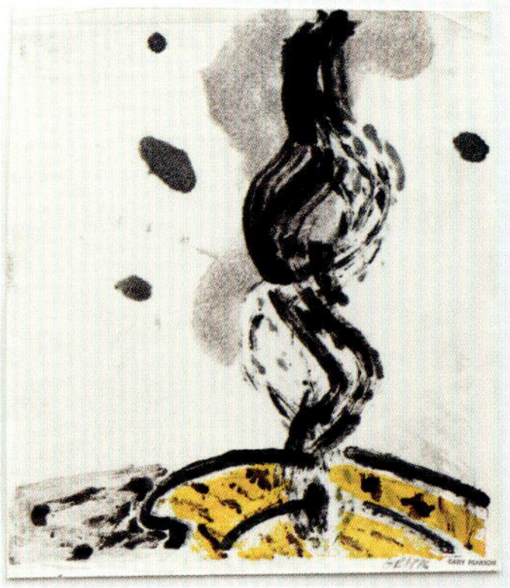
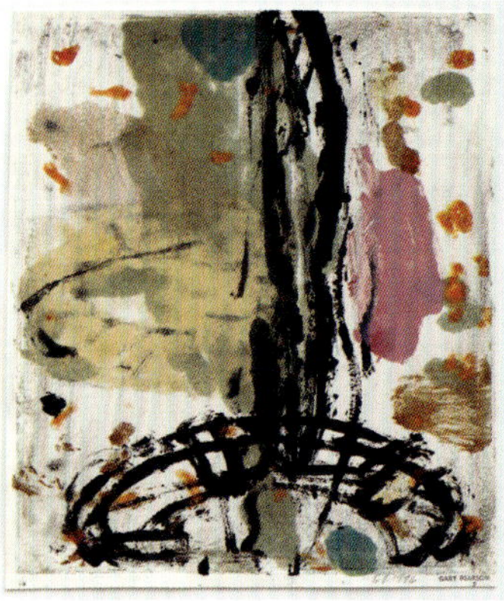
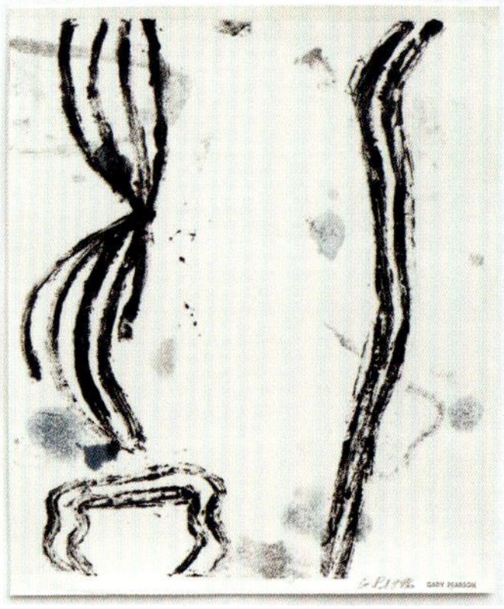
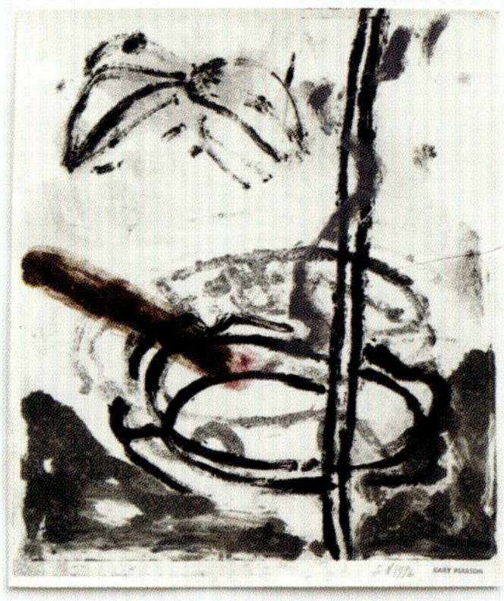
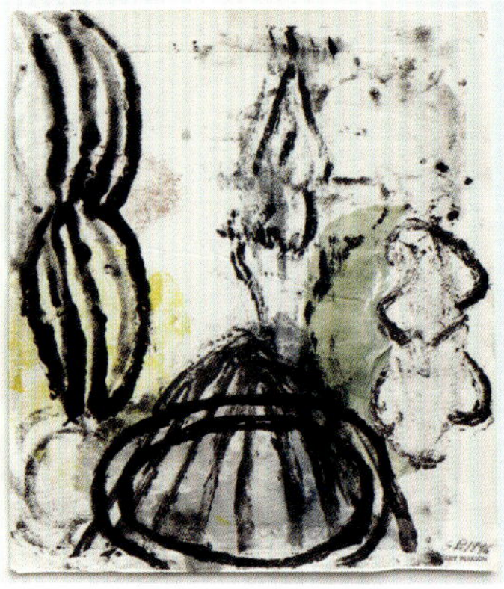
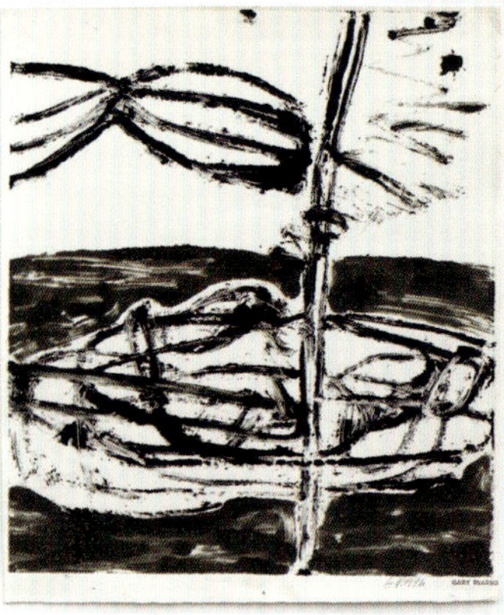
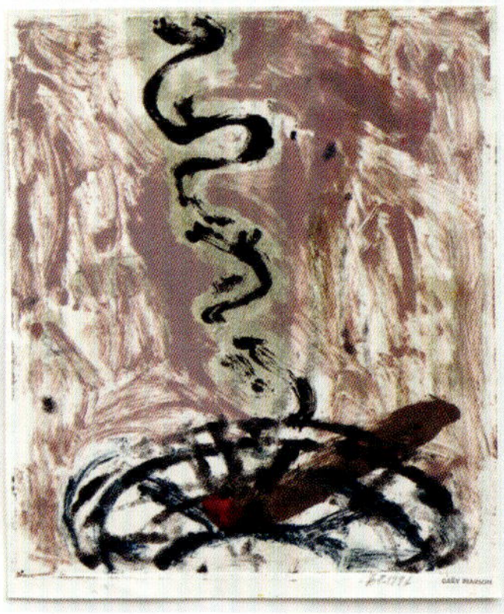
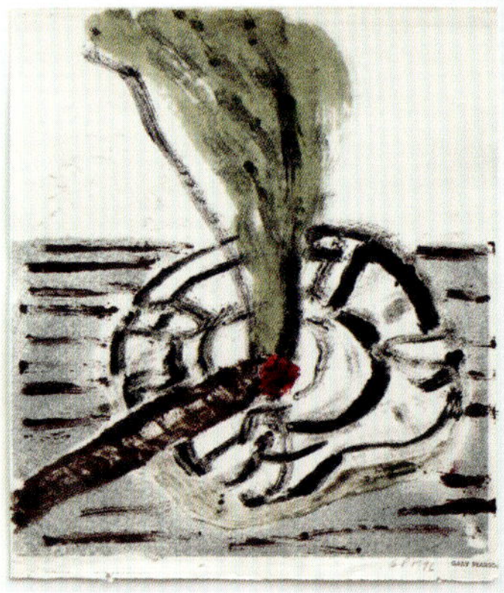
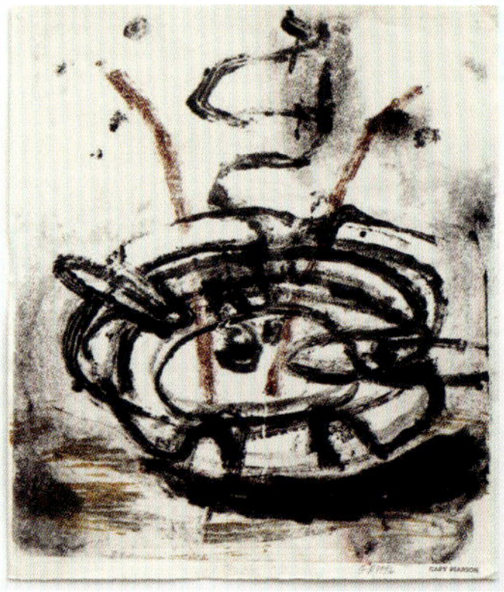
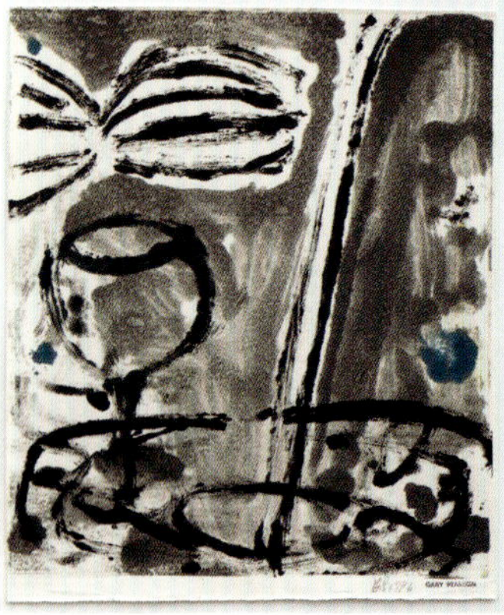
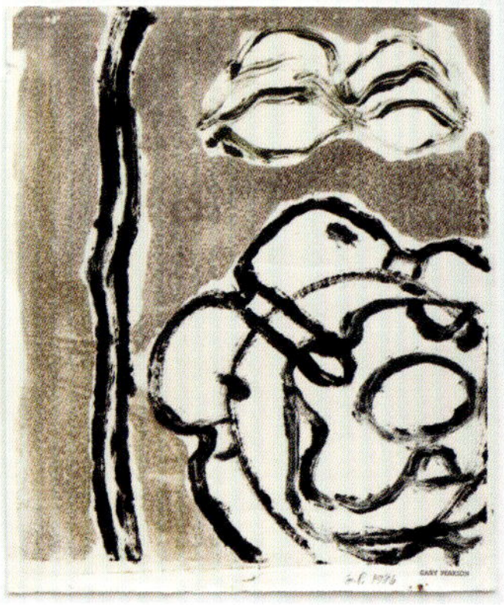
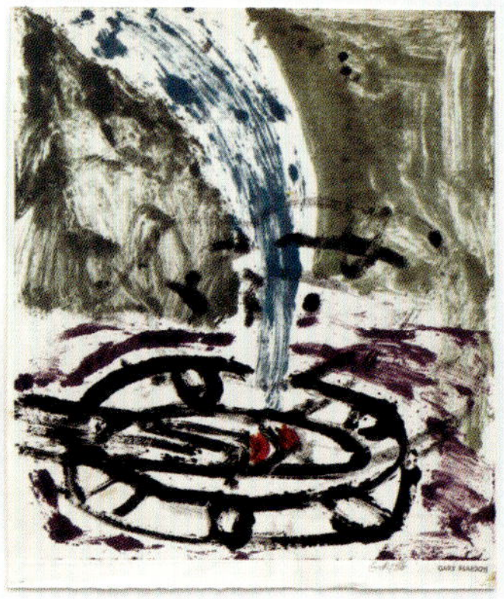
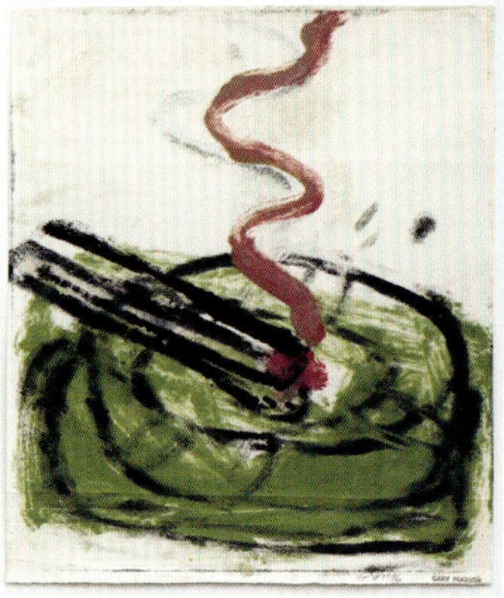

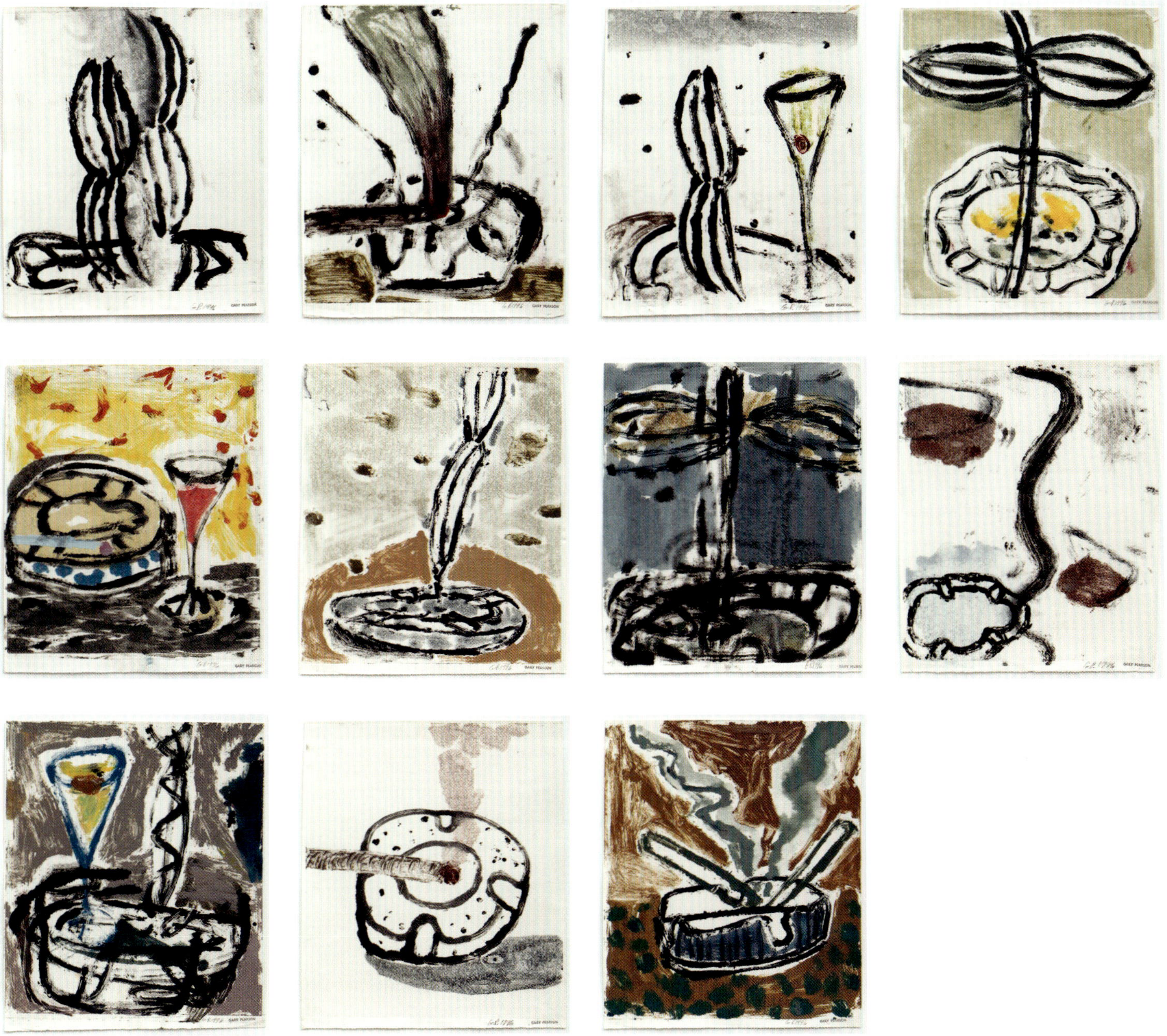

*Ashtray*, 1996

sort of thing in his works, depicting recognizable subjects observed dispassionately with an emotional distance.

The completion of the *Ashtray* suite brings us to the brink of 1998, and that fateful Diana Krall concert after which Pearson's work would undergo an extreme change. Up until this time, Pearson had been on his individual path as an artist, but was unknowingly (or perhaps knowingly at some level) ripe for a change. In 1998, abstraction was no longer the prow of art history (in the words of *New Yorker* critic Peter Schjeldahl) that it had once been, and street-wise, tough representation had come into play for painting, having started with the so-called New Image work of the 1970s and then the neo-expressionist work of the 1980s.

Sometimes it happens in life that we begin something that feels entirely new to us, but after we have begun, and happen at one point to look back, we can find antecedents that we neither noticed at the time, nor recalled until we went looking. So Pearson discovered, when looking back through images in preparation for this publication, that he actually had made a work on paper in 1979 that depicted sitters in a cafe.

This work is a small pencil drawing with collage. One person lolling against another sitter on a banquette has a mask-like face. Most of the work appears given over to patterns and contrasts between light and dark shapes. Pearson, the artist, is the unseen observer and chronicler of the scene, a momentary, maybe even unimportant, event. The subject of people at a table in a cafe or bar is an impressionist one, developed at the time when cafes were first beginning in Paris. At the same moment Baudelaire invented the notion of the flâneur, that dispassionate observer of this new, public, modern urban life. It was largely the Post-Impressionists of the day who turned the happy drinkers and diners into melancholic loners, gazing out over their glasses of poisonous absinthe, and this is the tradition Pearson draws upon for his many works depicting drinkers and smokers at tables—sometimes in couples, but many times alone. Even each customer who finds the fly in his soup in Pearson's 2016 video work *The Waiter Joke*, is a solo diner. In other works it would seem that Pearson himself plays the role of the flâneur, turning his dispassionate and neutral gaze over the scene at hand.

The full name for all the works that have stemmed from Pearson's night hearing Diana Krall in Berlin is *The Night of the Diana Krall Concert, Berlin, April 19th, 1998.* The main shift we see immediately in all these works from Pearson's earlier practice is the representational imagery. His so-called symbolic abstraction has been left behind, to recur only occasionally in his work from this point on. Pearson's first series depicting people in the Quasimodo at the concert dates from 1999, and is a suite of ten works on paper in vertical format, created in blue oil wash over black ink. This restricted palette works well to convey a nightclub atmosphere and demi-monde mood. Underneath each image of the two patrons Pearson has left a blank margin of white paper onto which he roughly inscribed some text in black ink, which doubles as the title for each work. He has also stamped each work with a commercial stamp ordered for this purpose with the series title.

Each of these pieces reads as a casual vignette, with the sitters posed as people used to for the old-time roving photographers, who would come around nightclubs taking photographs of patrons and orders for copies. It's hard to believe that Pearson created all these works from his memories of the concert. One might wonder whether the individual titles of the pieces are of Pearson's own creation, or were they perhaps based on snatches of conversation he heard that night? They read like lines from songs, or even song titles.

One big shift that occurred with Pearson's change in tack is that existential issues raised in his work are now meant for us to work out in the here and now, in lived reality, not through means of symbolic/abstract metaphors. The fragments of text that he so often includes

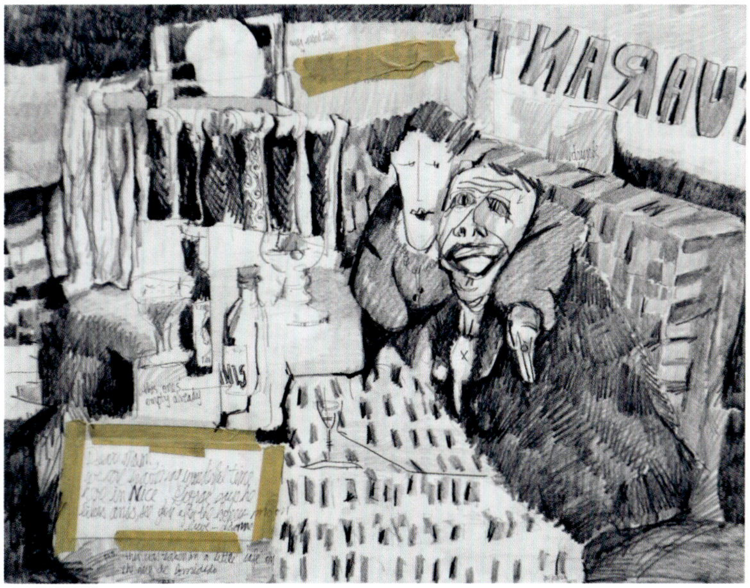

*Café Blues*, 1979

help to ground the images in what seems like some kind of experienced reality. We can all recall times when we overheard something said by a stranger as they passed us that coincidentally resonated with meaning for ourselves in our then current situation.

In his *Diana Krall* canvases Pearson continued to apply his paint thickly—in some cases it seems to have been used more as a paste than a liquid. His renderings are crude, sometimes awkward, and the figures are stiff and stolid. We would not term these works painterly or lyrical. The sitters' faces are generally pale white, with dark, strongly delineated features. In strong contrast with their darkly coloured settings, they look ghostly, or as though they have been caught in the blinding light of a flashbulb.

Pearson continued to produce *Diana Krall* works, but also worked on single pieces that only slightly related to the *Diana Krall* series. One outstanding example of these paintings is *The Toast*, 2001–2002.

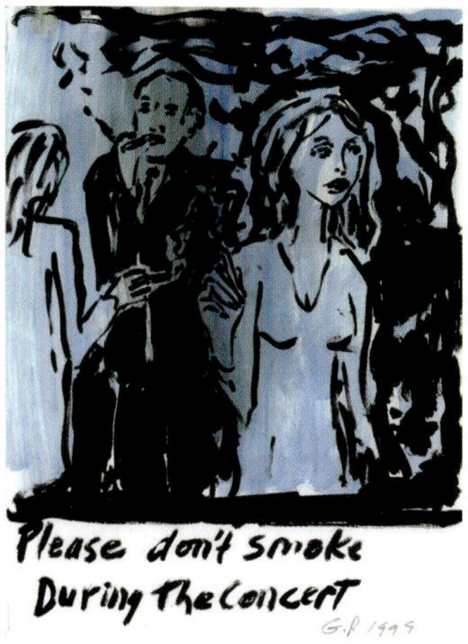


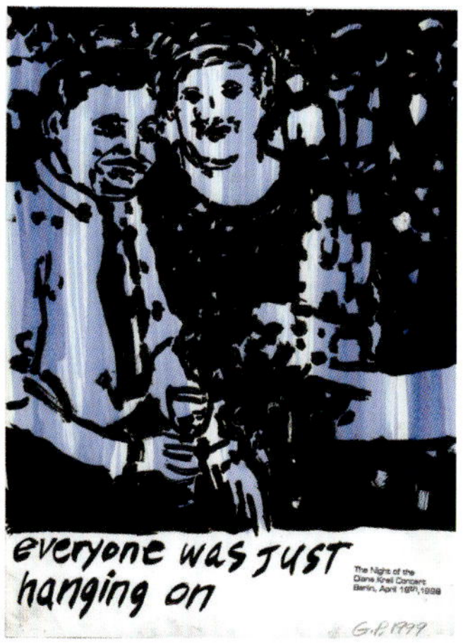


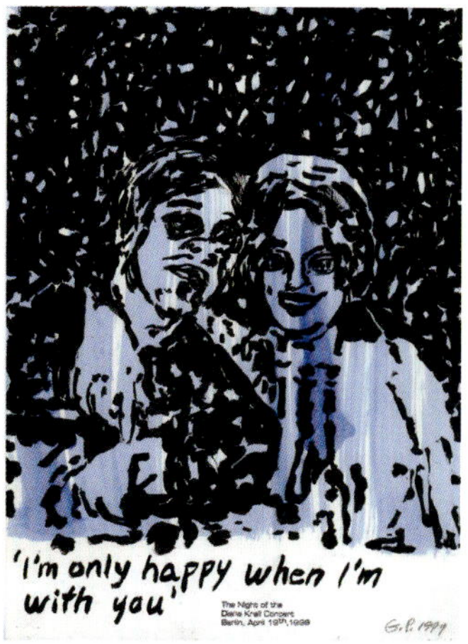


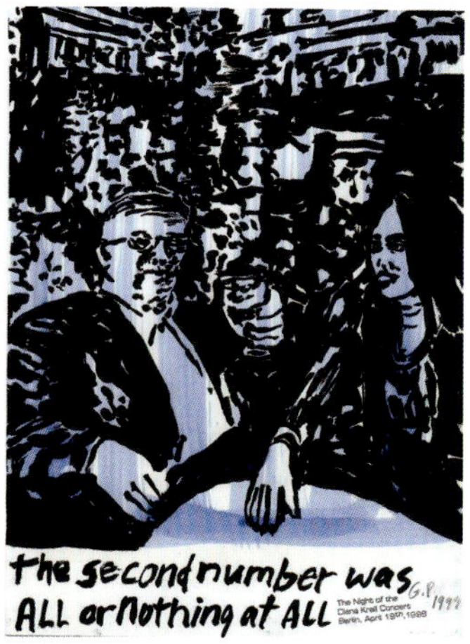


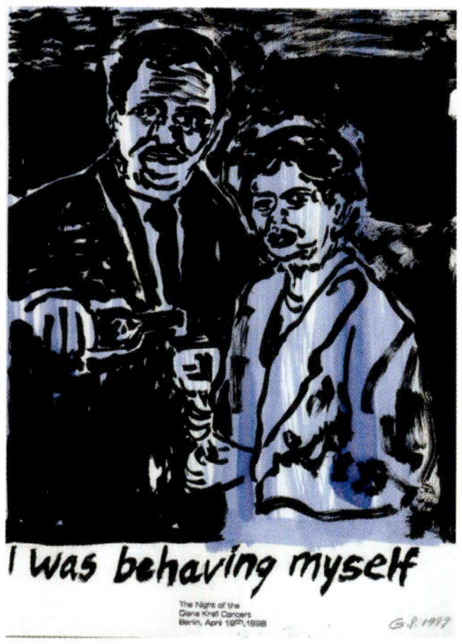

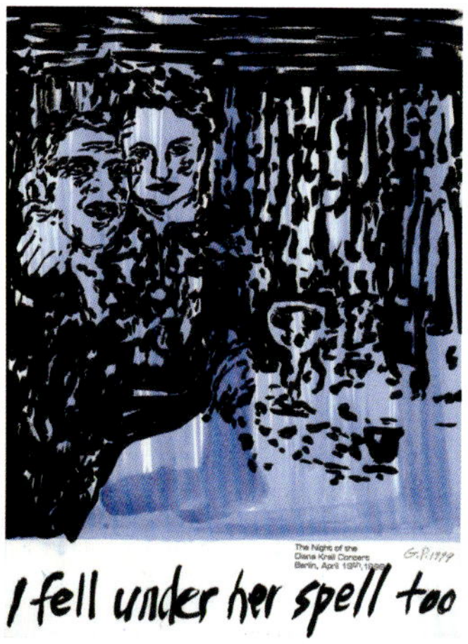


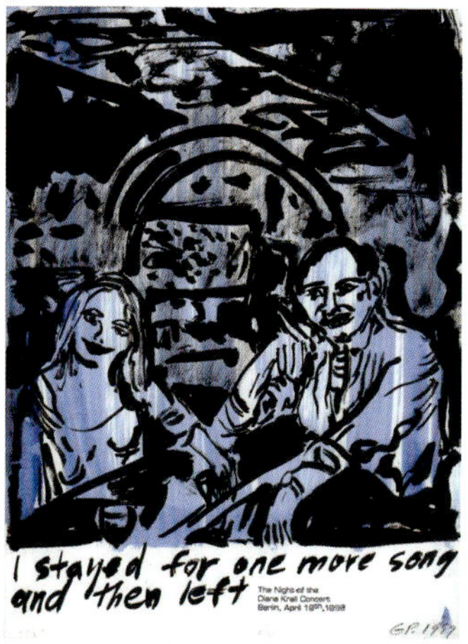


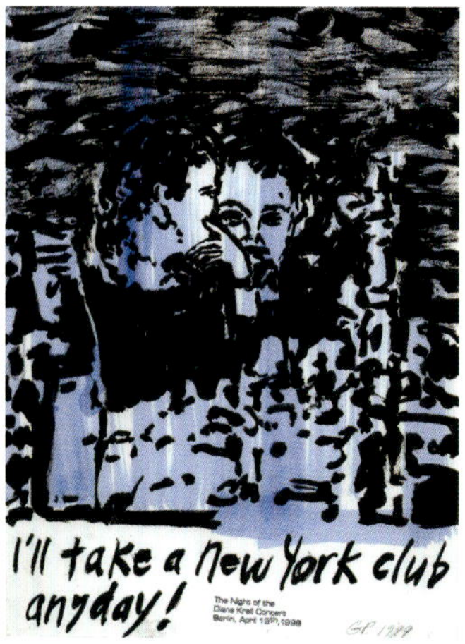


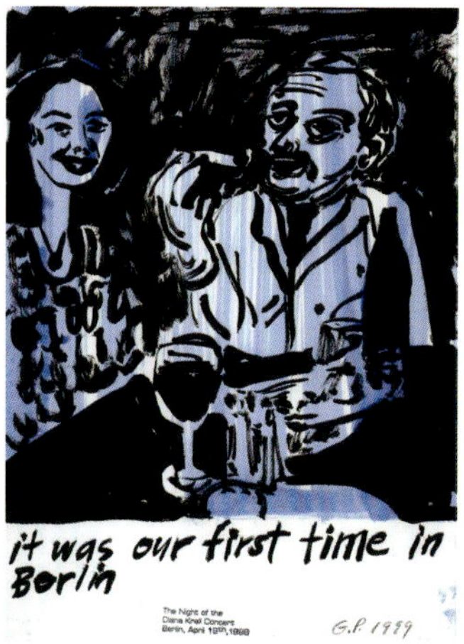


*Please Don't Smoke During the Concert*, 1999
*Everyone Was Just Hanging On*, 1999
*I'm Only Happy When I'm With You*, 1999
*The Second Number Was All or Nothing At All*, 1999
*I Was Behaving Myself*, 1999
*She Pushed the Limits on the Piano Solos*, 1999
*I Fell Under Her Spell Too*, 1999
*I Stayed for One More Song and Then Left*, 1999
*I'll Take a New York Club Any Day*, 1999
*It Was Our First Time in Berlin*, 1999

In this large painting a group of seven people is gathered at a table on which there are plates of food and bottles of wine. A hand holding a wine bottle extends into the work from the bottom right corner of the painting, which could be the artist's own hand—or has it been included and cropped to act as a repoussoir device, something entirely formal in purpose? On the surface of the painting random words have been printed out in brown paint: "Hello! Shit! Ok! Ohhh! Nice! Mommy! Tomorrow! Sunday!" These give the impression of snatches of conversation overheard, with multiple speakers overlapping, so that only nonsense emerges for a listener. The title of the work, *The Toast*, refers to the figure at the head of the table, raising his glass. But, otherwise the work overall is enigmatic and a tour de force of Pearson's arsenal: the paused moment, random pieces of text, an ambiguous setting and pale-faced, frozen personages.

Pearson continues to utilize overheard conversational fragments in his work. For example, in a short video he made in 2016 called *The Cocktail Bar (4 Vignettes)*, pairs of actors have brief dialogues that are conversations overheard by Pearson.

In 2004 Pearson received a half-year sabbatical from teaching and made a road trip with his wife in their VW Westfalia down to the southern

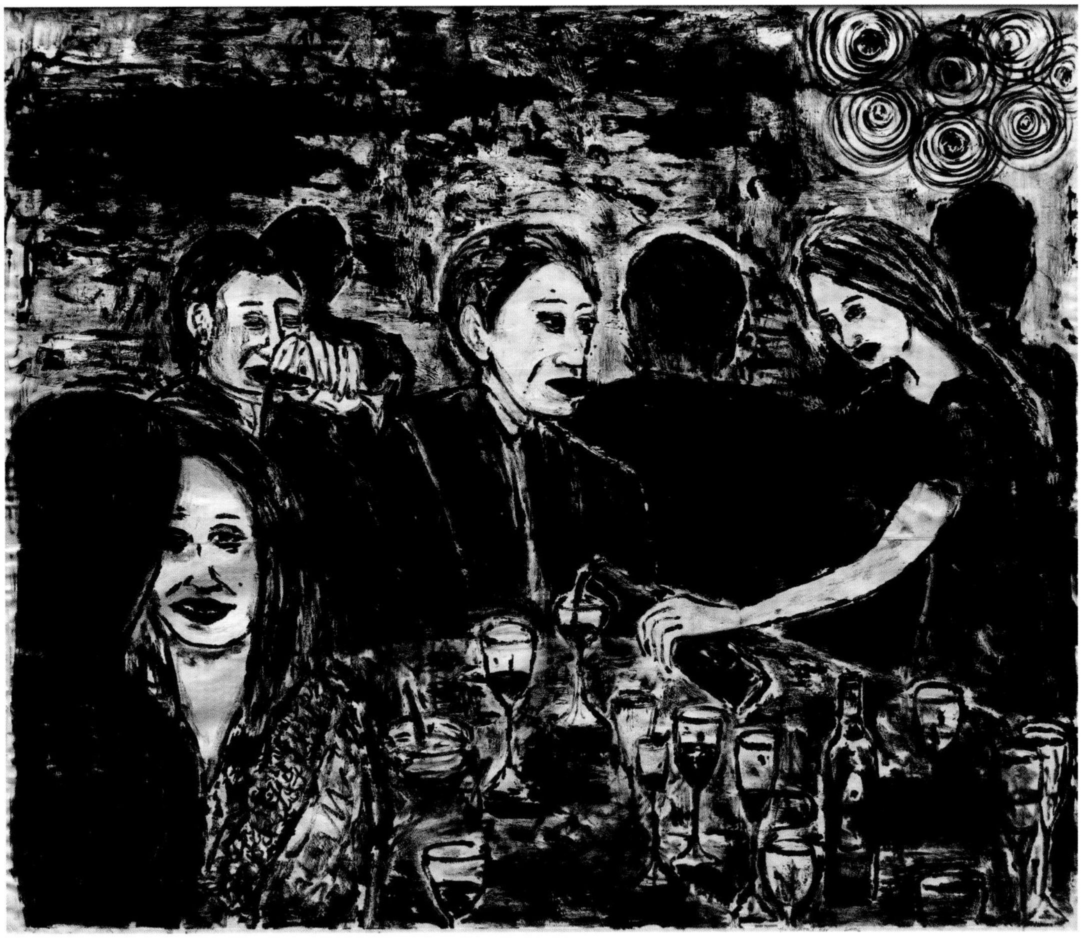



*The Cocktail Bar*, 2007

states. In one sense the artist was on the trail of the country-blues singer and songwriter Lucinda Williams. Her lyrics and this trip provided the material for a new series of paintings (that to some extent carried on with the *Diana Krall* series motifs) called *Going back to Greenville*. The artist explained: "The title for the *Greenville* series is a reworking of a line, 'I'm Going Back to Greenville,' from the Lucinda Williams song

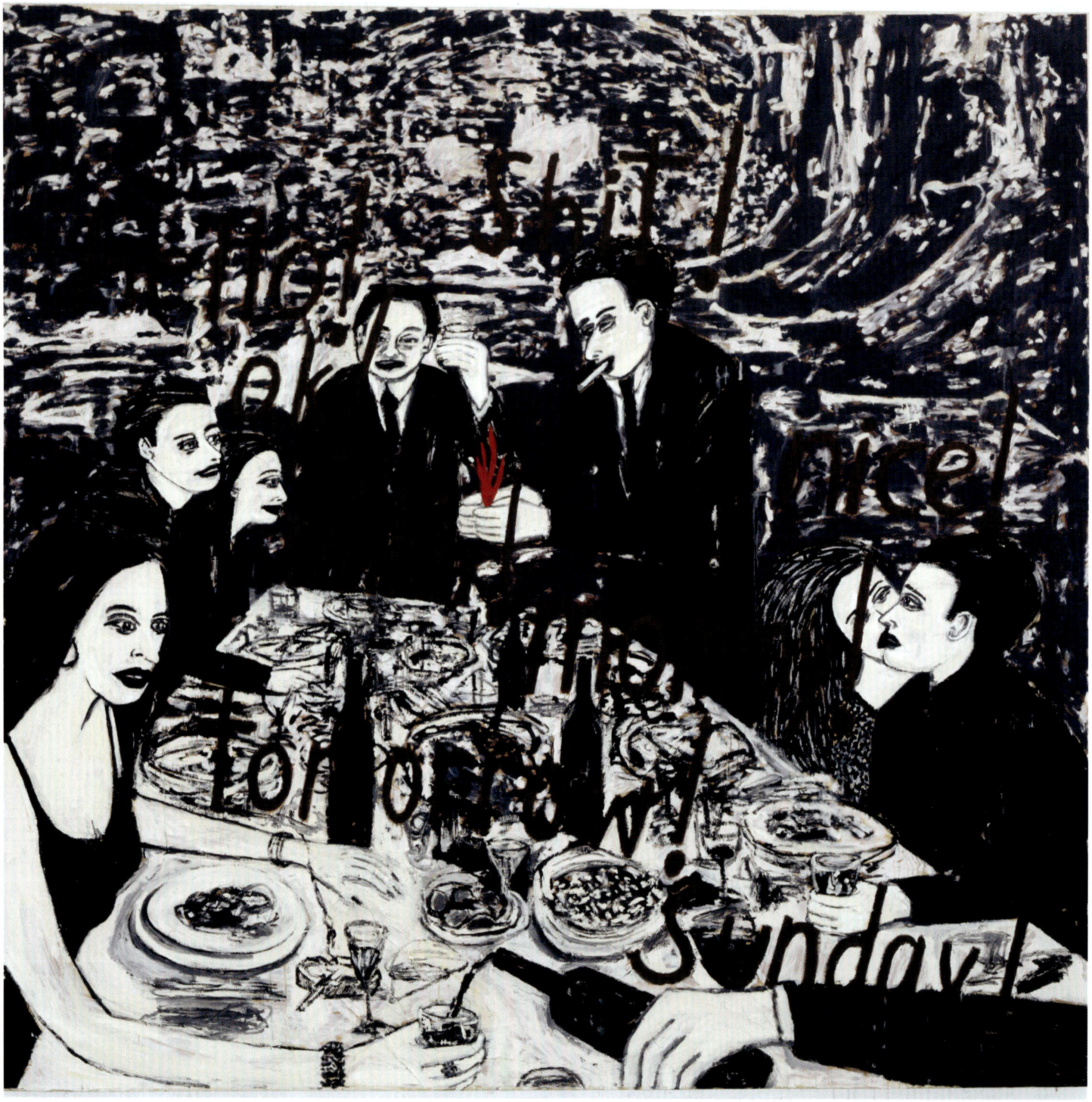


*The Toast*, 2001–2002

'Greenville' on her 1998 album *Car Wheels on a Gravel Road*. The series got underway after a five-month road trip through the US and Canada in the first half of 2004." Pearson went on to explain that Greenville is a fictional place that he invented in order to tell a story.[5] Yet, once again, we're not given the full story but provided only single unrelated glimpses, like random photographs taken from a moving car on a road trip or vignettes that do not tie together into any sort of cohesive narrative. Pearson painted and drew images of trees; paintings of a single man at a table being served a drink by a waitress in a short dress and heels; and in one case, a self-portrait. These works ooze a feeling of mournfulness, a kind of intensity of melancholy, such as the best blues music conveys. It is interesting to note, that it was two very different female singers who were both muses to Pearson, providing him with vital inspiration for his work.

In Pearson's self-portrait he is at a bar with a cigarette burning in an ashtray and a half-full/half-empty drink in front of him. He looks away from the viewer, and five people in masks, like those painted by the Belgian James Ensor, leer in through a window on the right-hand side. It is weird to see Pearson as seen by Pearson. The idea of seeing oneself in or as the third person is mentioned in another passage from literature about smoking, in this case from Anton Chekov's *The Seagull*: "Wine and tobacco destroy the individuality. After a cigar or a glass of vodka you are no longer Peter Sorin, but Peter Sorin plus somebody else. Your ego breaks in two: you begin to think of yourself in the third person."[6] Travelling, I would think, has something to do with this phenomenon also, as when we are on a trip away from home we often feel a quickening and an intense feeling of life that becomes dulled by the day-to-day routine of our workaday lives. We begin to observe ourselves as travellers. So Pearson creates tropes from his perceptions of the American South just as he did with the Diana Krall patrons inside the Quasimodo nightclub. The places and things seen become types, signifiers, not noteworthy as singular examples in and of themselves. This is even extended to his depiction of himself at the bar, where he becomes just a man, as in the start of a joke: a man walks into a bar. In the later years of the 2000s and moving into the 2010s, Pearson felt compelled to include references to current events in his work, such as the 2010 ash cloud in Iceland that grounded aircraft flights in much of the world for days and the NASA missions to Mars in 2011 and 2013.

Some of these paintings were completed as single works—expressions of the artist's reactions and responses to events in the news. A more generalized group of four paintings was named for the ancient elements (earth, water, fire and air) and was also painted in 2010. These subjects/themes could have been sparked by articles in the media about the threat of climate change.

Only rarely has Pearson ever addressed the place where he actually lives: Kelowna, BC. It is a small city in a bucolic setting, with exquisitely clear light (except during the winter months). In 2007 Pearson

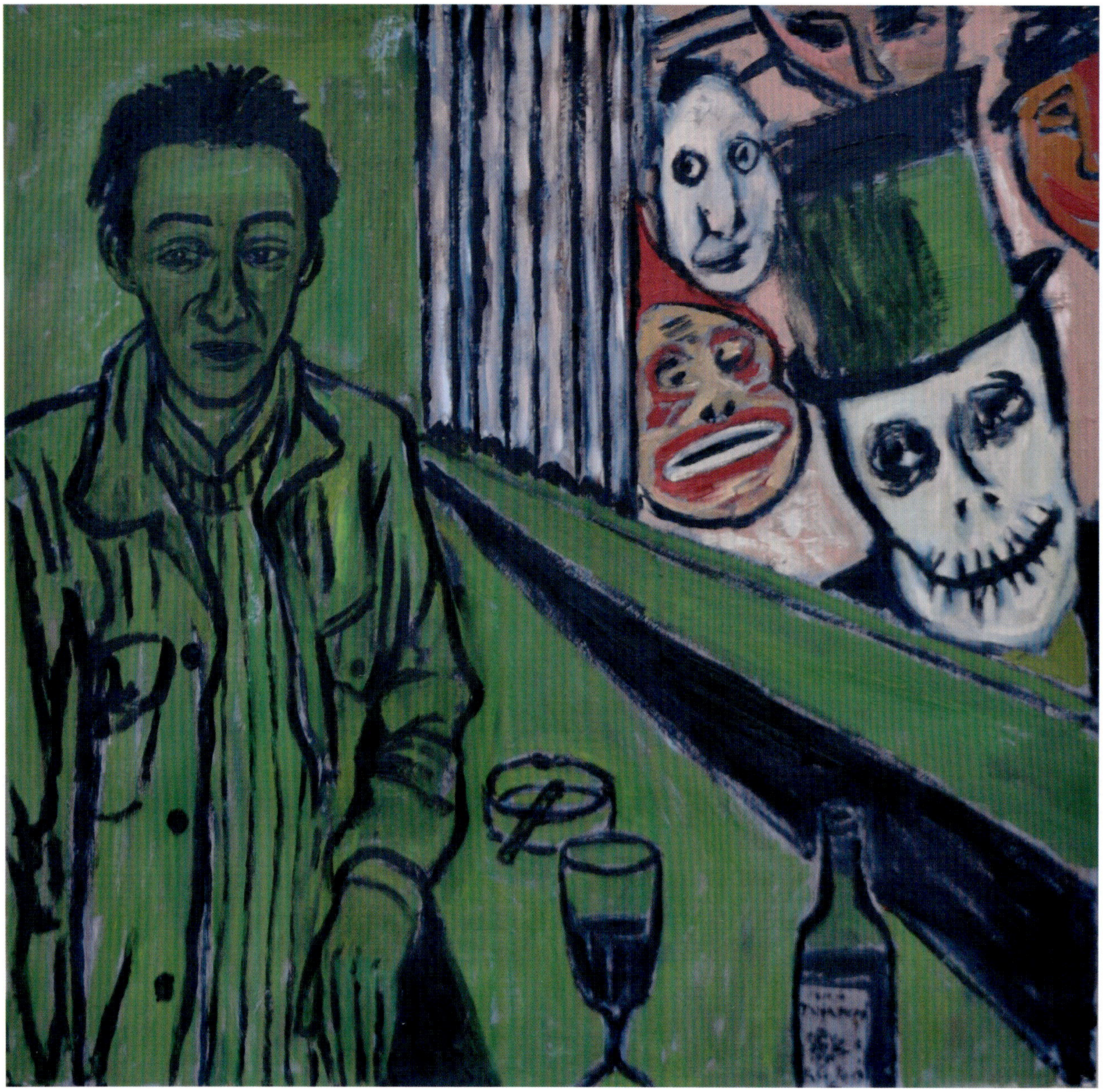

*Self-Portrait, New Orleans, LA*, 2004

painted a depiction of a potted bay leaf tree on his deck, set against Okanagan Lake below, with a huge, invented waterspout in the centre of the lake. It is interesting he felt compelled to turn the mundane subject into a dramatic, if not horrific one, rather than keep it as a straightforward depiction of the view from his studio.

Six years later, Pearson painted a work of Ponderosa pines sprouting vertically on the sun-bleached flank of Knox Mountain in Kelowna, a view only steps away from where he lives. In neither of these canvases is the scenery of the Okanagan painted as beautiful or welcoming. It would seem that Pearson is most inspired to paint and draw foreign subjects, seen when travelling away from home, not when ensconced in his own environment.

The artist has participated twice in the Bus from Guadalajara Artist's Residence Project in Ajijic, Jalisco, in Mexico; once in 2010, and again in 2015. Both of these visits provided him the opportunity to work prolifically on works on paper while there, depicting various trees and shrubs, views of the walled garden of the residency and the statues, fountains and parks of the town. Once back in his Kelowna studio, some of these drawings formed the starting points for works on canvas. But the canvases are not just scaled up versions of his studies and sketches—they are filtered and mediated by Pearson into otherworldly meditations.

Created at and inspired by his residency in Mexico, both Pearson's works on paper and the drawn elements in his paintings look incised, or etched, rather than just drawn. The subjects have a static quality, much in the manner of some medieval and folk art. There is an expressive power to be found in this approach, despite the limitations set upon verisimilitude. Even when Pearson opts to depict a statue, a fountain, a potted plant or tree in these drawings, his subjects read as portraits, and have some of the feeling of a human being—as though the outward characteristics should be overlooked, and we should consider the living inner ethos of

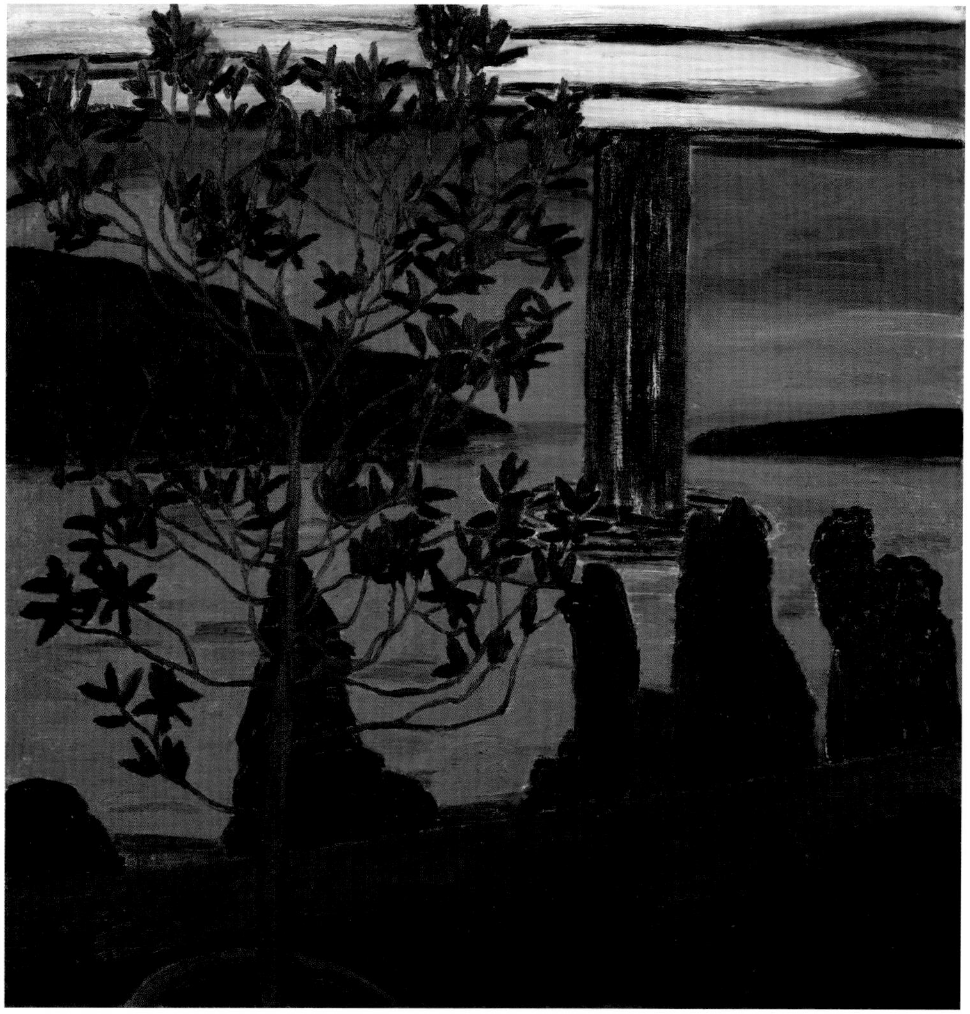



*The Bay Leaf Tree*, 2007

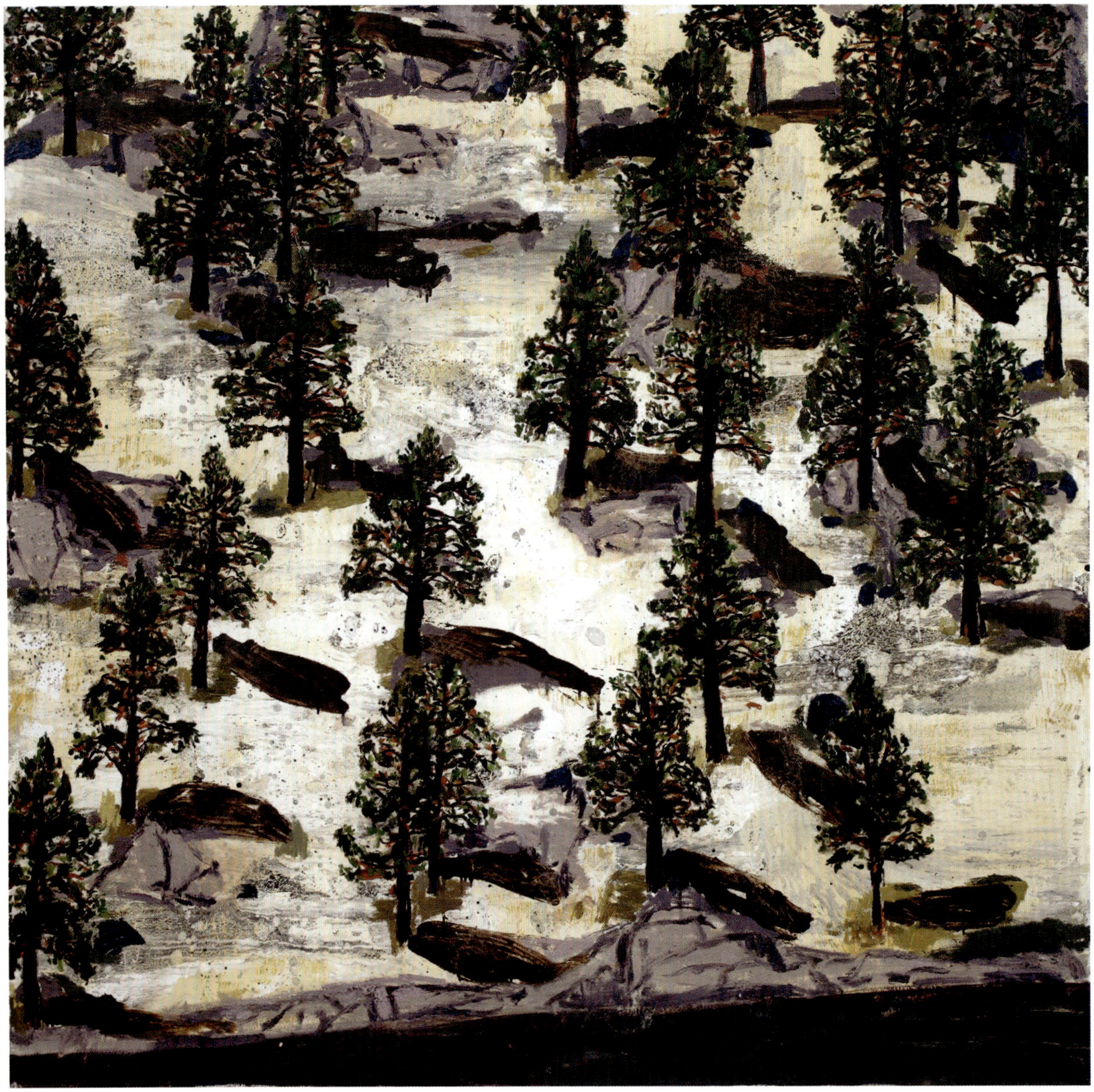

*Knox Mountain*, 2013

each one. His pleasure and enthusiasm in these works are both palpable, and the mood of these pieces is less sombre than usual, instead bordering on a bizarre sort of exuberance.

In 2014 the artist worked on a suite of 20 works in pen, ink and oil that he called *Rise and Fall*, referencing an opera from the late 1920s written by Kurt Weill, with a libretto by Brecht, called *Rise and Fall of the City of Mahagonny*. Its creators wanted this work to be a criticism of traditional opera as it existed at the time. Thus some tropes of opera are subverted and become the mirrored opposites of their originals, and there is great human degradation and debasement. It is hard to fathom the specific appeal to Pearson of illustrating this work, other than its exciting contrast to his cultural environment in Kelowna. His graphic sensibility comes to the fore, and each of the works pack a dramatic punch. Pearson exhibits great compositional inventiveness, and excellent judicial use of spot colour. The sheets are small, only 40 centimetres tall and wide, making them perfect to hold in the hand. One can imagine this suite functioning as something of a graphic novel, or a portfolio, to be opened up from time to time by a collector in his library and pored through in private.

In the following year, 2015, Pearson worked on another suite of small-scale works on paper, in this case a single view, rendered in red wash of the planet Mars from the rover sent by NASA to explore its surface in 2013 and interspersed with black-and-white works in ink, taken from news and talk show footage. So events being discussed in the daily news are juxtaposed with barren images of the red planet next door. What could reveal our petty obsessions and conflicts in a more glaring light than this juxtaposed contrast in scale and distance.

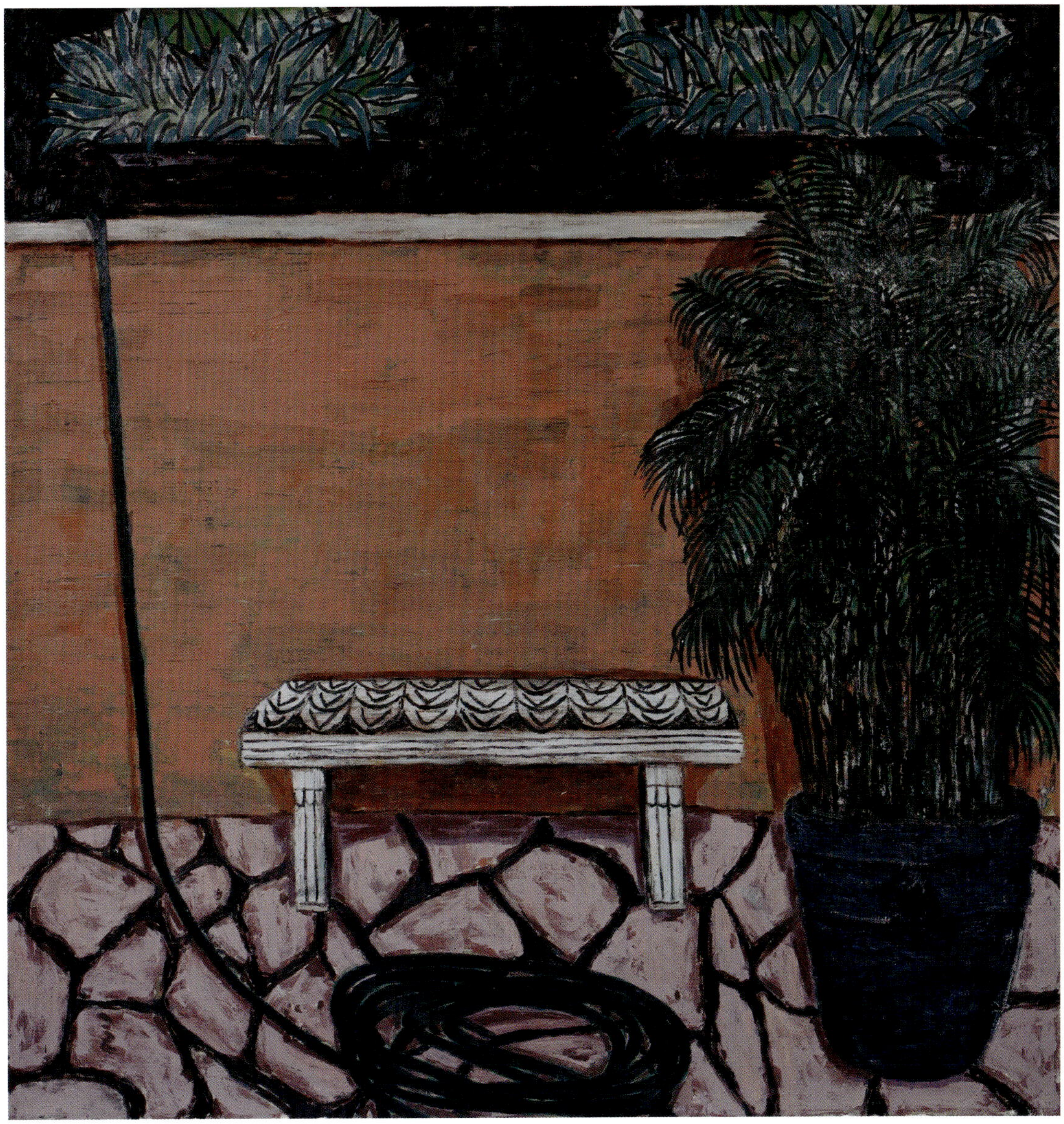

*The Garden Hose*, 2011

Pearson produced his *Trees on Knox Mountain* for an invitational exhibition of large drawings at the Kelowna Art Gallery in 2016. It is made on 12 sheets of paper that butt together to form a work almost 4 metres high and 10 metres long. Created with black ink and paper collage, the work is impressive, and not only for its gigantic scale, but for its overall success in internal scale: the size of the elements as related to the whole. In passing, Pearson termed this piece more of an inventory than a scene, and one gets a sense of that; the passages from one sheet to another are not always smooth and contiguous. One's vision becomes interrupted, suspended, as though we are receiving data through a malfunctioning instrument. Finally—a paean on Pearson's part to the landscape in which he lives, and he obviously knows it well: the various species of trees, for example, could be identified from his depictions as though from diagrams.

Gary Pearson is a protean artist, full of restless creativity. As well as his work in painting, drawing and printmaking, he writes critical reviews and short fiction, and makes art videos. In Kelowna for the last 25 years or more he has been both a beacon and a one-man band for promoting and supporting art, both in terms of the local artists in the area and bringing in visiting artists from other places. In 1998 he wrote a book on artists in various disciplines living in the Okanagan region.[7] As well as having taught studio courses at the University of British Columbia Okanagan since 1991, he has curated exhibitions at the Kelowna Art Gallery (and elsewhere) and has sporadically acted as an impresario for cafe events, poetry readings, musical evenings, etc, in various Kelowna venues. With the example of his ambitious work he has set the bar high for local artists.

Pearson is a singular artist, not a member of any group or movement and who has no artistic peers in terms of style, approach or subject. He has not set out to have his work engage with the tradition of painting per se, as his interest is more specifically in expression, and the depiction of an intensely imagined life. It has been people observed and overheard, the places visited and the music embraced that have provided him a quickened feeling of engagement, as referenced in the epigram that began this text, such that Pearson could "race away with it in some great and enthralling pursuit".

1 Pearson, Gary, Autobiographical writings (unpublished), shared with the author 2016.

2 Pearson, Autobiographical writings.

3 Robin Laurence, "Gary Pearson: The Geometrics of Conjecture," in *Gary Pearson: The Geometrics of Conjecture*. Kelowna, BC: Kelowna Art Gallery, 1991.

4 Wilde, Oscar, "The Picture of Dorian Gray", *The Collected Works of Oscar Wilde: The Plays, the Poems, the Stories and the Essays*, Hertfordshire: Wordsworth, 1997, p 57.

5 Pearson, Autobiographical writings.

6 Chekov, Anton, *The Seagull*, New York, NY: Dover Publications, 1999, p 19.

7 The book is an anthology of 35 interviews with artists, writers, musicians and filmmakers in the Okanagan. *The Creative Voice: Art and Life in the Okanagan*, Prince George, BC: Caitlin Press, 1998.

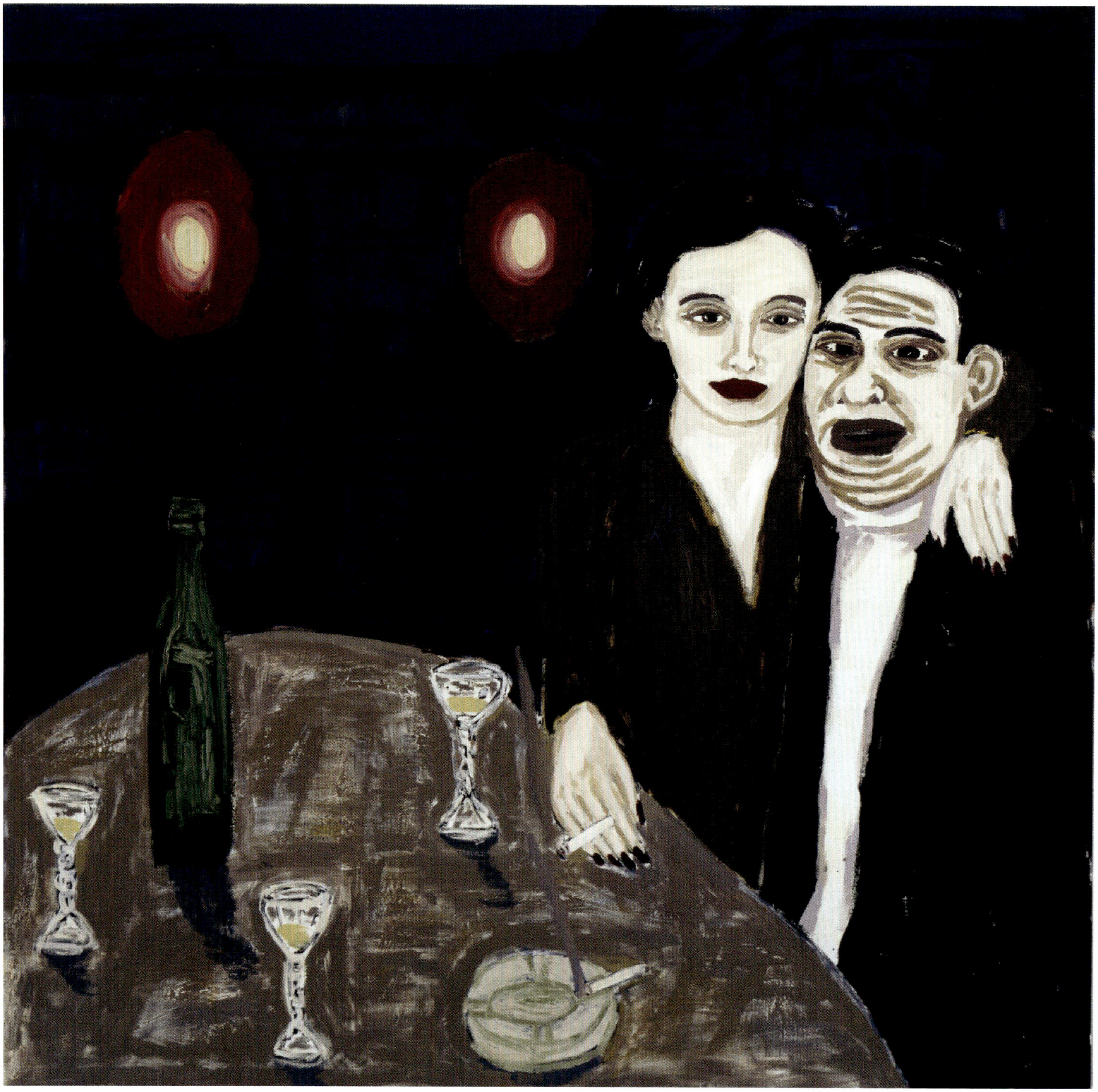



*I Stayed For One More Song And Then Left*, 2000

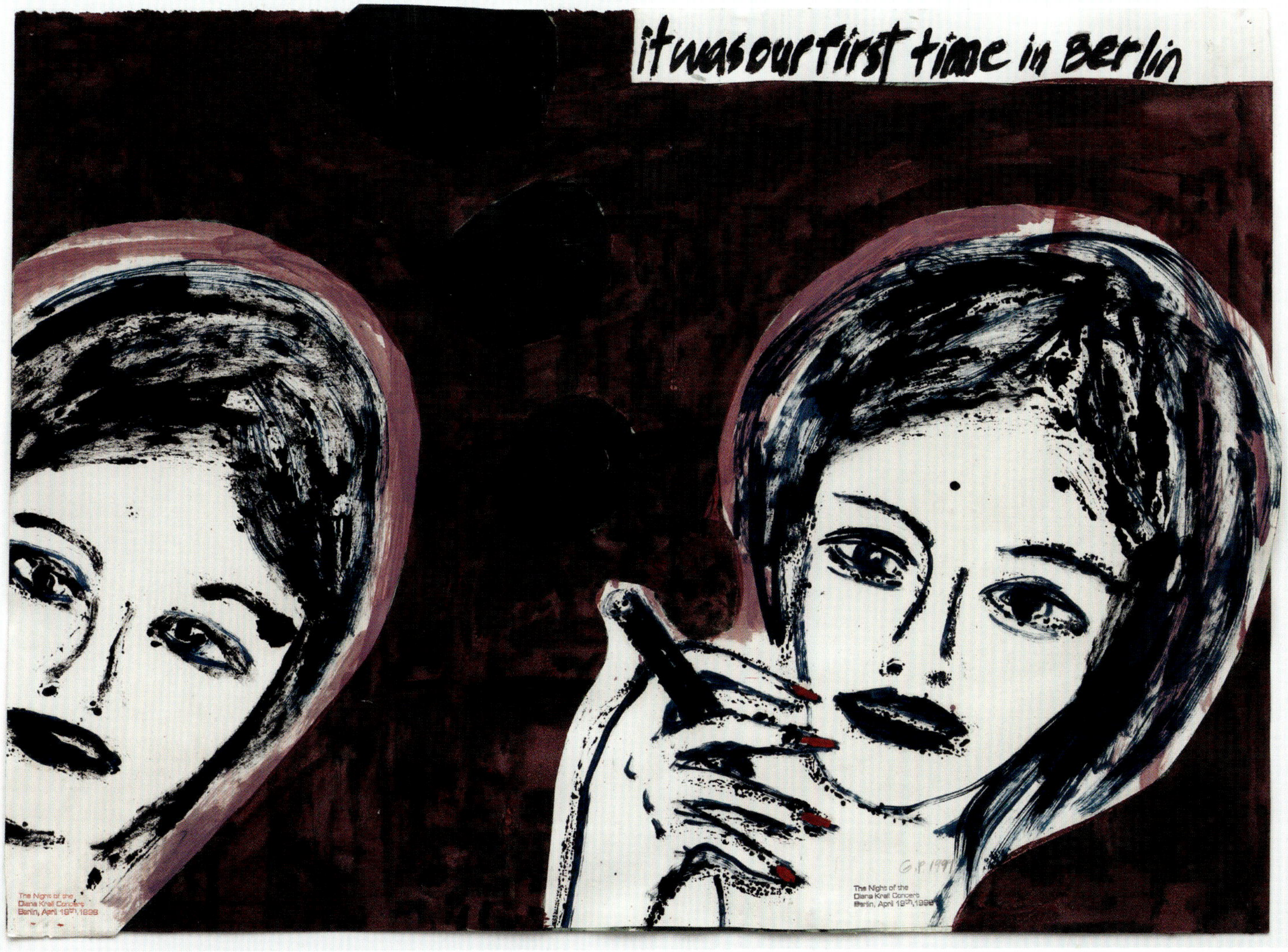


*It Was Our First Time in Berlin*, 1999

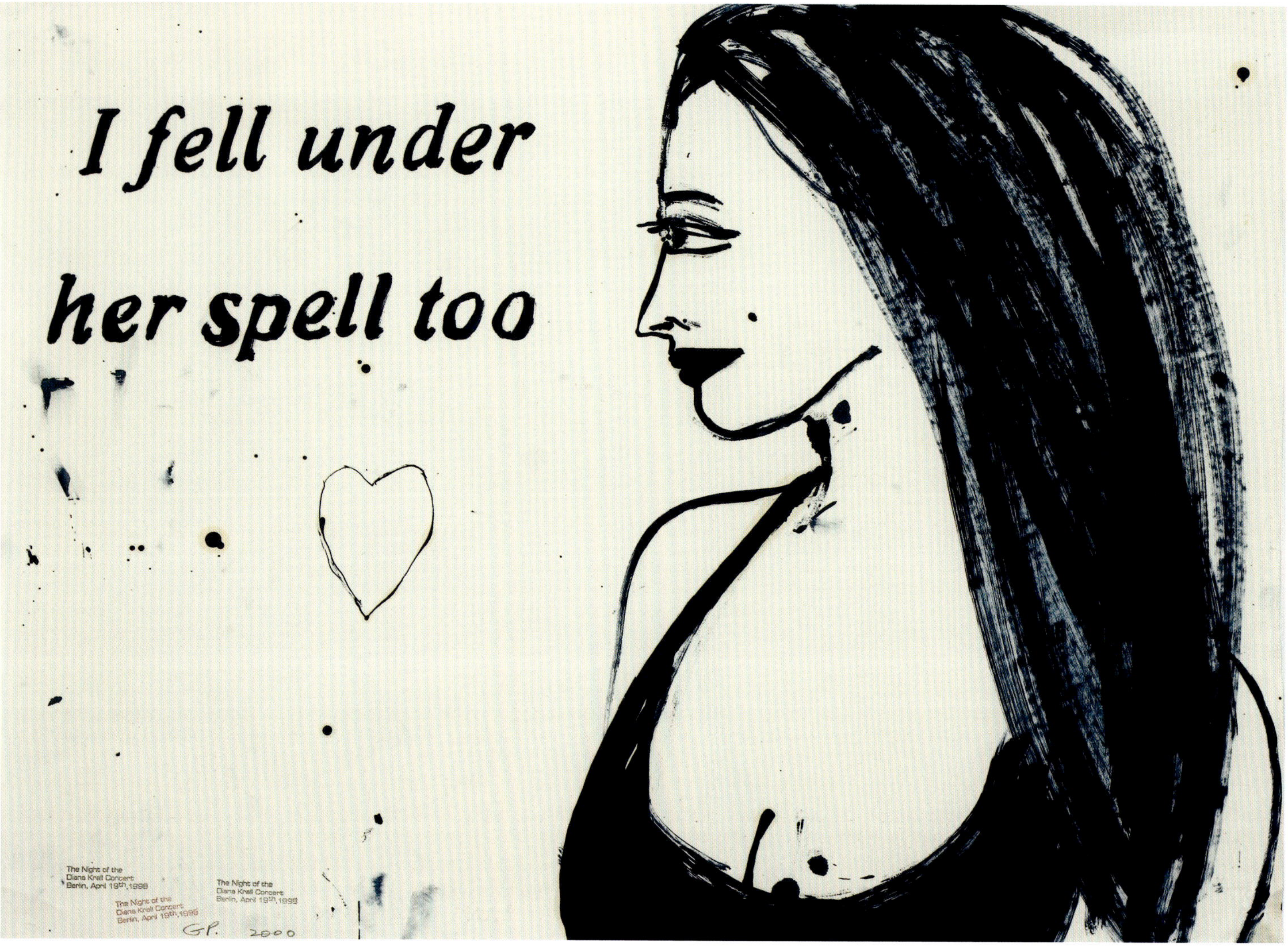


*I Fell Under Her Spell Too*, 2000

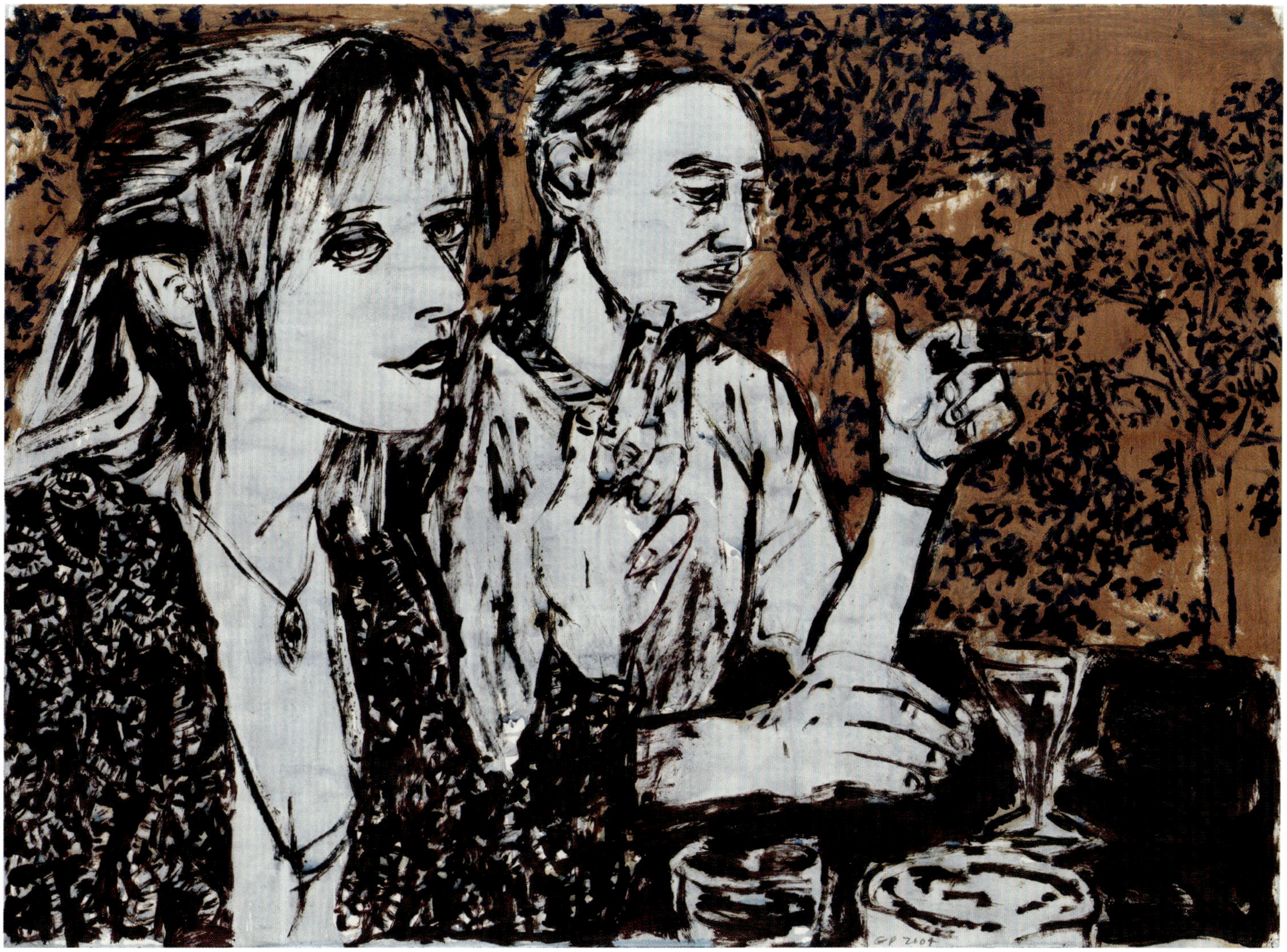

*Lori and Joshua*, 2004

A man in his late thirties, or early forties is sitting on a chair behind the wrought iron railing of a second-floor balcony. He gets up from the chair and retreats inside through an open door to a dark interior room. He emerges from inside about ten seconds later, and sits back down on the chair, only to rise again after about ten seconds, and return inside. Moments later he comes back out on the balcony again.

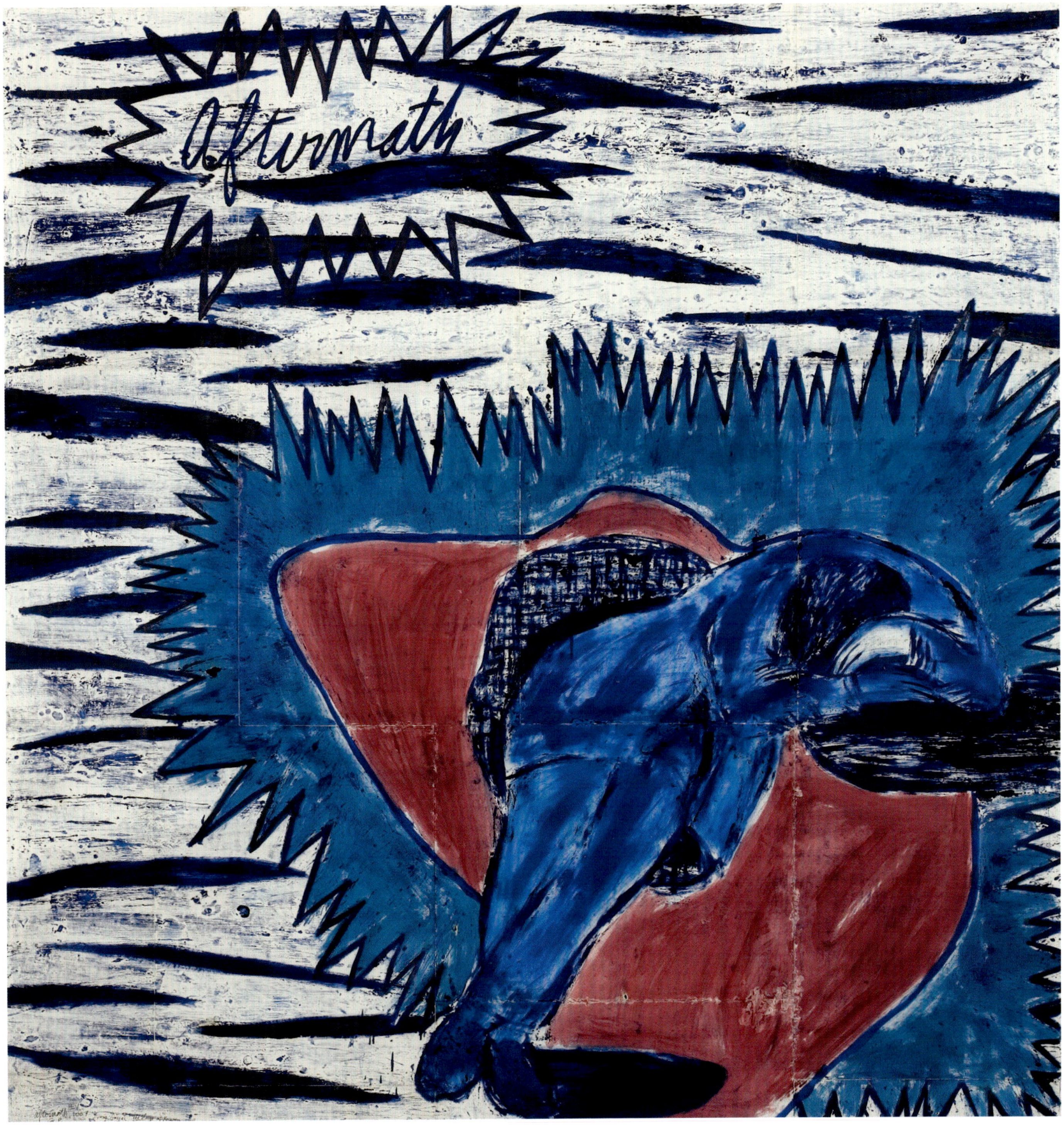


*Aftermath*, 2007

A man about twenty years old is standing at a traffic intersection crosswalk. He is dressed in dirty work clothes. In one of his rear pockets is a crescent wrench, in the other pocket a ball cap. His right hand is placed at the walk signal button. One of his fingers repeatedly massages the concave surface of the button. For the most part he restricts the finger action to the button itself, but at times he rubs the palm of his hand over the entire signal mechanism.

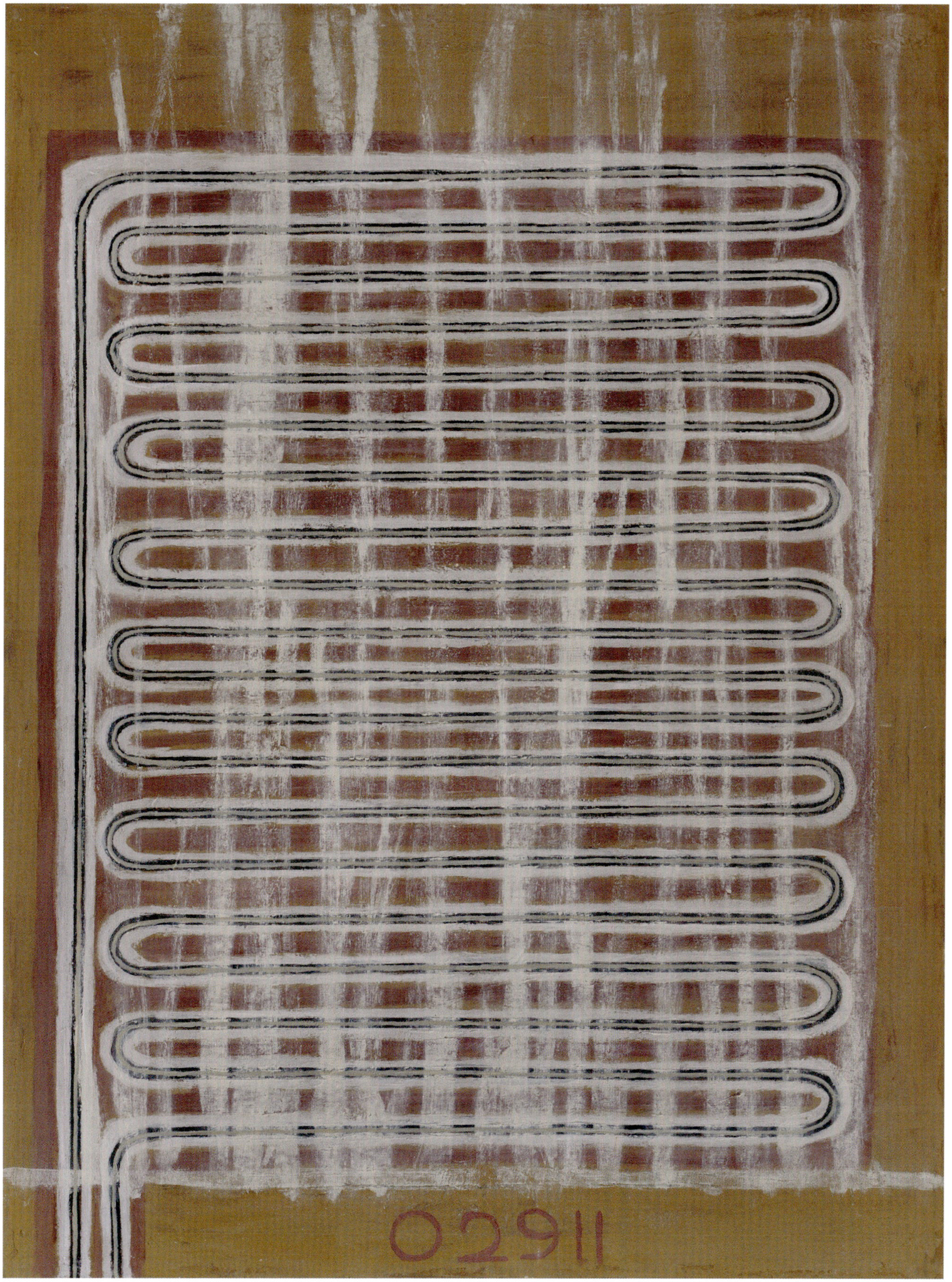




*02911*, 1991

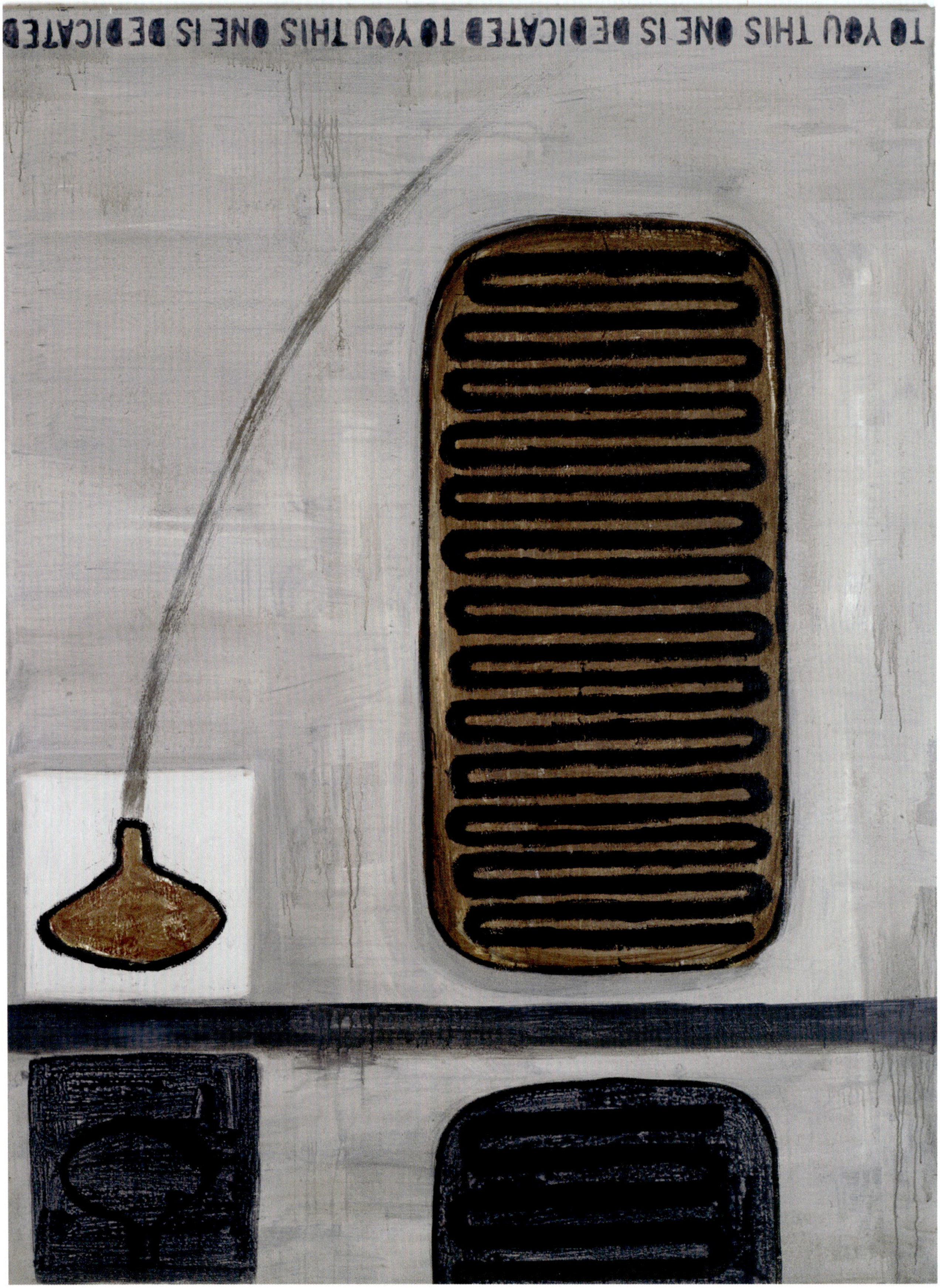


*This One Is Dedicated To You*, 1990

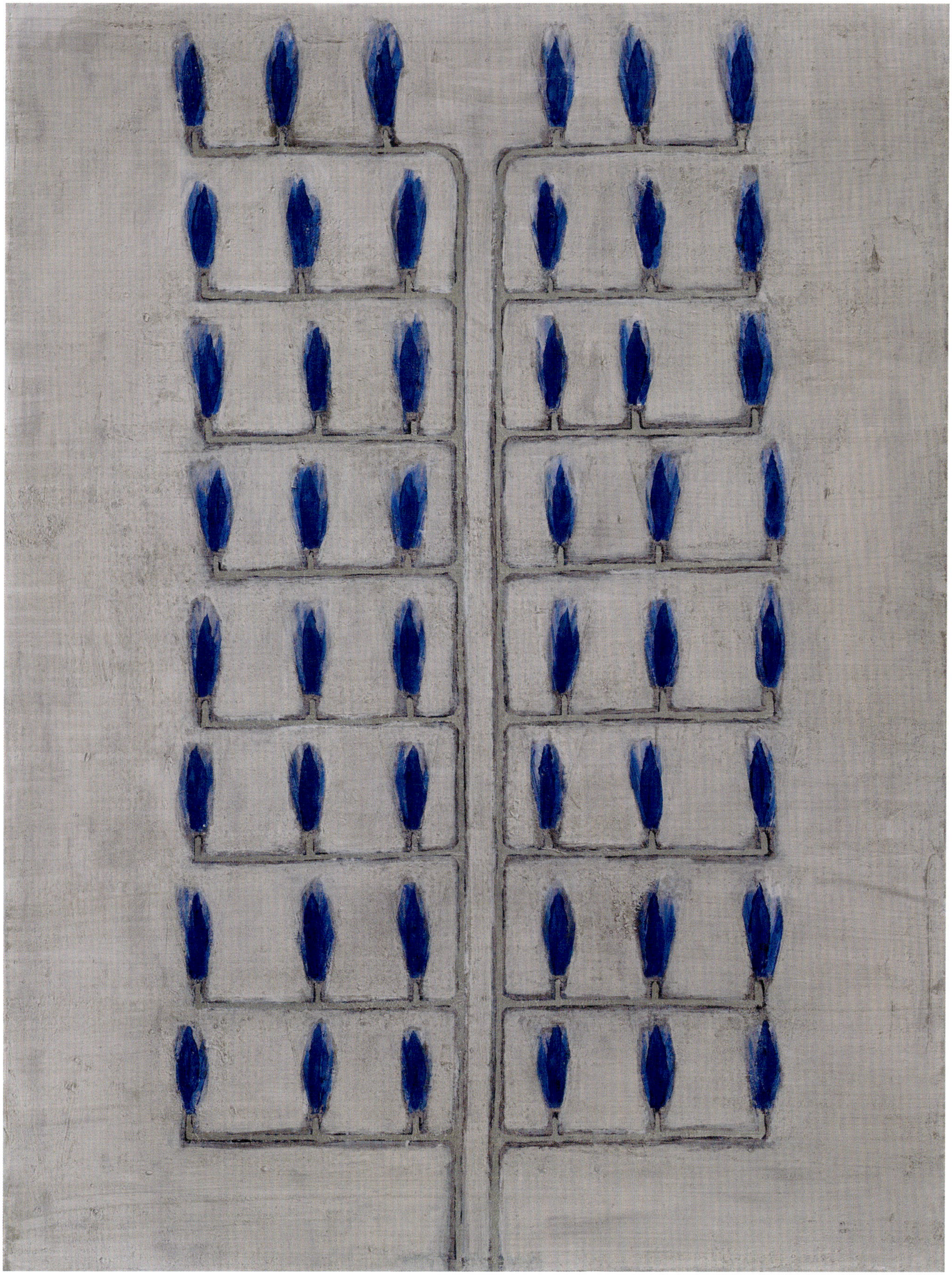

*Forty-Eight Blue Flames*, 1991

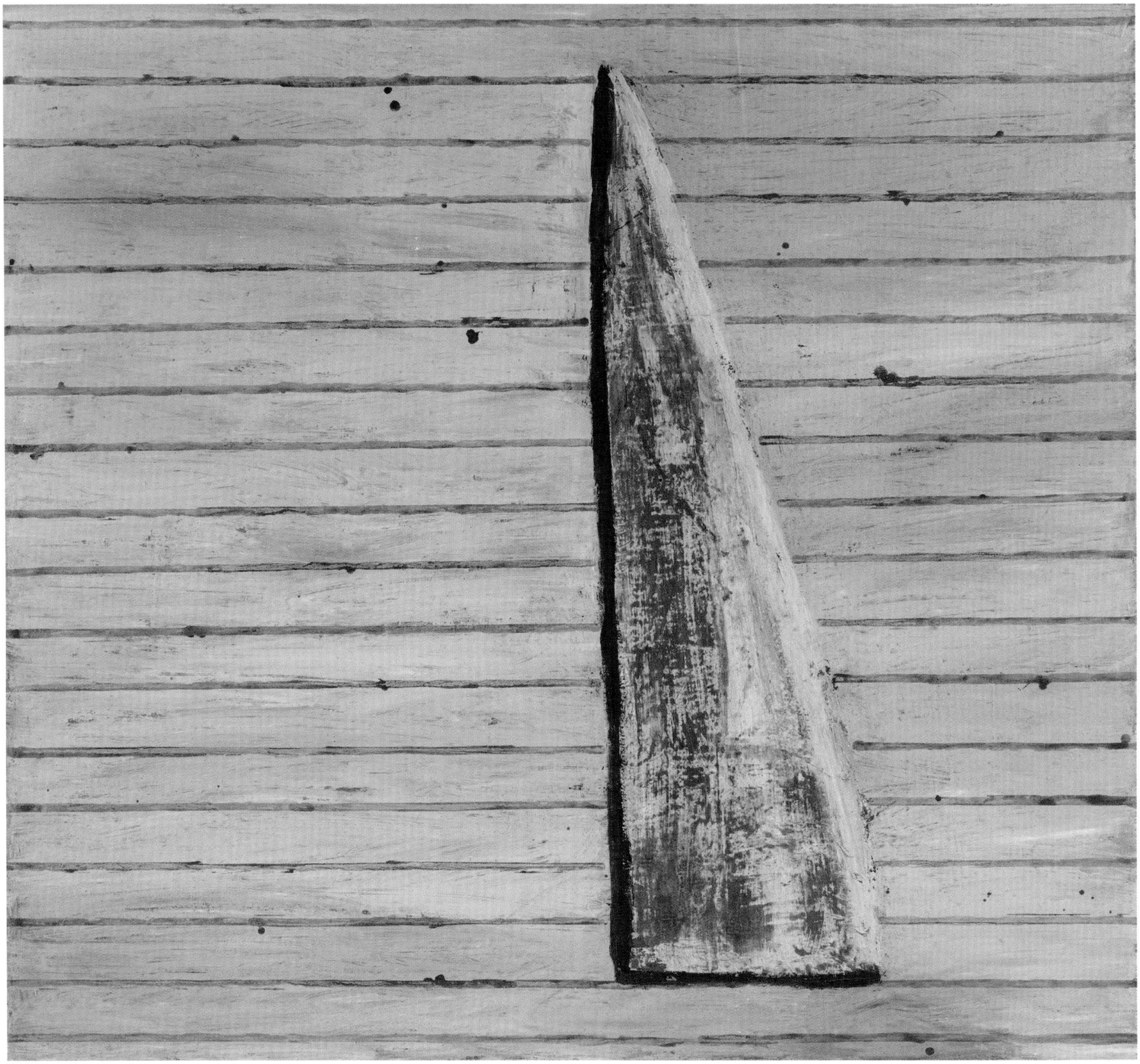



*Untitled*, 1992

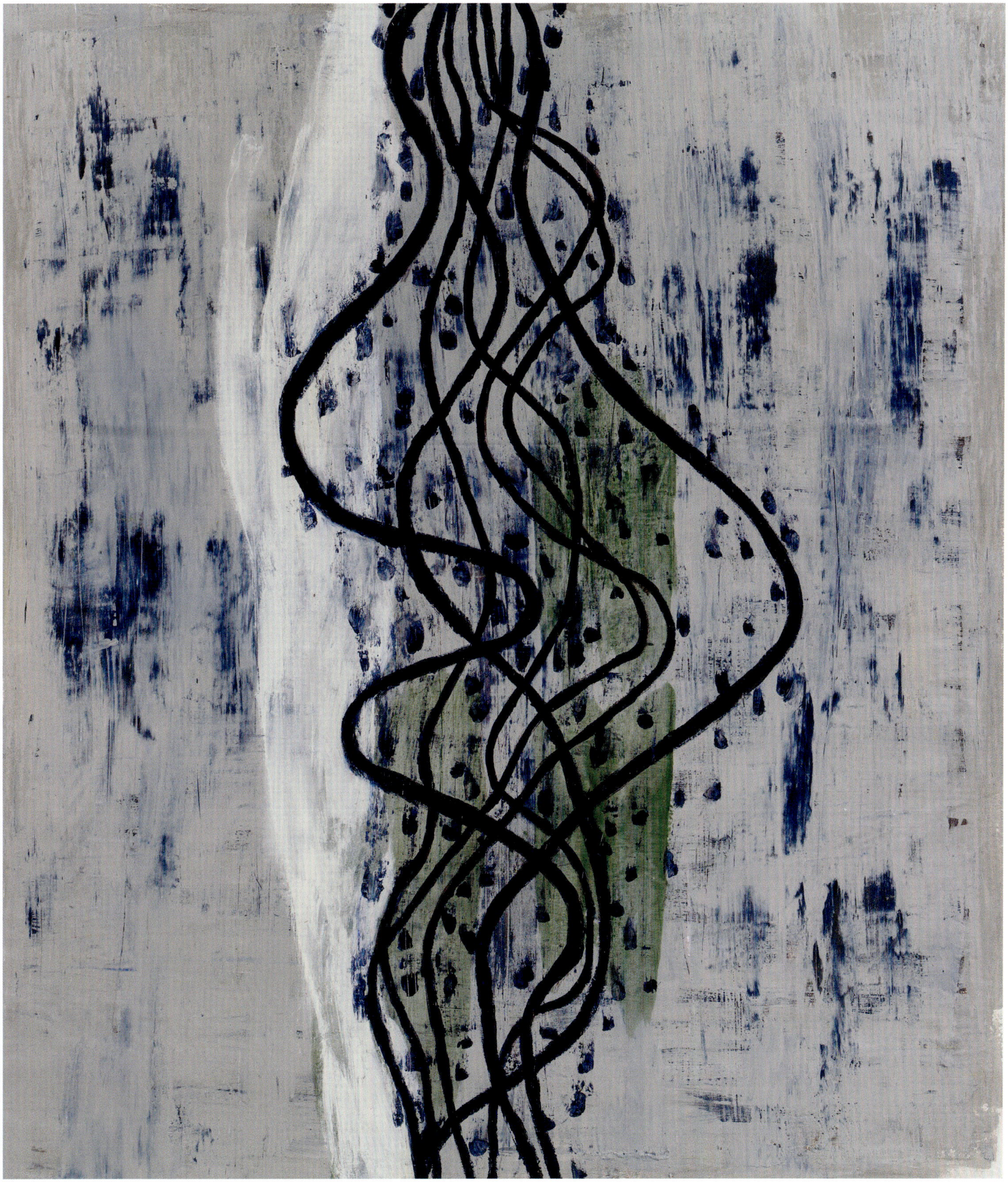

*Untitled*, 1992–1993

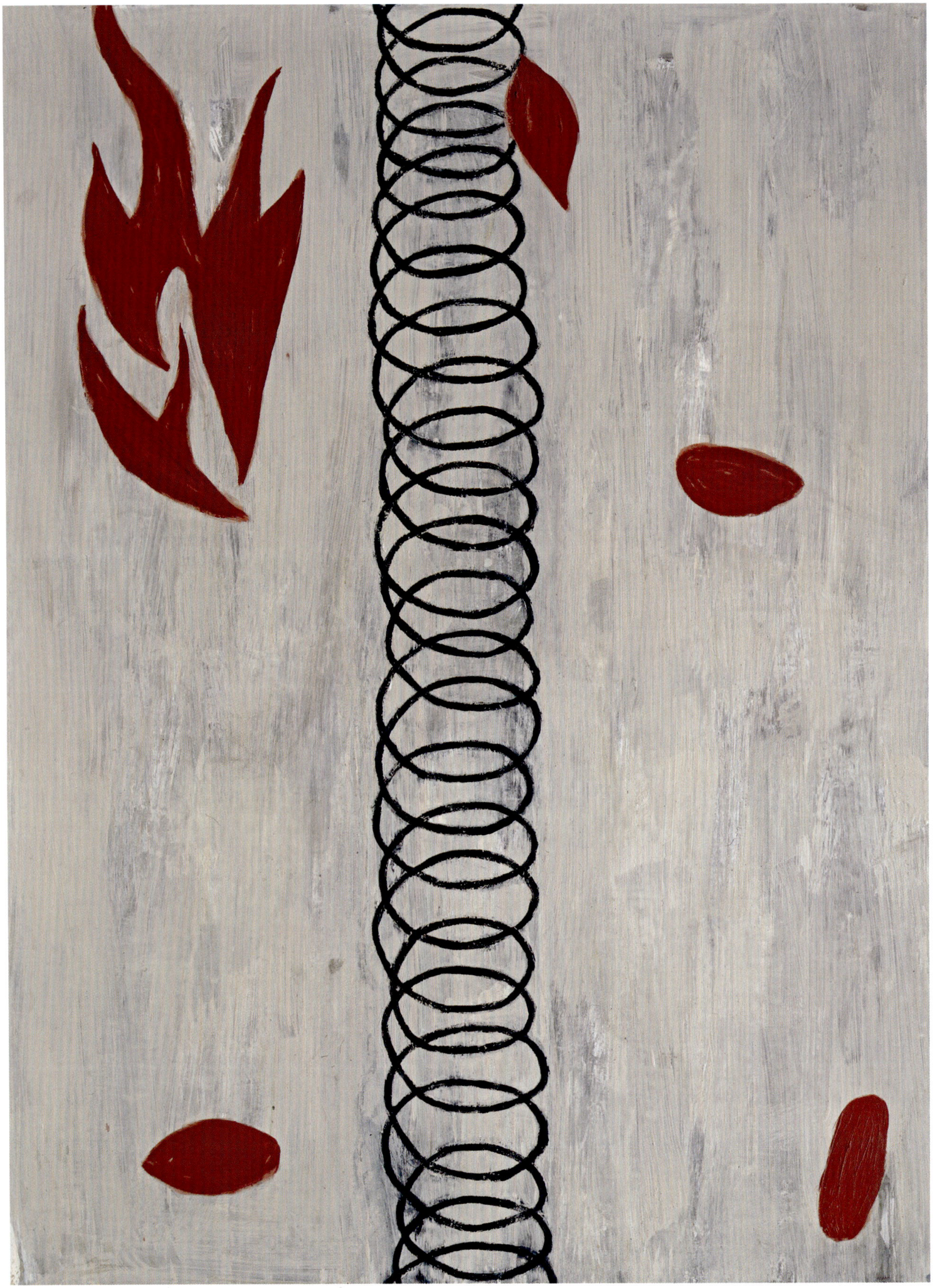



*Zündergeben*, 1994

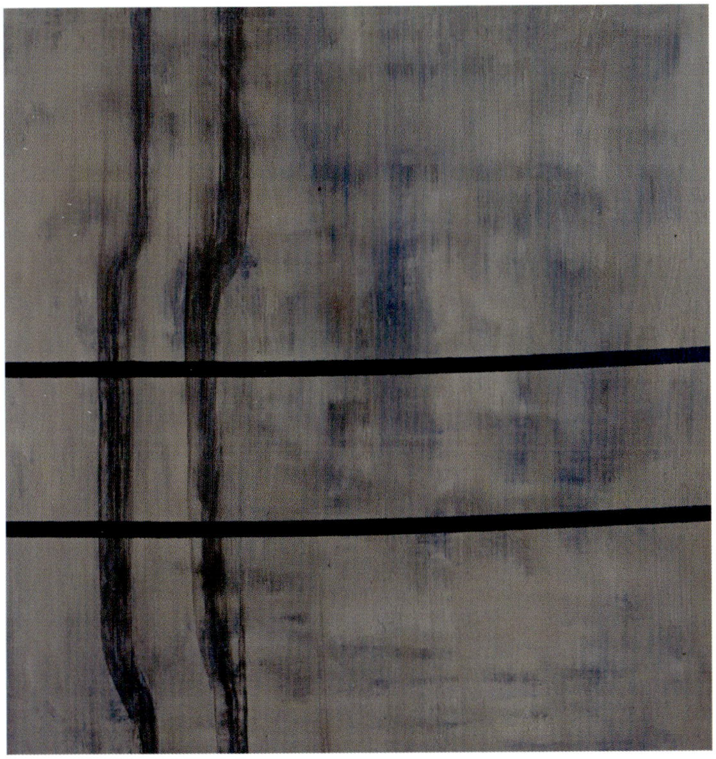

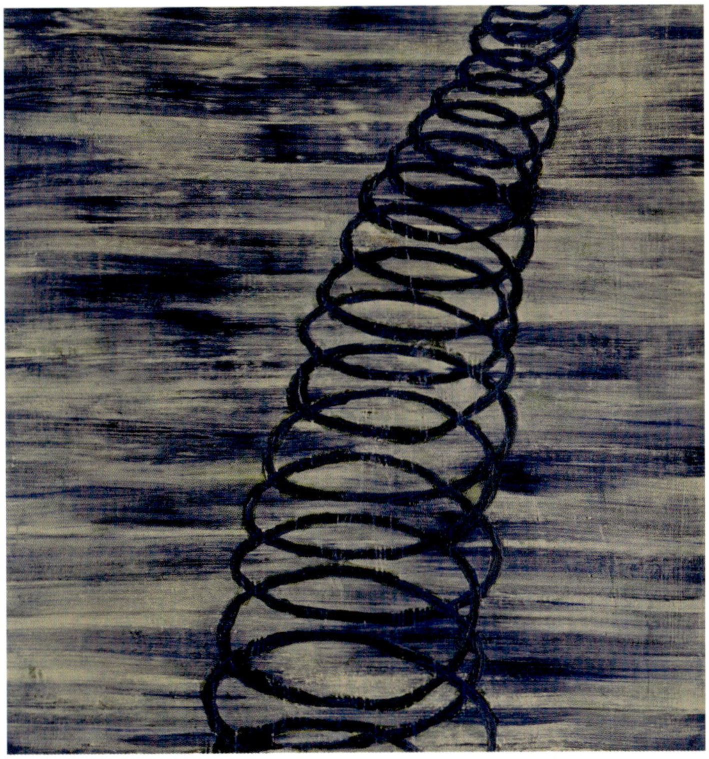

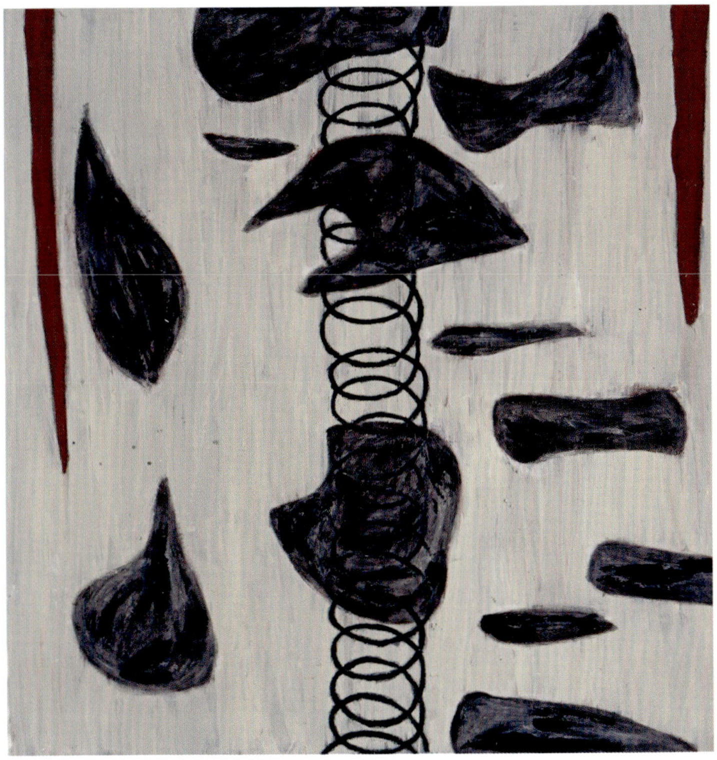

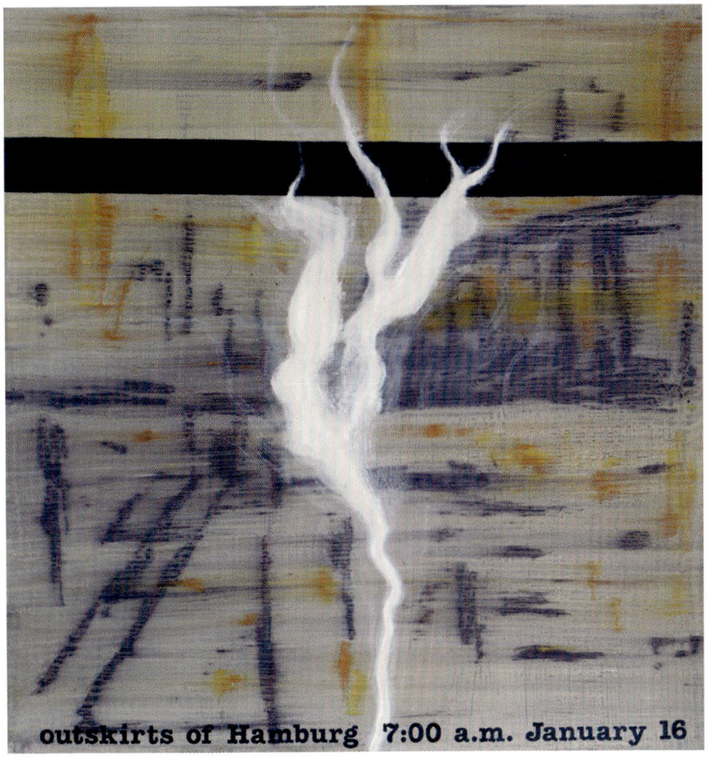



*Landscape Between Poznan and Kutno*, 1993
*Night Sky over Poznan*, 1993
*Ashes*, 1994–1995
*Hamburg*, 1994–1995

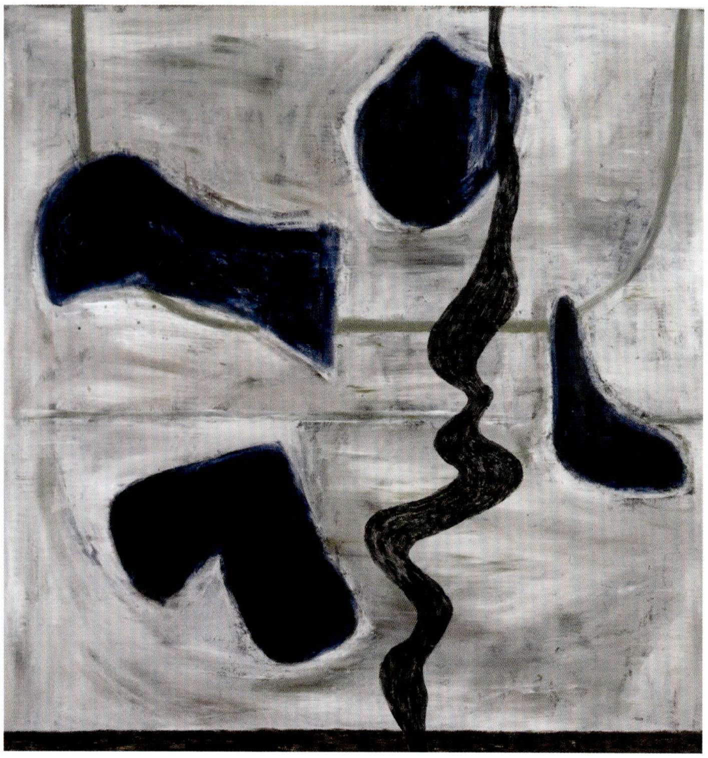

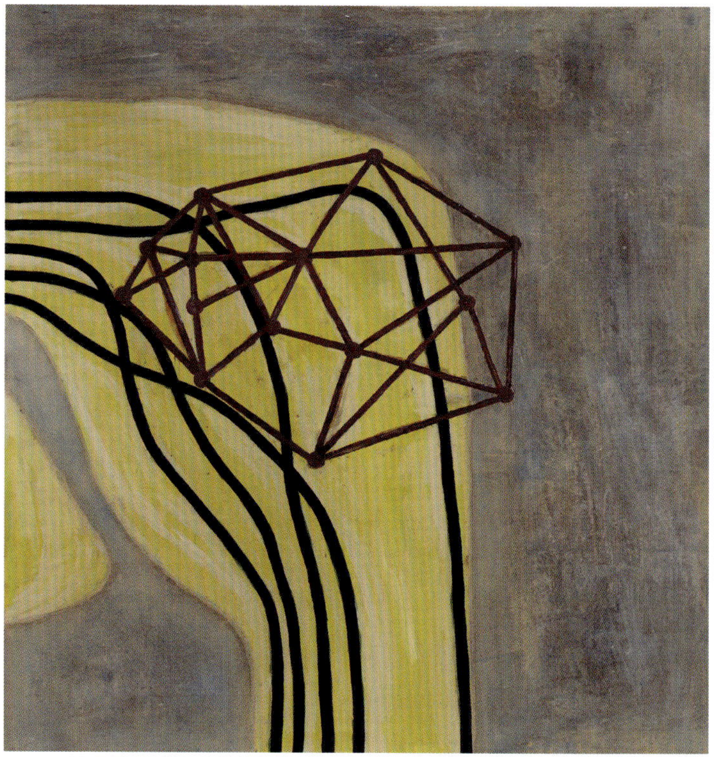

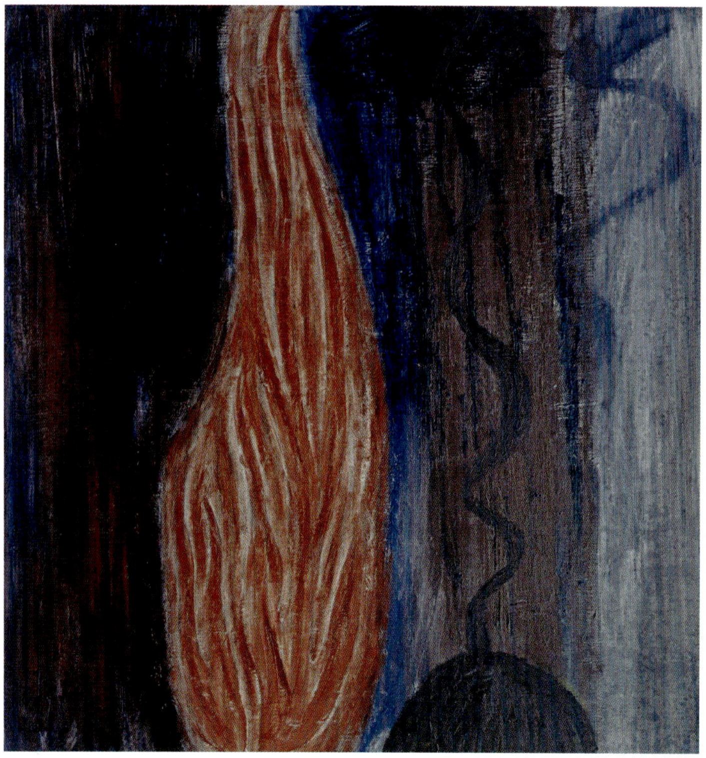

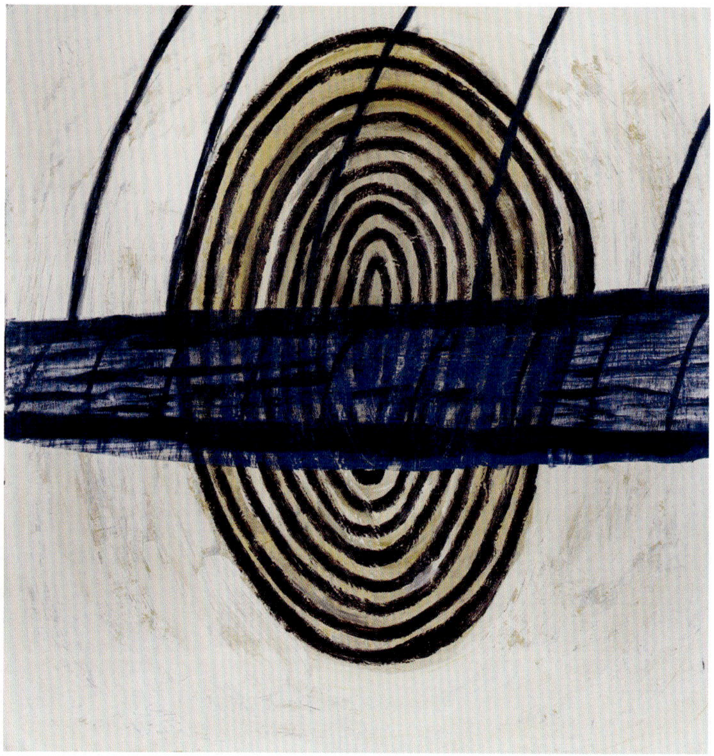

*Conversation*, 1994–1995
*Untitled*, 1994–1995
*Victim of Anonymity*, 1994–1995
*Untitled*, 1995

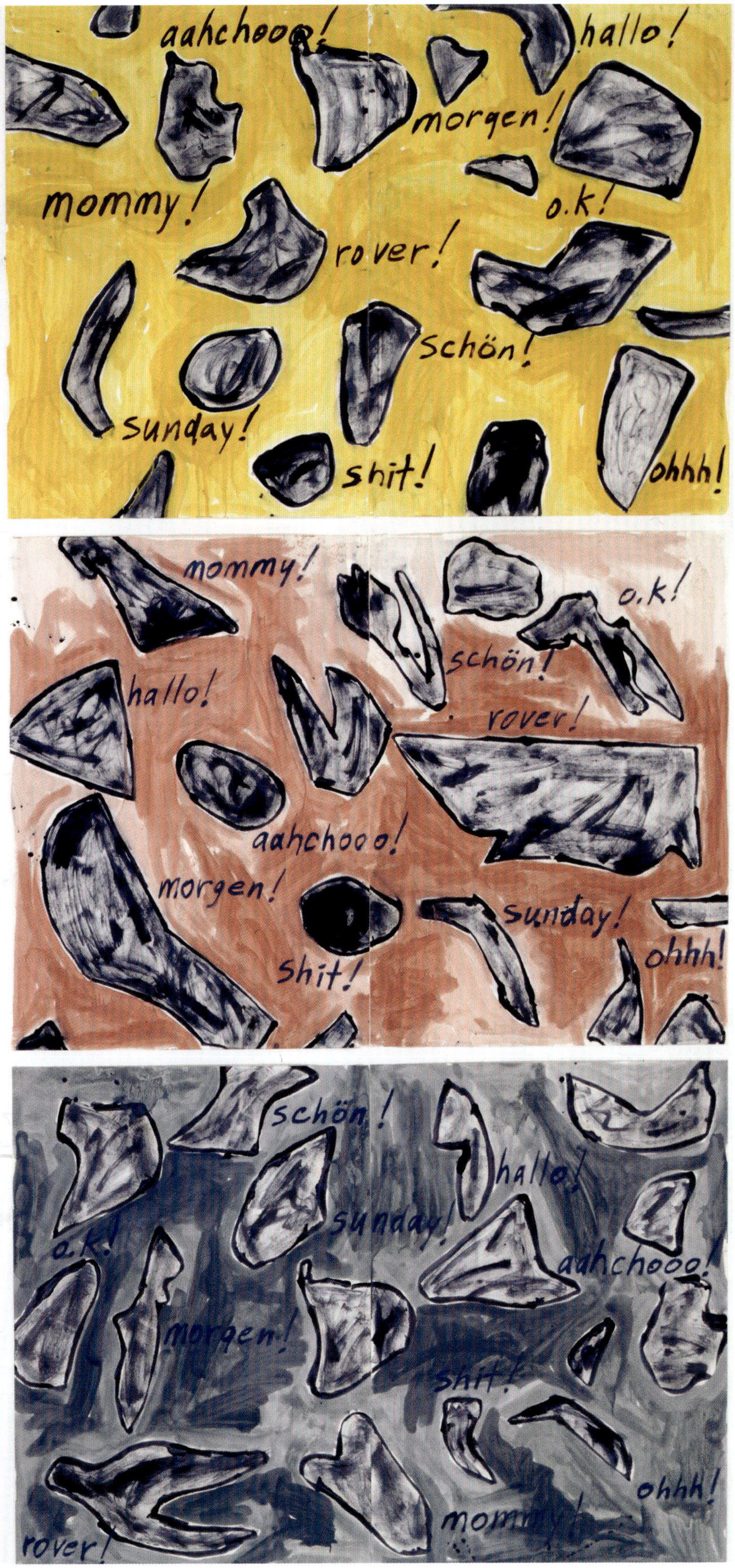


*Heinrichplatz in Berlin Kreuzberg, April 17, 1998*, 1998

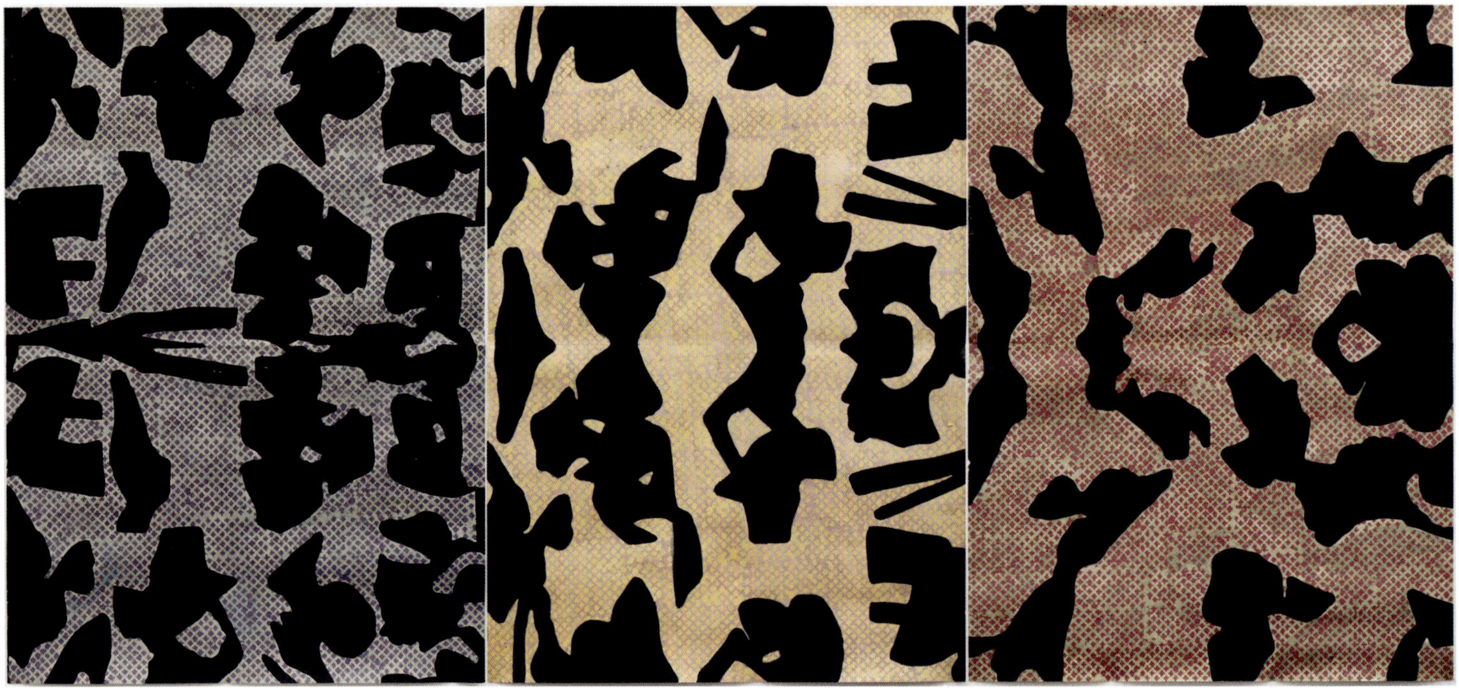



*Two of Everything*, 1998

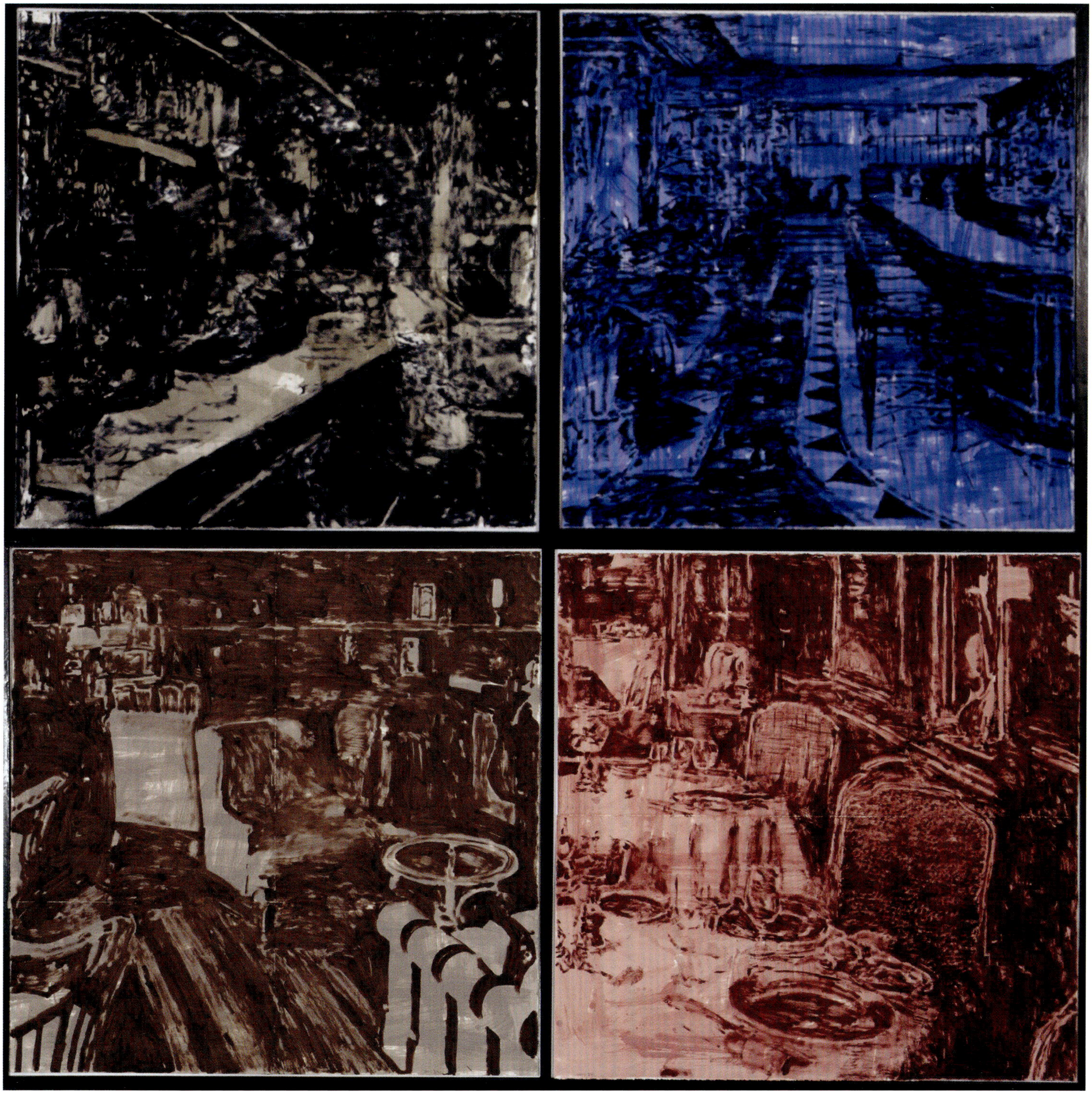

*After Hours*, 2000

I stopped in every little honky tonk along the highway and asked the bartender if I could bring my old guitar in. They said sure and I put my case out and at the end of the night I'd had all the beers I could drink, money for a motel, and gas to get me to the next town.

Once in a while I'd ask some pretty little blonde if she'd like to sing a song, and you wouldn't believe it but some of them could yodel and sing traditional songs from the 40s and 50s like *Honky Tonk Angel*.

There's a lot of talent out there.

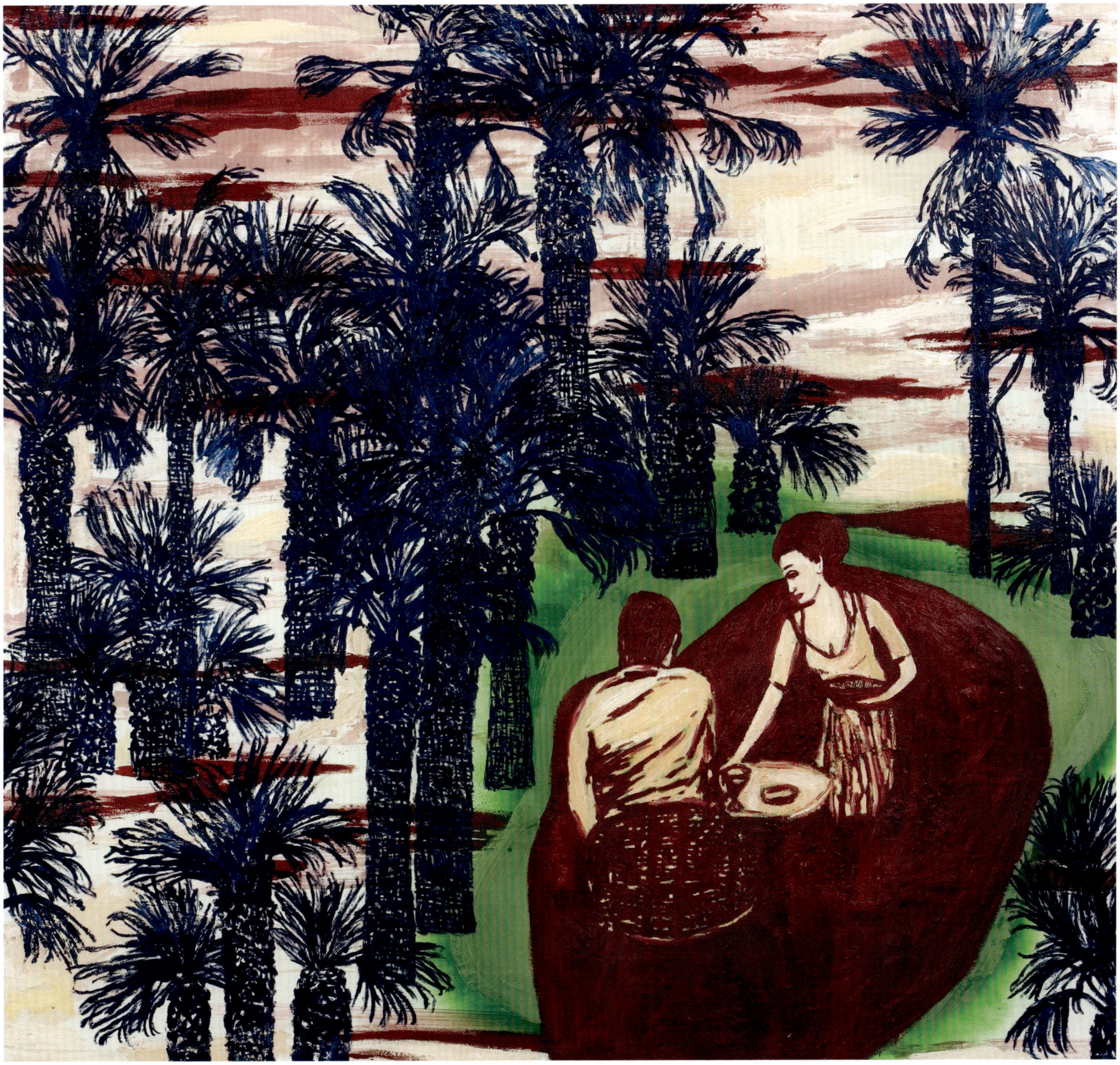



*Under The Blue Palms*, 2005

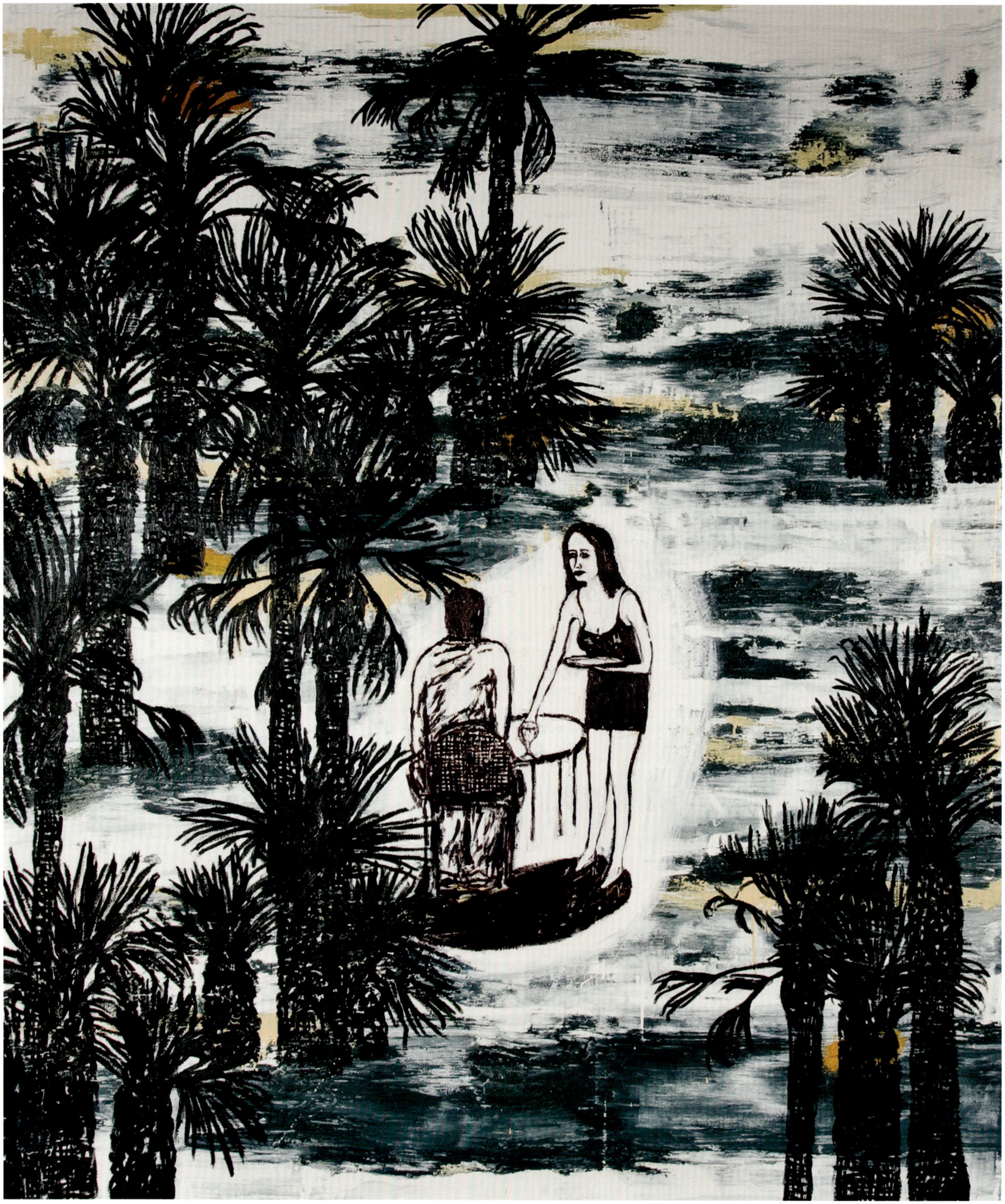



*When I Get To Baton Rouge*, 2005

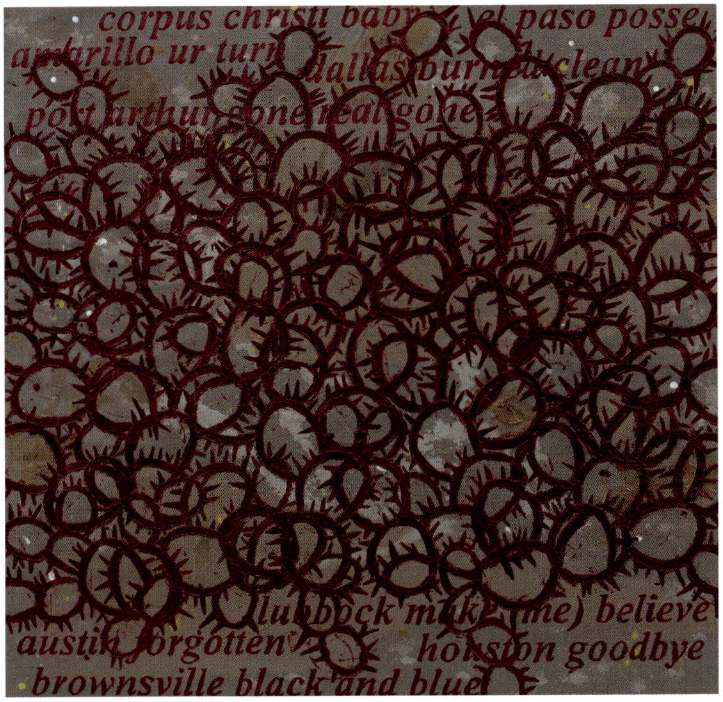


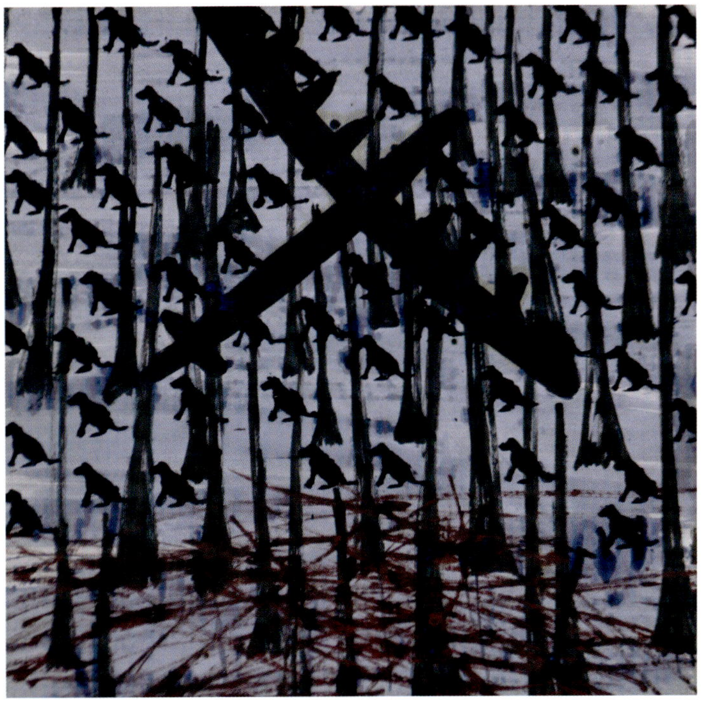

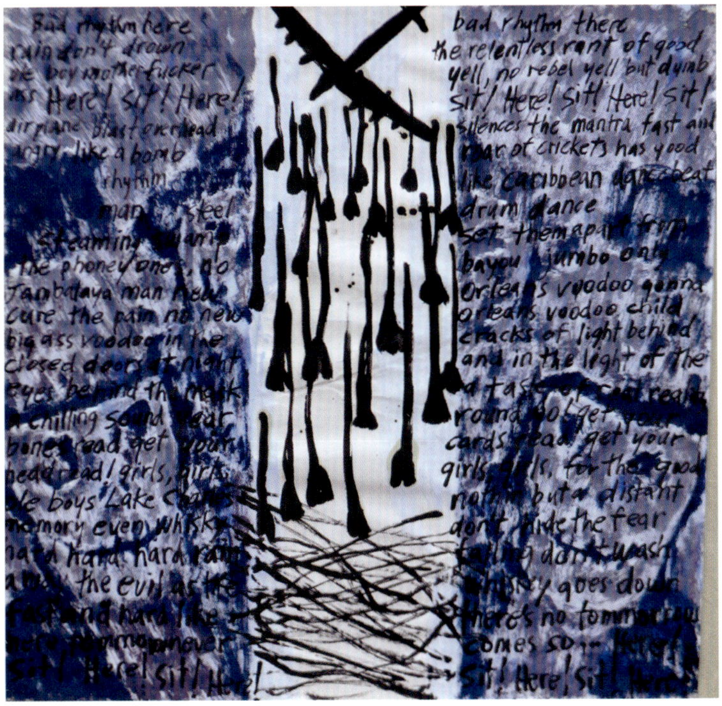


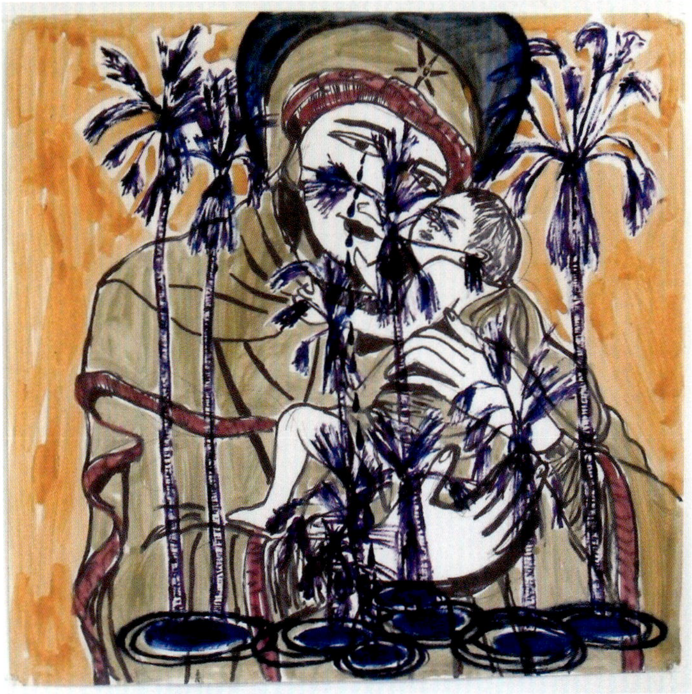

*Texas Tattoo*, 2004
*Here Sit (study)*, 2004
*Bad Rhythm Here*, 2004
*Yuma, AR*, 2004

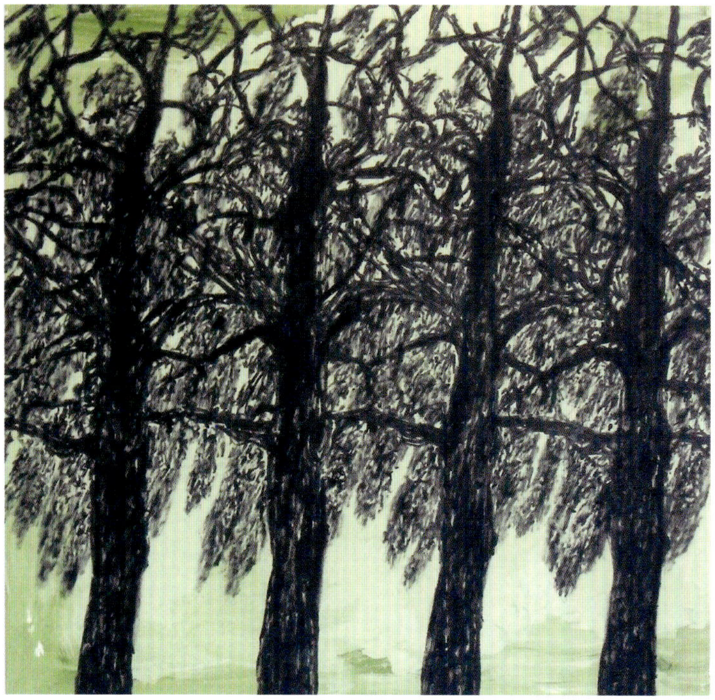

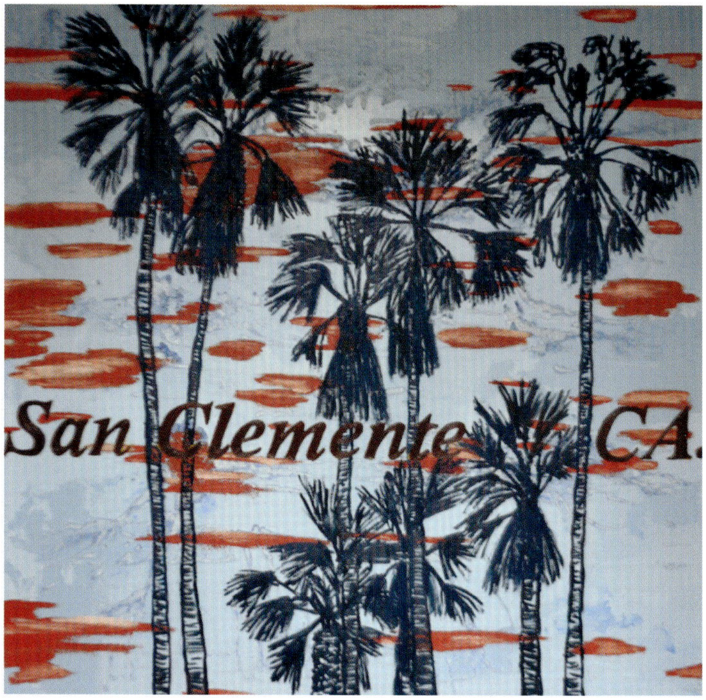


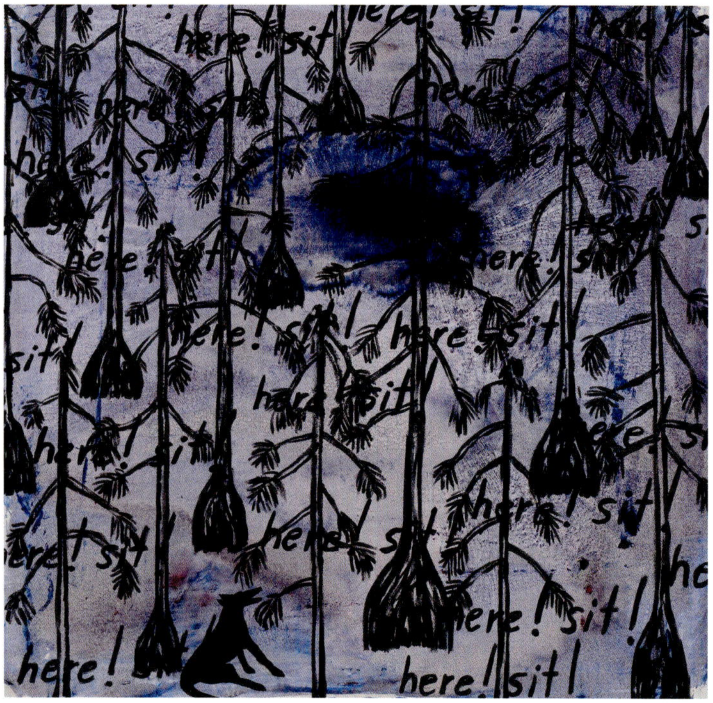


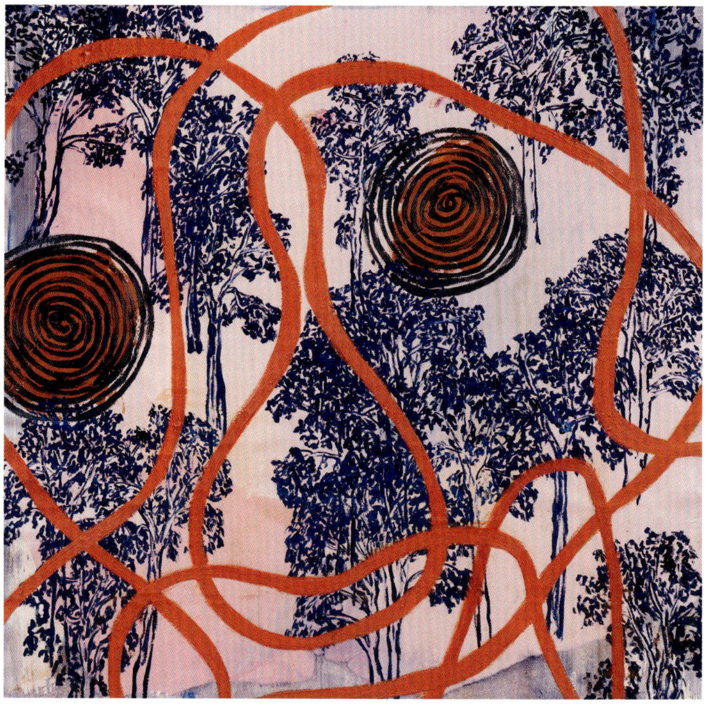

*Savannah, GA*, 2004
*San Clemente, CA*, 2004
*Near Lake Charles, LA*, 2004
*Eucalyptus Trees, CA*, 2004

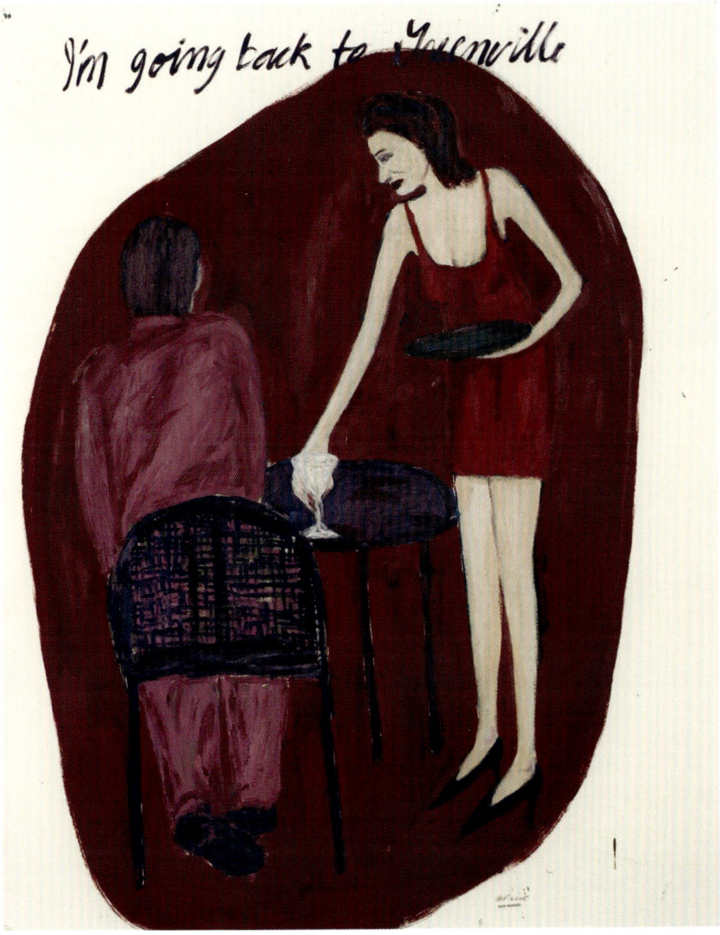


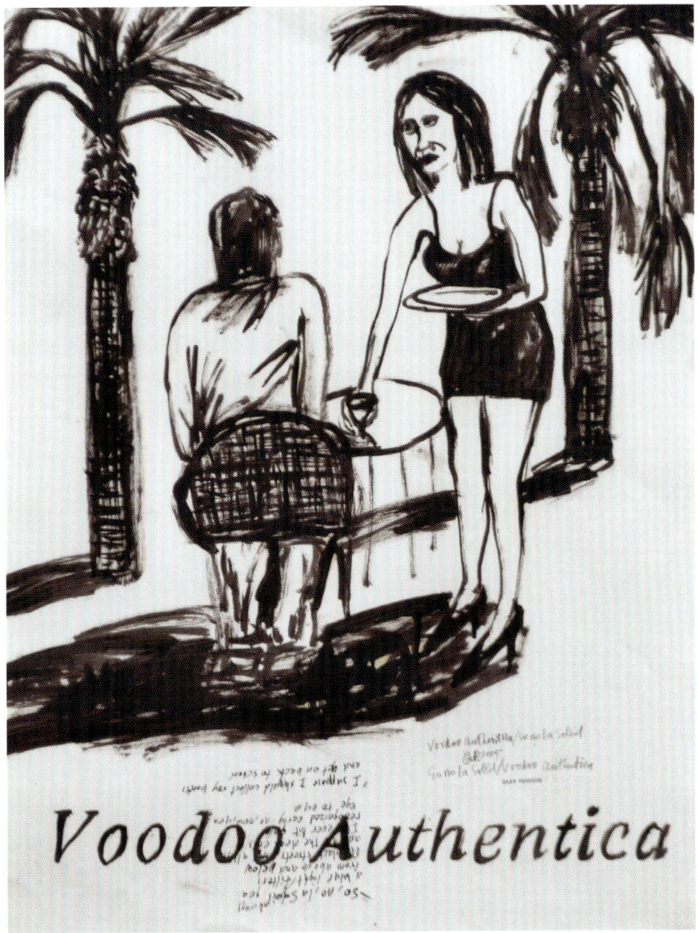


*I'm Going Back To Greenville*, 2005
*Voodoo Authentica*, 2005

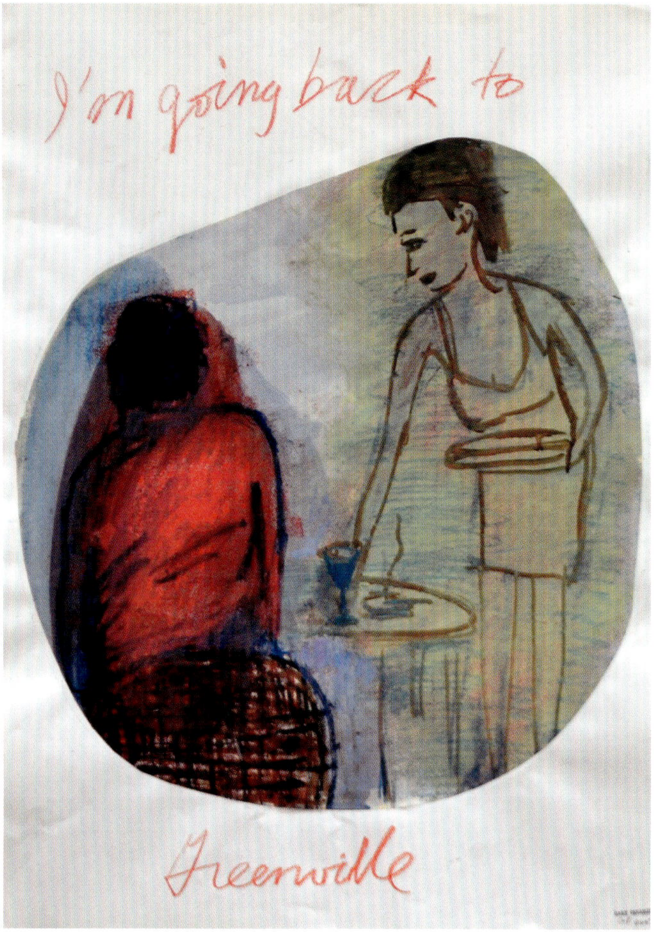


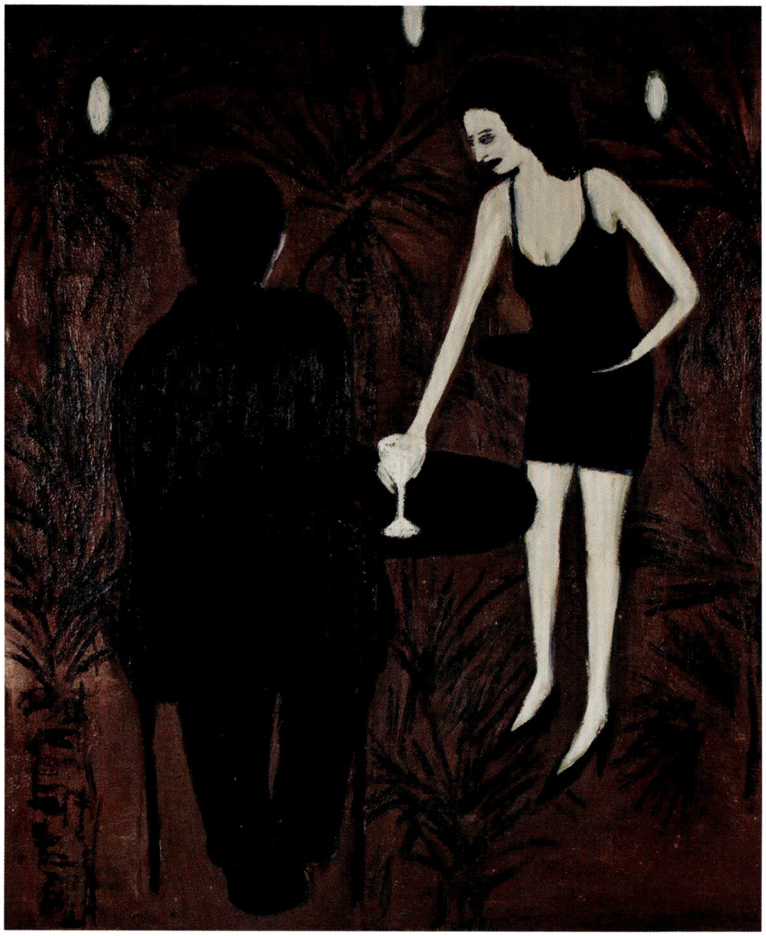

*I'm Going Back to Greenville*, 2005
*I'm Going Back to Greenville*, 2005

Three young women are sitting in a trendy bar. They are all drinking cocktails, but only one of the women seems to be talking. The other two are nodding their heads and laughing. The woman who does all the talking has dark hair, long and straight.

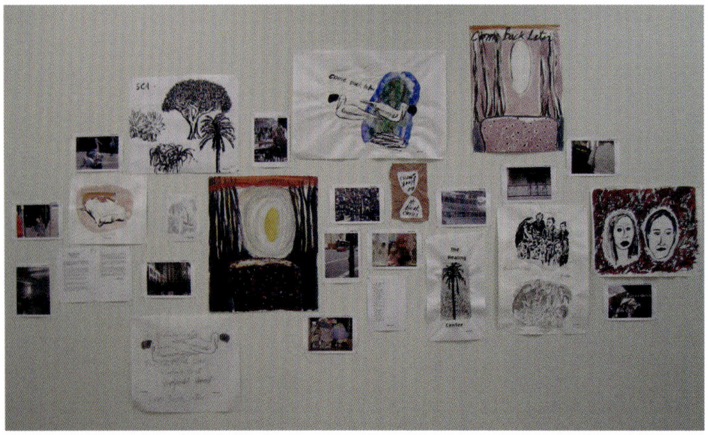

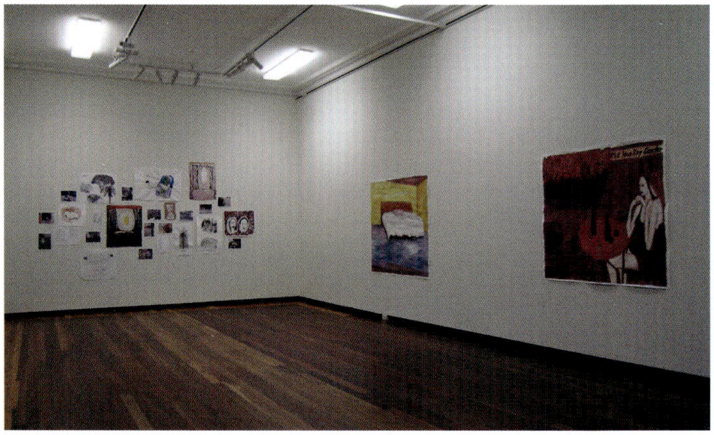

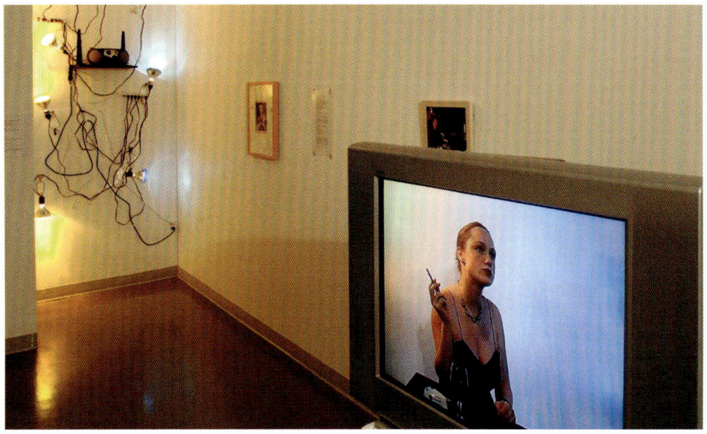

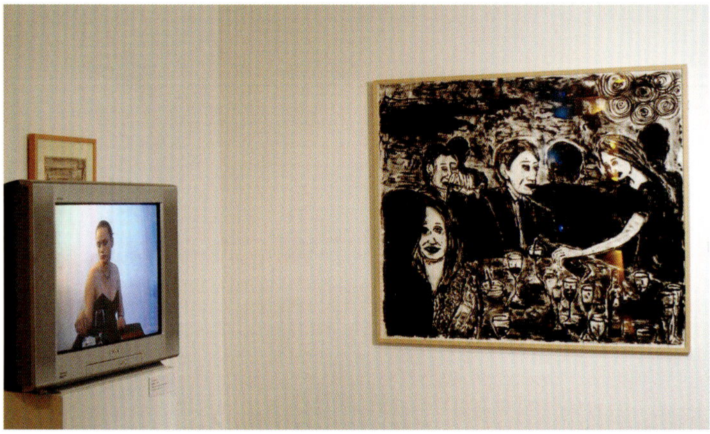

Installation views: Oblique Stories, 2005, SCA Gallery, Sydney College of the Arts, University of Sydney, Australia. Photograph by Kate Major.

Installation views: High Early, 2006, Art Gallery of Greater Victoria, BC.

## Conversation between Gary Pearson and Ihor Holubizky

The following conversation took place by correspondence between curator-historian Ihor Holubizky and artist Gary Pearson in early 2017. In the context of wide-ranging and ambulatory dialogues on topics of mutual interest that have gone on for the past 16 years in Kelowna, BC, Brisbane, Australia, Hamilton, ON and Edmonton, AB, one thing leads to another, moving back and forth.

**Gary Pearson**

I recently premiered my latest video, titled *The Cocktail Bar (4 Vignettes)*. It is the fifth in a loosely defined group that are tied to a bar/restaurant social setting and subject. The others are *Berlin Jazz Story*, 2000, *Soliloquy*, 2006, *Soliloquy2*, 2008, and *The Waiter Joke*, 2011. I'll show all five in the Kelowna Art Gallery exhibition in 2018.

**Ihor Holubizky**

Let's jump into that terrain—video work 'by a painter' that is not (or is it?) 'video art' per se, but informed by? In turn, what ideas inform your paintings—and do you make a distinction between paintings (medium on canvas) and painted drawings?

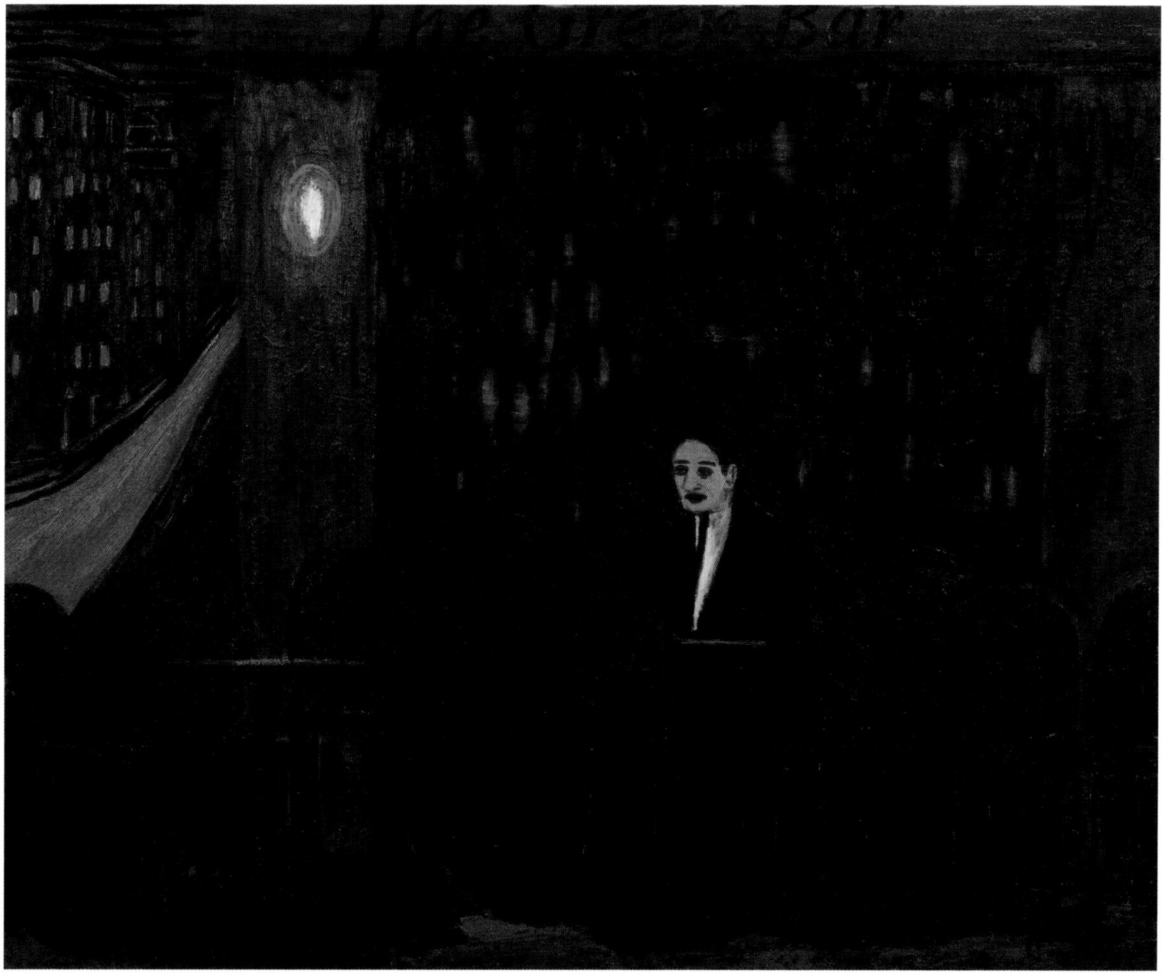



*The Green Bar*, 2007

**GP**

I would say that video art is video made by an artist. Or specifically—to paraphrase Marcel Duchamp—for a video to be designated as a work of art, it would require the author of the work to be an artist, or to have designated him or herself an artist. A problem might lie with the audience and preconceptions about what 'video art' is or what it looks like.

My videos are produced 'by a painter', but since 1996 I've only produced 12 videos. *The Cocktail Bar (4 Vignettes)* will be the thirteenth, excluding documentaries. Had I only produced 13 paintings over 20 years, we probably wouldn't be having this conversation. So I'm a painter in the first place, and my videos are definitely informed by the ideas that inform my paintings.

I've recycled a lot of images over my career. One is a photograph that the mother of a friend of mine in Germany gave to me in 1975. I have used it as a source and re-worked it as a motif in painting and drawing a number of times. The photograph is by an unknown photographer and is of an unknown couple sitting in an unknown bar or restaurant in an unknown city at an unknown time. However, I suspect the photograph was taken in Germany in the 1920s or 1930s, or maybe the 1950s.

The image has clearly had an impact on me and even haunted me for over 40 years. I could probably draw it blindfolded. They're a very attractive couple who appear to have carved out a remarkable, even enviable, space of their own in that—however transitory—place and time.

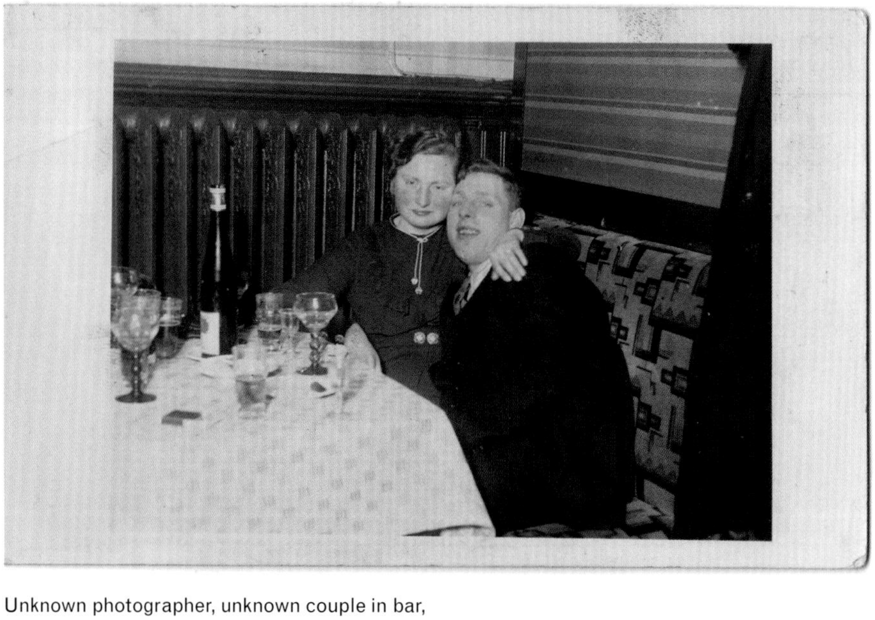

Unknown photographer, unknown couple in bar, undated, black-and-white photograph, 9 × 14 cm. Courtesy of the artist.

The ideas that inform my paintings come both from visual source material and direct experiences, as well as verbal expressions or statements and even songs. To give one example, the painting *The Incident at the Guadalupe Bar*, 2011, is based on some written observations I made while sitting in a restaurant in Mexico.

My *Greenville* series was in part inspired by the lyrics of Lucinda Williams. I act upon these sources, and they trigger plot lines for lack of a better description. The Penguin reference guide *Dictionary of Literary Terms & Literary Theory* defines 'plot' as character development and organization of incident (to induce curiosity and suspense). In the space/time continuum of plot the continual question operates in three tenses: Why did that happen? Why is this happening? What is going to happen next—and why? (To which may be added: is *anything* going to happen?).[1]

If you look at the photograph of the couple in the bar/restaurant, all of these questions can come into play. This is a natural product of representation in visual art or in the literary and performing arts. The suspense surrounding the question "Is anything going to happen?" is especially important to me.

In answer to your other question related to making a distinction between paintings and painted drawings, I find the canvas works far more challenging in the resolution of composition. Typically, my canvasses are large (part of the difference and challenge), yet I've always self-identified as a draughtsperson first. I've been drawing all my life so I'm not intimidated by it in any way, whereas with painting, in spite of the years I've been at it, I still experience a level of uncertainty each time I start a new canvas. That in itself makes it a challenge worth taking on.

**IH**

Your thoughts about the traffic between video work and your 'not-video' work brings to mind an Edvard Munch comment about photography: "The camera cannot compete with painting as long as it cannot be used in Heaven and Hell."[2] Munch used his camera work as a source, but not necessarily to replicate and/or illustrate.

**GP**

Munch's paintings appear to have been partially influenced by his own photograph of Rosa Meissner. Munch also occupied a unique position in the origins of Modern art. Widely considered the father of Expressionism, Munch was also influenced by Symbolism, so it was the latter personality, the symbolist one, which would have been responsible for his metaphor for painting.

The days of painting competing with photography (at least in the historical sense) are over. Not many artists today are producing sketches at the pace of Edgar Degas, for example. Instead, many painters rely heavily on photographs for the information that sketches from life used to provide. Working from a photograph constantly reminds you that you are engaged with an interpretation and translation of the photograph so that, unlike working with sketches, you are more consciously compelled to create your departures from the photograph in the art and craft of painting or drawing from the photographic source. Unless you're what I call a copy artist, that is an artist intent on mimesis for its own sake only, or a photo-realist, which would mean that your primary challenge would be the technical crafting of the mimetic subject in a non-photographic medium. Granted, as in the relationship between the Munch painting and his photograph of Rosa Meissner, the elements of composition may also be changed regardless of your stylistic approach.

In my case the relationship between painting and photography can also be illustrated by my painting *Girl and Dog*, 2014, which is based on a photograph I shot in Leeuwarden in the Friesland state of the Netherlands in 2013.

The cafe-bar sign comes from another photograph I took, also in Leeuwarden. Upon seeing this street scene I knew immediately that it was something I wanted to paint. I asked the young woman if I could take the photograph and happily she consented. I changed the colour

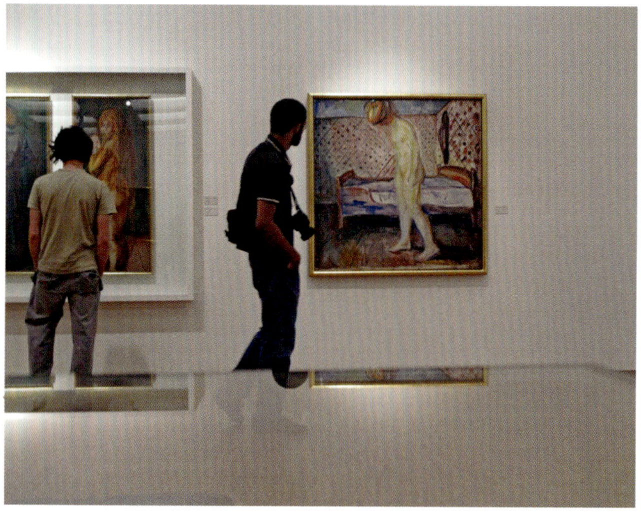

Installation view with painting of Rosa Meissner, 2010, Munch Museum, Oslo. Photograph by Ihor Holubizky.

and light quite a bit from the photograph, and modified the appearance of the street to create more drama.

First and foremost, I'm interested in the composition and the possibilities of a story line—something that grabs me in a scene or a figure grouping that I'm able to verbalize. It is from that point that I begin to translate what I've seen, heard or captured in a photograph into a painting, or a video, or text works such as my *Short Fictions*. Another example is the spoken parts in my video *The Cocktail Bar (4 Vignettes)*, which are all drawn from my *Short Fictions* series. In tandem with these lines I attempted to cast actors who supported the verbal characterizations. And as in my *The Waiter Joke* video, the actors (all of whom were non-professional) function in a greater or lesser way as caricatures. Similarly, the actors in *Soliloquy* and *Soliloquy2*, while less caricatured in the conventional sense, represent the subject type and plot line. In that sense there is a close relationship among my canvasses and drawings, my videos and my short text pieces.

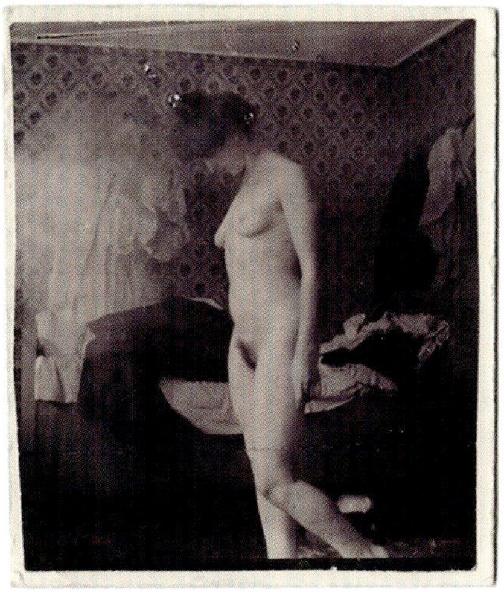

Edvard Munch, photograph of Rosa Meissner, circa 1907.

**IH**

Back to Munch. His photograph of Rosa Meissner seems more interesting to me than his painting of her, but Munch painted at least four versions of the image between 1907 and 1909, and he did a lithograph of the subject in 1930. Yet each is different enough. So this one photograph fed his imagination enough to return to it—if not to 'achieve' the photograph, but what it offered.

On the other hand, I would say that your painting *Girl and Dog* is more interesting than its source photograph, even if the 'alterations' are somewhat 'minor'—or as you say, to create more drama... but still not to switch the scene from a 'come across' to a dramatic scene. As I might in a moment jump to a Beckett 'question'.

The Munch paintings are all (I think?) titled *Weeping Woman*. Curious. I don't see any weeping in the photograph—nor does it lead me to 'think weeping'—whereas your *Girl and Dog* has no ambiguity. Had you titled it *Girl Weeping over Dog*, then drama-emotion could not be ignored. (That's not a question, but an observation, but may be a question about your titles?)

You spoke of interest "in the composition and possibilities of a story line" from something captured or grabbed, and with respect to plot: "is *anything* going to happen?" It brings to mind Susan Sontag's commentary on Samuel Beckett and his contribution to the realisms of the nineteenth century. Referring to *Waiting for Godot* in her 1977 essay "On Art and Consciousness", she wrote:

> Normally people on the stage reflect on the macrostructure of action. What am I going to do this year? Tomorrow? Tonight? They ask: Am I going mad? Will I ever get to Moscow? Should I leave my husband? Do I have to murder my uncle? My mother? These are the sorts of large projects which have traditionally concerned a play's leading characters. Beckett is the first writer to dramatize

the microstructure of the action. What am I going to do one minute from now? In the next second? Weep? Take out my comb? Stand up? Sigh? Sit? Be silent? Tell a joke? Understand something?[3]

We don't often think of Beckett as a 'jokester', yet *Waiting for Godot* has funny—absurd and discursive—passages... where 'nothing happens'. What are your Beckett thoughts with respect to your text and enactment works?

And then your thought about the microstructure with respect to your *Ashtray* monoprints: the cigarette itself is 'seen smoking', yet not needing to see or know the smoker, nor 'about' the consumption of the

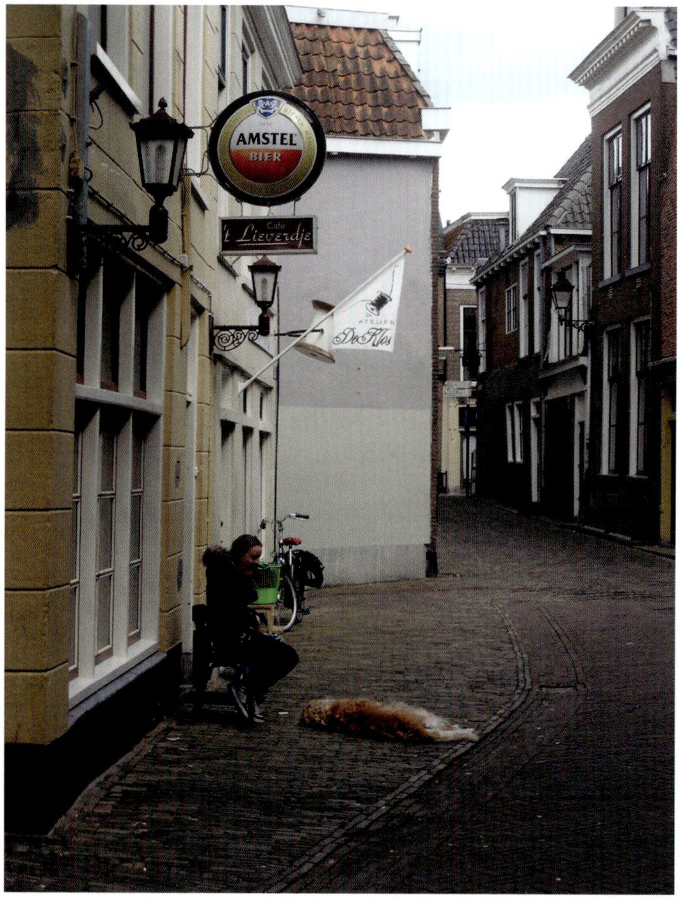


Leeuwarden, the Netherlands, 2013.
Photograph by Gary Pearson.

cigarette either. Neither dramatic, nor a portent. Yet not necessarily a 'quiddity'—the is-what-it-is. Can this be reflected on in a Beckettian way?

**GP**

When you're watching a film or reading a book you are conscious of all the supportive and peripheral activities and visual information in a shot or scene, and are calculating their contribution to the narrative—you're reading everything. Which is to say that you assume the information, whether primary or secondary, macro or micro, is all part of what you should be following to fully grasp the meaning of the narrative. Let's say a crow landing on a tree branch, leaves blowing across the street, a man in the hotel lobby reading a newspaper, a tipped over garbage can. The artist Jeff Wall said, "Seeing something where you might expect not to see anything worth looking at is a sort of gift that art gives us."[4]

Audience response, that is, how the audience responds or reads the work, is largely in the hands of a film's director; how the story is told stylistically, and in an either 'readerly' or 'writerly' voice. How you watch a Hitchcock film is different than how you watch a film by Jean-Luc Godard.

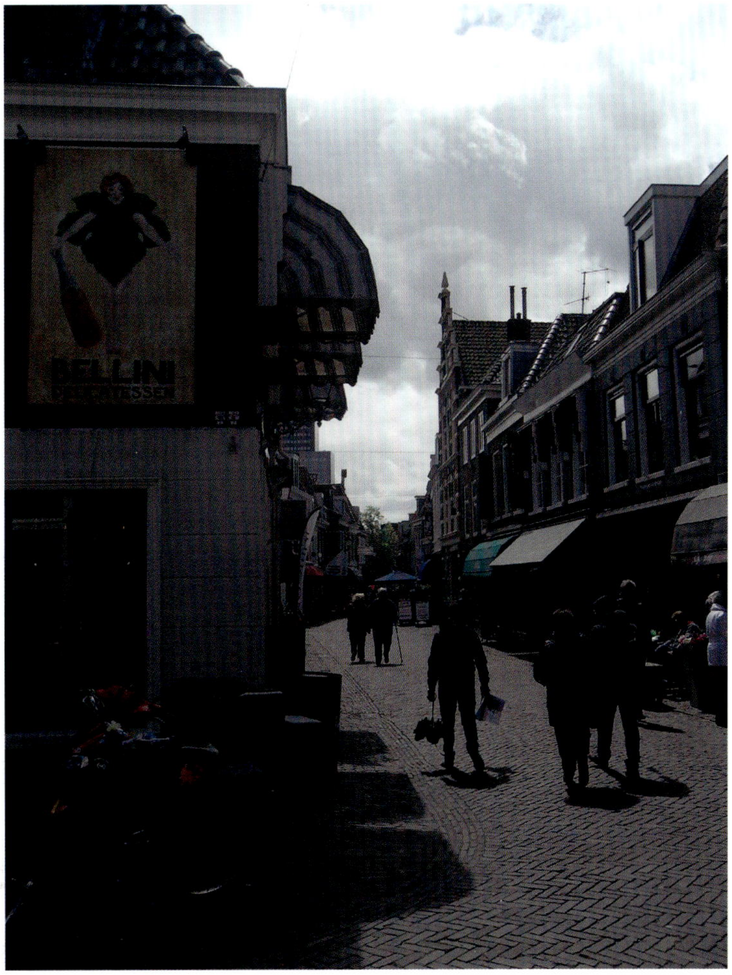


Leeuwarden, the Netherlands, 2013.
Photograph by Gary Pearson.

Looking at a Jonathan Meese painting is a different viewing process and experience than looking at a Kerry James Marshall.

Godard's production style and techniques, such as jump cuts, chaptering and episodic structures, voice-over, direct address to the spectator, use of signs, writing, background and contrasting sounds, were indebted to much earlier filmic innovations, and to playwrights such as Brecht and Beckett. All things considered, a crow landing on a tree branch with leaves blowing across the street below doesn't sound like a bad idea for a painting composition. If you were to do a film or a

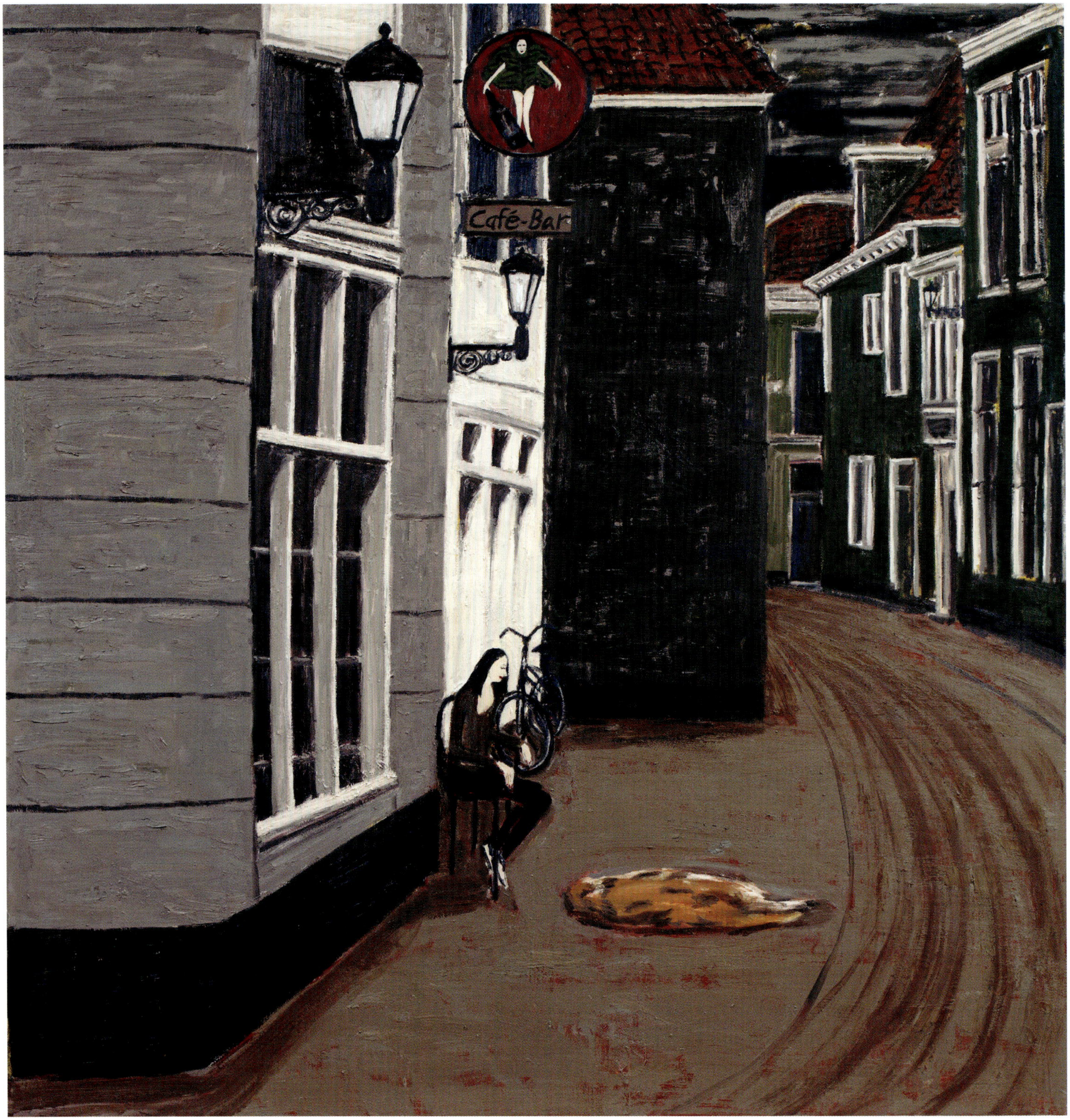




*Girl and Dog*, 2014

video work, adding the man in the lobby and the tipped over garbage can would supply you with ample subject matter for a screenplay or video script. But there's always that lingering question of meaning, of making meaning—what does it mean, does it mean anything?

From my standpoint I guess I'm 'Beckettian' in that I'm more attracted to the poetics and artistic potential in 'taking out my comb'. As you pointed out, my *Ashtray* series is something like that. Regarding my painting *Girl and Dog*, I had thought of titles that might lead the viewer toward a certain interpretation, as I had various interpretations of the painting myself. Artists have to have something in mind that motivates them toward some level of achievement, and as in this painting I felt I had accomplished that. It seemed unnecessary to advertise it through its title, so I kept the title simple. On the other hand, my short fiction below appears simple and direct. The text of it reads:

> Three young women are sitting in a trendy bar. They are all drinking cocktails but only one of the women seems to be talking. The other two are nodding their heads and laughing. The woman who does all the talking has dark hair, long and straight.

What I have attempted to do here is to create a scenario with lots of incompletions. I have partially described the woman who does all the talking as an incentive to the audience to imagine or visualize a description of the other two, or even to imagine what they were laughing about. This short fiction could be seen as simple, but in fact it's not.

**IH**

Backtracking—how different directors direct and orchestrate. While working on a Hitchcock exhibition for the MCA Sydney in 1999, I retrieved some (facsimiles) of original storyboards—one was for *The Birds*, 1963. Not sure who did the drawing, but I made a note of the framing and that the 'scene' drawing extended beyond the frame, beyond the (final film) framing—what is to be seen, and need not be seen, yet is there nonetheless if we are to exercise our imagination, as it relates to the creative act and process, and as you spoke of the poetics—a "scenario with lots of incompletions".

Your painting *Face of the Earth, the Surface of Mars*, 2015, reads as a storyboard (is a story board?). The cuts between dramatic/body-language action on Earth and the monocular eye of a 'Mars Rover' move in one direction, in silence. On Earth, a cast of characters—types and combinations—repeat only one line of text-dialogue: "my hands are clean."

A passage from film editor Walter Murch comes to mind—either as a second question or a contextual thought—if you see that for yourself/your thinking and working: "It is frequently at the edges of things that we learn most about the middle." I believe he is referring to the edit cut as 'the edge of things'.[5]

**GP**

As I see it, the Murch quotation relates to the role of the imagination. The edges can give up a lot of information that may contribute to the middle. It might be understood as a kind of asymmetrical balance that may bring an equilibrium or perhaps disequilibrium to the composition. Henri de Toulouse-Lautrec was a master at activating the edge. I think he created some of the most dramatic compositions in the history of art.

My painting *Face of the Earth, the Surface of Mars* does read as a storyboard. It is the model for this type of sequential composition. And to follow the film analogy, viewing this 40-part set of images is analogous to viewing the effects achieved in crosscutting. The images could be compared to screen grabs from television. Basically there are 40 'blocks' each measuring 11 × 15 inches. They are not intended to be placed in any particular order. The 20 Mars images are variations on a single-source photographic image, establishing a distinct repetitive pattern, which when combined with the 20 singularly different images of Earth underscores contrast and juxtaposition (the 'jump cut'). The visual dominance of the repetitive Mars images is in part intended to direct a closer reading of the Earth image-scenes, and to provoke the idea of the existence of a correlative pattern of repetition in these works. If the audience even considers a correlational and interdependent formal thematic as a compositional structure (through repetition) throughout the 40 pieces, then the door opens for interpretation, and the viewers' search for meaning. What does an artist's representation of Mars and Earth mean?

Nobody I know has been to Mars, whereas we all know being 'on Earth'. In this way, the image-scenes have a certain universal level of recognition and resonance, from which viewers can draw their own assumptions. But if I were to ask you to describe the meaning of life, or the meaning of death, I'm pretty sure that you'd find the first question easier to respond to, or at least to contemplate, than the latter one. So the combination of familiarity and mystery, the known and the unknown, Earth and Mars, while not new, is an interesting juxtaposition.

In his 1909 text "An Essay in Aesthetics", the English art critic and painter Roger Fry talked about our "double lives" and "the possibility of a double life; one the actual life, the other the imaginative life". He described art as "an expression and stimulus of (this) imaginative life". Fry illustrated the distinction between these 'two lives' in a number of ways, including references to dreams, and the 'cinematograph', but I especially enjoyed his comparisons in reference to the mirror:

> A somewhat similar effect to that of the cinematograph can be obtained by watching a mirror in which a street scene is reflected. If we look at the street itself we are almost sure to adjust ourselves in some way to its actual existence... but, in the mirror, it is easier to abstract ourselves completely, and look upon the changing scene as a whole. It then, at once, takes on the visionary quality,

and we become true spectators, not selecting what we will see, but seeing everything equally.... The frame of the mirror, then, does to some extent turn the reflected scene from one that belongs to our actual life into one that belongs rather to the imaginative life. The frame of the mirror makes its surface into a very rudimentary work of art, since it helps us to attain to the artistic vision.[6]

**IH**

Your work *Face of the Earth, the Surface of Mars* offers everything—and what we experience as 'inbound images'. The film is in our head that need not be filmed? In popular science and fiction it is the Earth 'other'—dangerous things come from Mars, in films such as *The Angry Red Planet*, 1959, and *Mars Attacks!*, 1996, (and of course, the Roman God of War, but also... which I didn't register, an 'agricultural guardian'!) But even when it doesn't attack—as in *The Martian*, 2015, or *The Space Between Us*, 2017—we are the Martian. Perhaps in this way 'we've been to Mars'... and Mars to us. Is your group of works *Rise and Fall* a direct-reference storyboard? Or a discursive board through Brecht and Weill?

**GP**

It is the mysterious things, the unknown, that often gives rise to the imaginary, and the imaginings are often unpleasant and disturbing—which in turn promotes all kinds of inventions. *Rise and Fall* is a discursive board through Brecht and Weill. I can't recall my first encounter with Bertolt Brecht's work but I do remember reading the *Threepenny Novel* when I was an undergraduate student in the late 70s, and saw a Fire Hall Theatre production of *The Threepenny Opera* in Vancouver in the early 80s. Since then I've seen numerous productions of his plays, and have read many of them, in addition to other writings by him and about him, particularly by the Brecht scholar John Willett.

Brecht insisted that an actor in his plays not become "completely transformed on the stage into the character he is portraying". To create the alienation effect he said the actor should speak "his part not as if he were improvising it himself but like a quotation". He identifies "three aids which may help to alienate the actions and remarks of the characters being portrayed: 1. Transposition into the third person. 2. Transposition into the past. 3. Speaking the stage directions out loud."[7]

In my video *Berlin Jazz* Story, I've adopted the three A-effect techniques of Brecht. The principal mechanism for the transpositions is the voice-over and the timing delays between the narration and the actors speaking parts and actions. I've also used this in my *The Waiter Joke* video. In *The Cocktail Bar (4 Vignettes)* I intentionally included behind-the-camera production activities that reinforce the staged production. Of course in painting achieving this effect is not as easy, although I do attempt it through captioning and other elements in works such as *Anna's Piano Bar and Smoking Room*, 2011, *The Incident at the Guadalupe Bar*, 2011, and *Speak Low*, 2013. Brecht's influence, and also that of Kurt Weill,

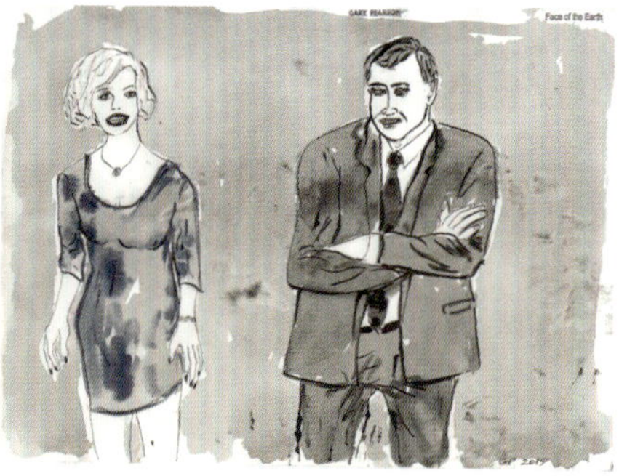
GARY PEARSON
Face of the Earth

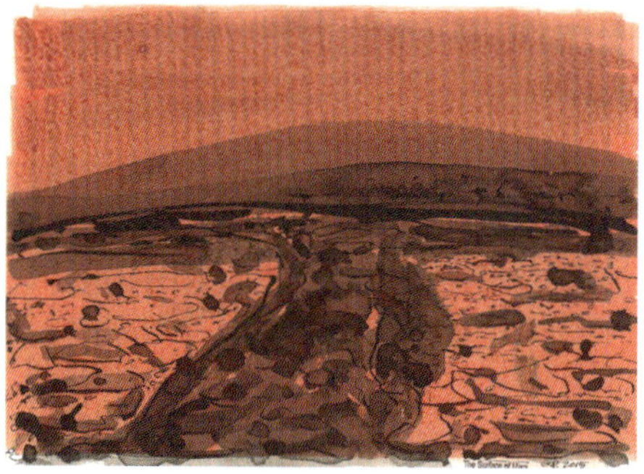

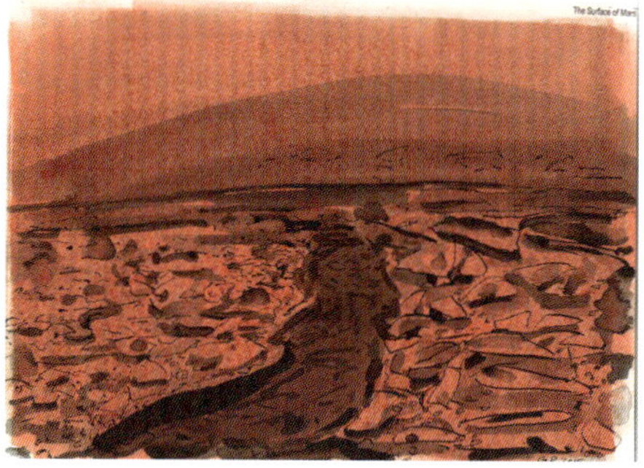
The Surface of Mars

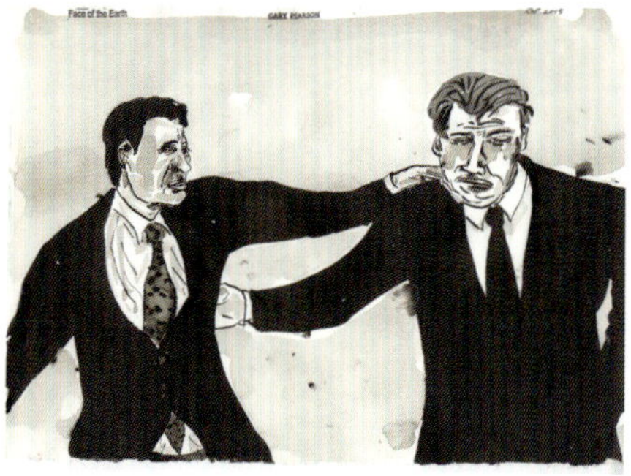
Face of the Earth
GARY PEARSON

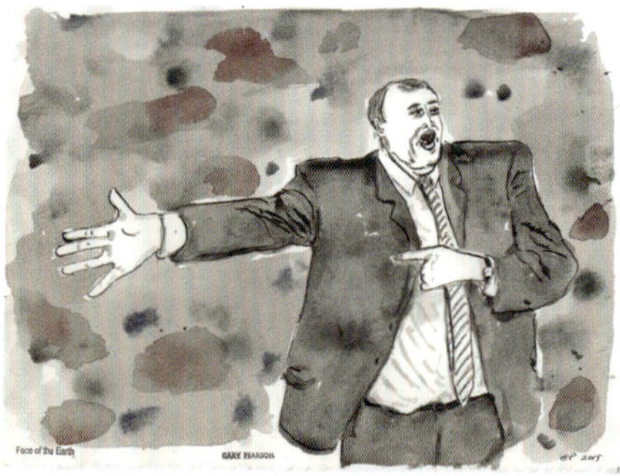
Face of the Earth
GARY PEARSON

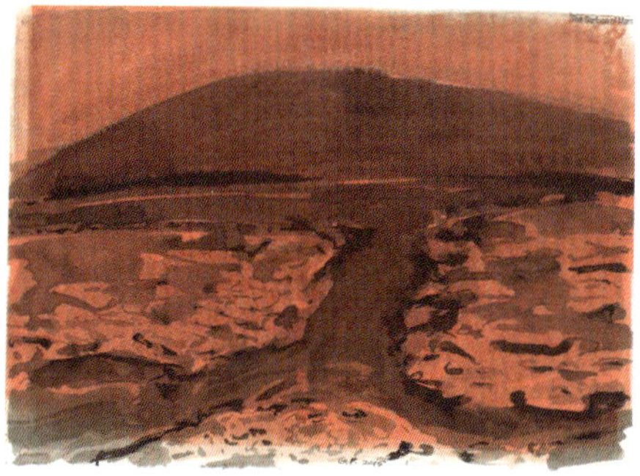

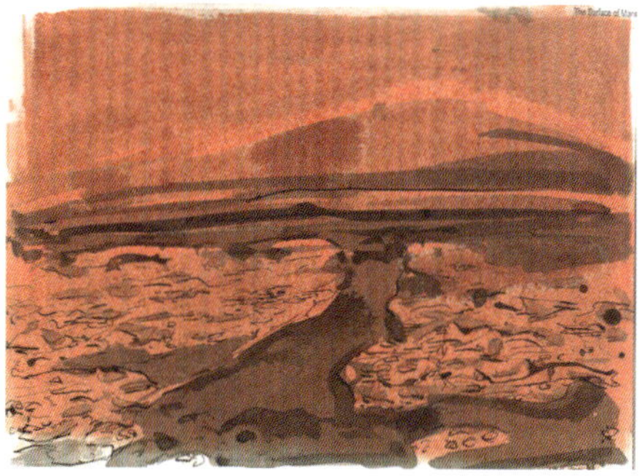
The Surface of Mars

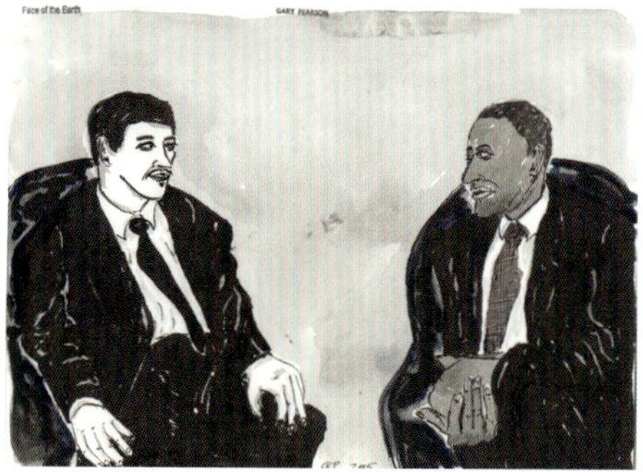
Face of the Earth
GARY PEARSON

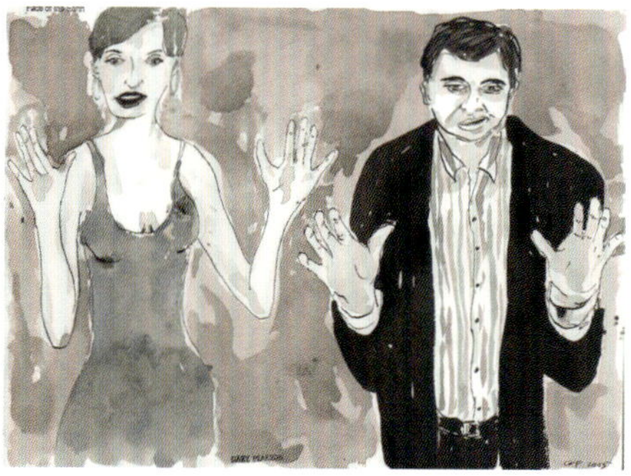

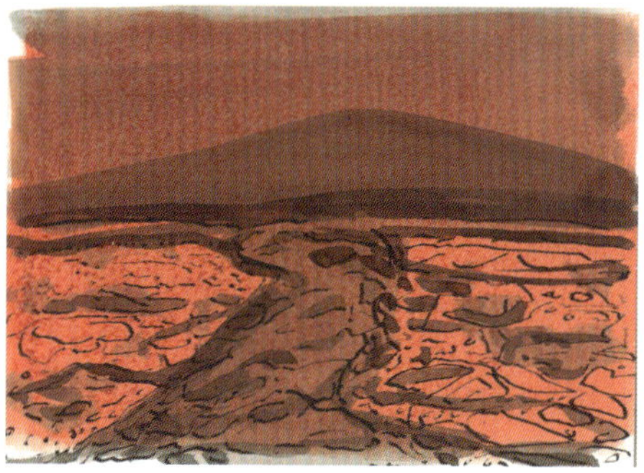

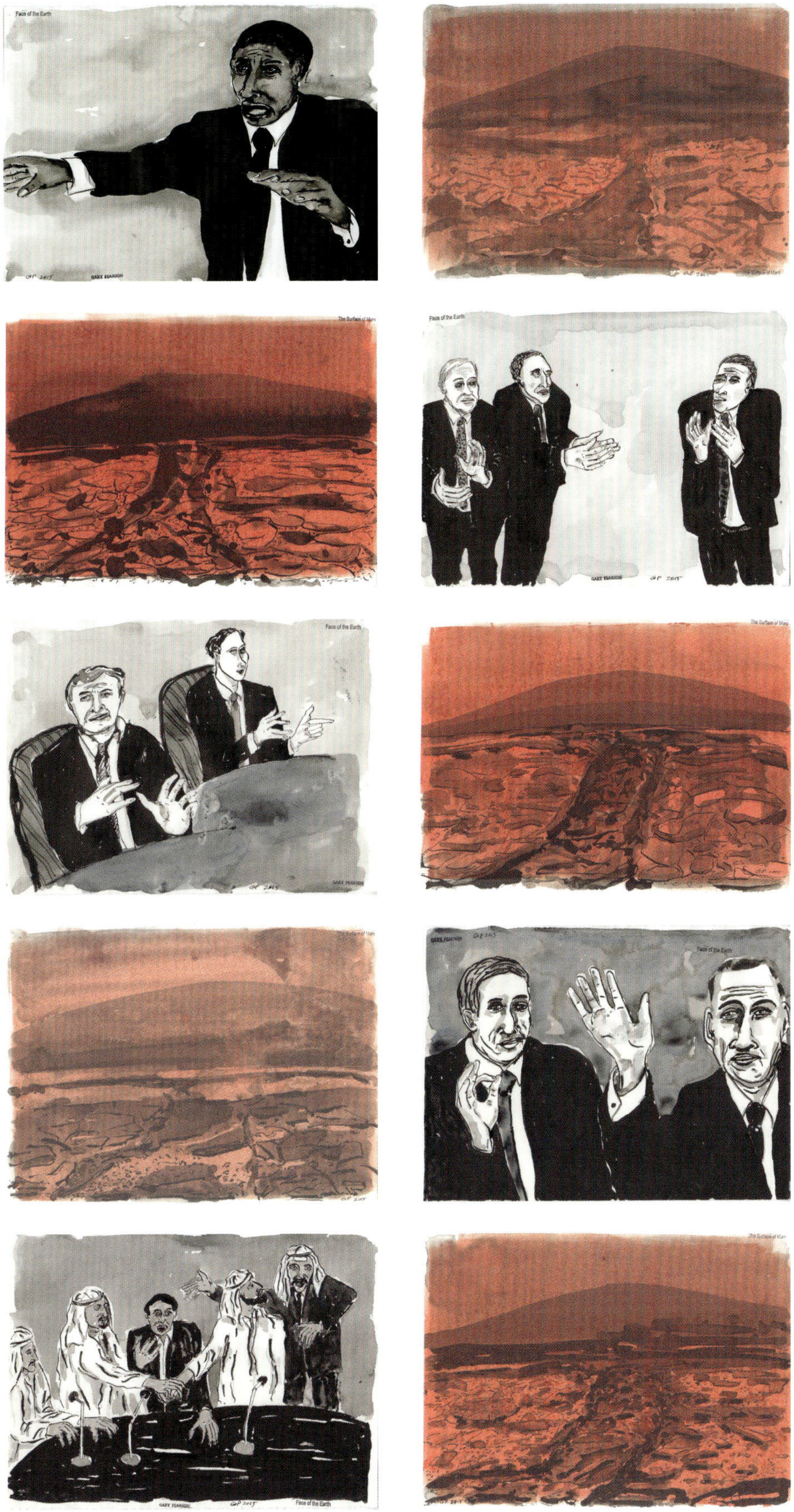


*Face of the Earth, the Surface of Mars*, 2015

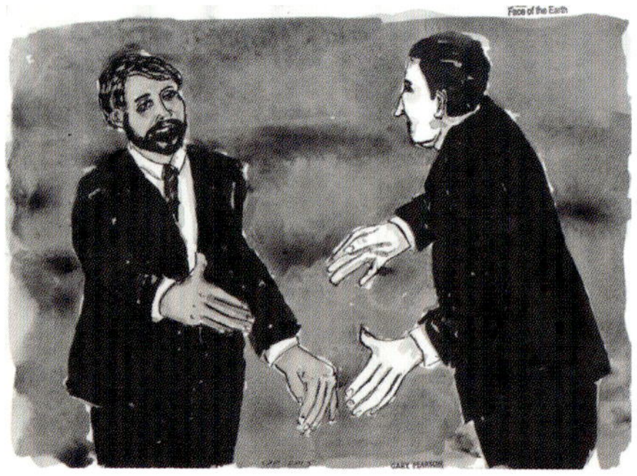
Face of the Earth
GARY PEARSON

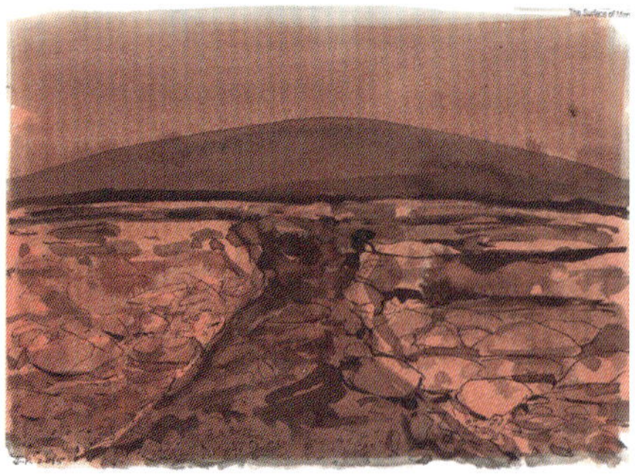
The Surface of Mars

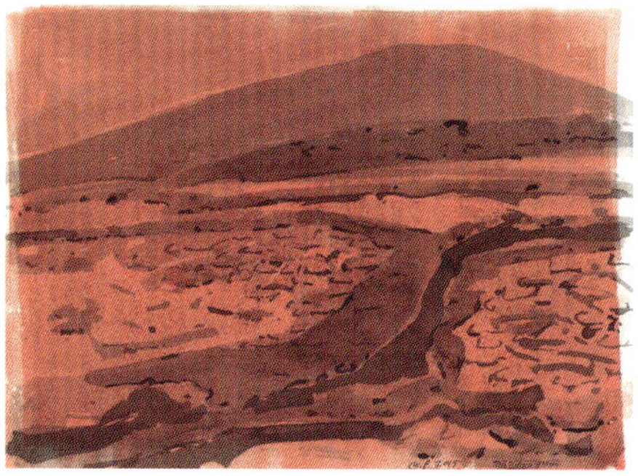

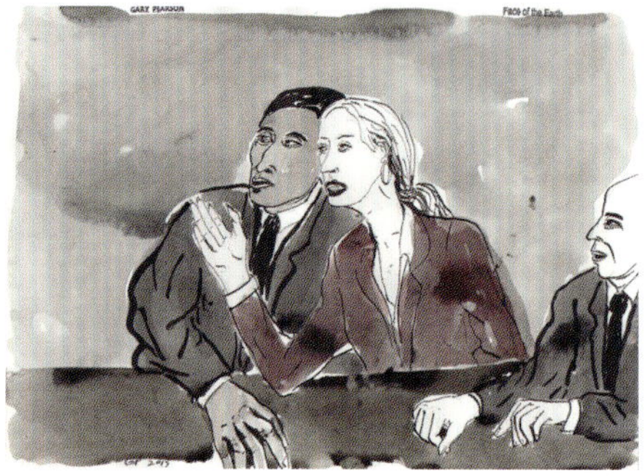
GARY PEARSON
Face of the Earth

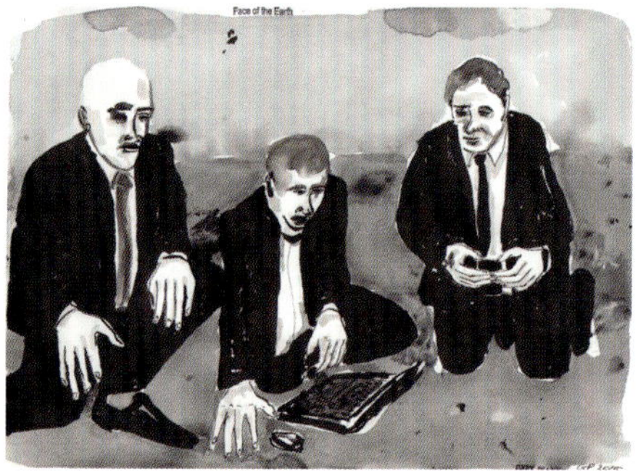
Face of the Earth

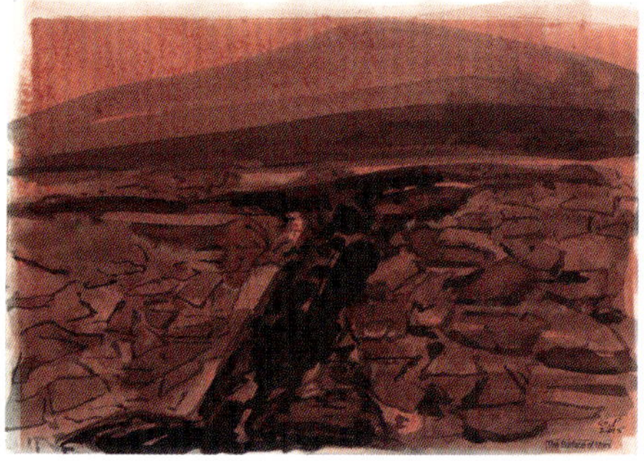
The Surface of Mars

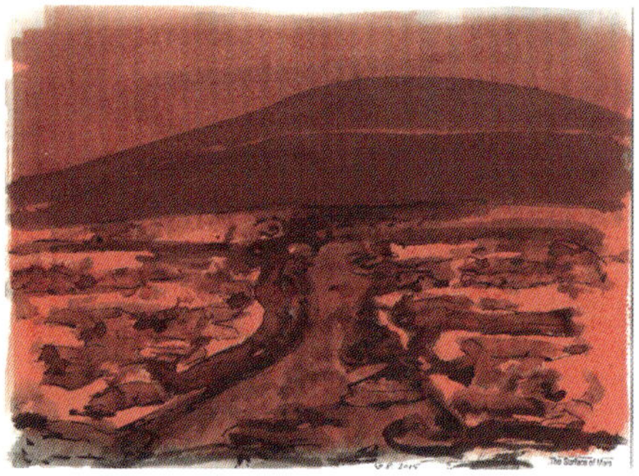
The Surface of Mars

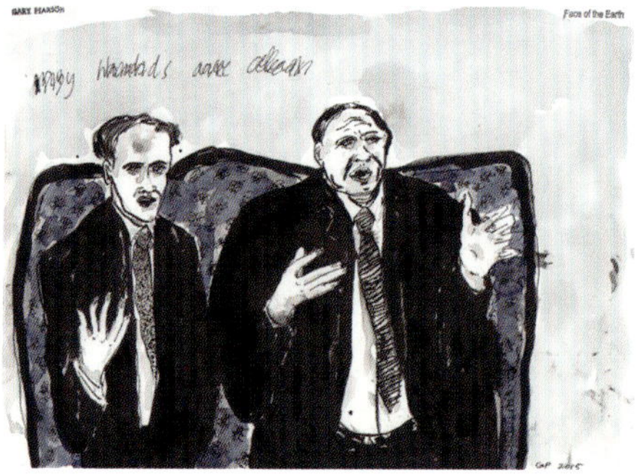
GARY PEARSON
Face of the Earth

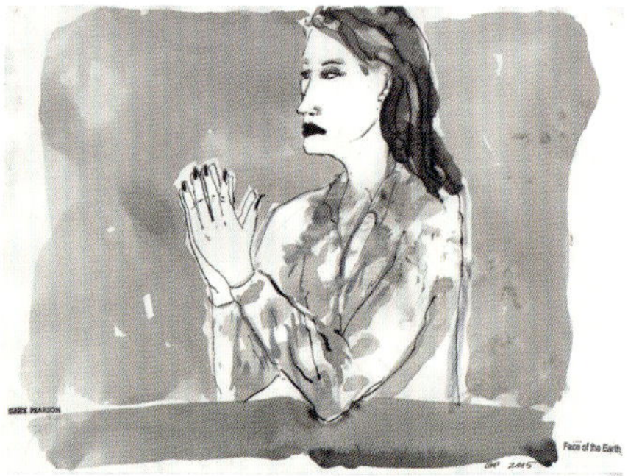
GARY PEARSON
Face of the Earth

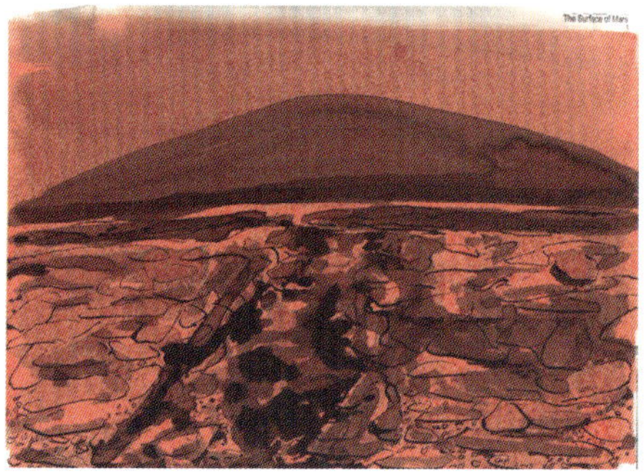
The Surface of Mars

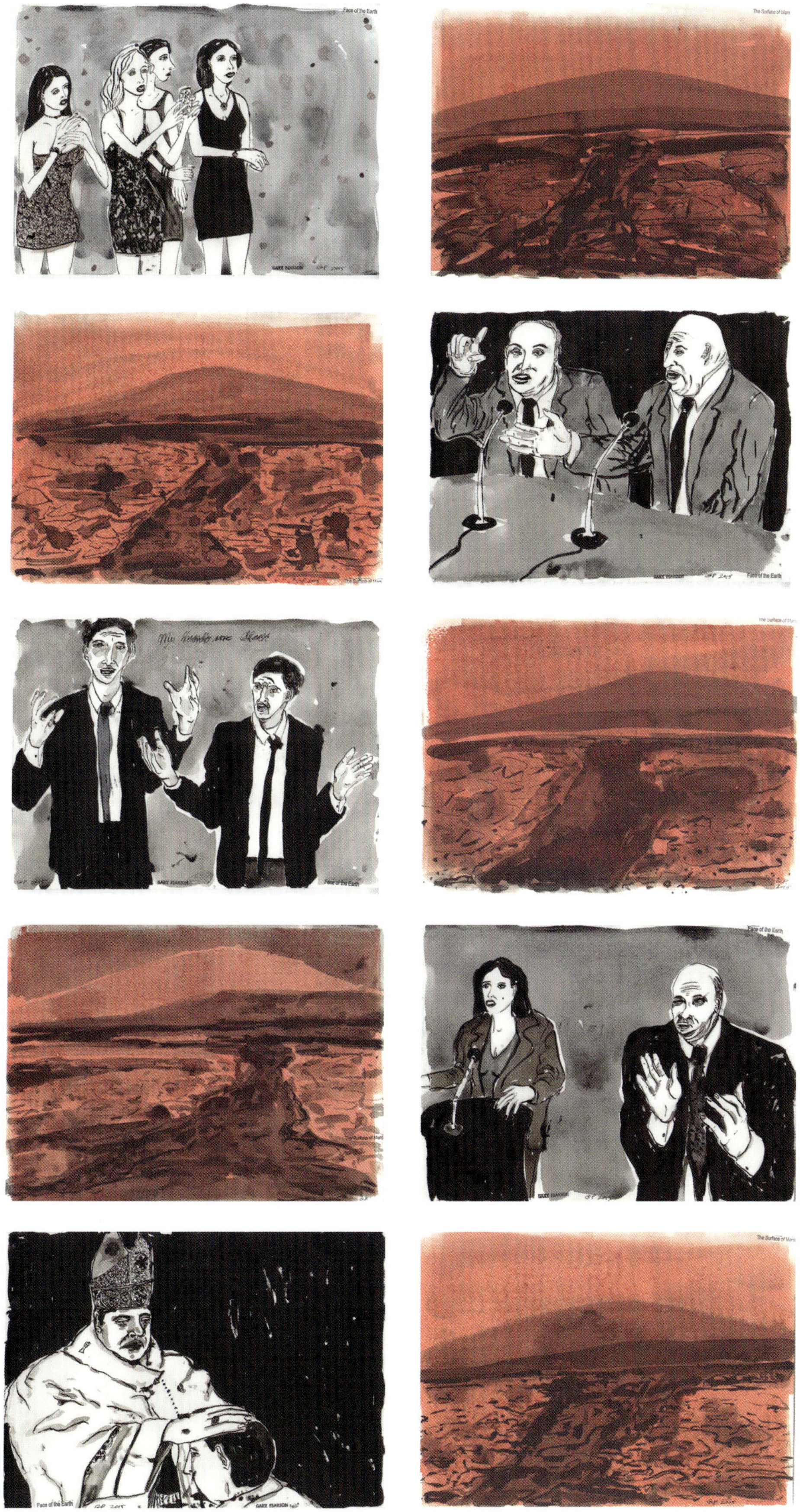

*Face of the Earth, the Surface of Mars*, 2015

can be seen in a very recent painting of mine titled *Honky Tonk*, 2017. Weill's discordant harmonies, eclectic instrumentations and rhythmic emphasis are very inspiring. In the end, I saw creating my *Rise and Fall*, 2014, series of drawings as a great opportunity to visually interpret Brecht's libretto the *Rise and Fall of the City of Mahagonny*. There are 20 principle scenes in the opera, so I did 20 drawings.

**IH**

Returning to your quotation from Roger Fry—does that sit in your working thoughts? Always adjusting to reality? A moment registered—your *Girl and Dog* as a cited example—and what sits with you over time, as in the vintage photograph of the couple given to you in 1975?

**GP**

I think many people, artists particularly, are always wary of becoming habituated, so we have a kind of built-in alert mechanism that would differ from person to person that promotes different ways of seeing. You could walk down the same street a hundred times, and each time you would see at least one thing that could be said to be different from all the other times. Each time this happens it may offer the right moment to truly grasp the meaning of that street, and your particular connection in time and space on that street, and to the formation of that meaning. So if you're alert to that you could store that mental image, or write down some notes that might be the basis for a painting or other work. To follow Fry's line of thinking, it is the imaginative life intervening into the actual life that makes these opportunities and experiences possible.

Sometimes an experience of seeing or hearing something or reading something makes a significant impression on your imagination. There are always big events that are thrust upon you, and there are those that, in the bigger picture, would be considered insignificant. I've gone back time and time again to the vintage photograph of the couple; it is in the latter category, and that is why I have been able to return to this image, each time feeling inspired to re-create their likenesses in another paper work, or another canvas. If you add to this my adoration for artists such as Toulouse-Lautrec, Goya, Munch and German Expressionist artists and their subject matter, it doesn't surprise me that this photograph has offered up such a wealth of information and inspiration.

**IH**

Let's talk about your fountain works; fountains originated in the practical, a source of water, but then morphed into the spectacle. What draws/drew you to them?

**GP**

My *Fountain* series consists of four major canvasses and many works on paper. My wife Dagmar and I spent a month in the village of Ajijic, Jalisco, Mexico, in 2015. Ajijic is about a half-hour drive south of

Guadalajara on Lake Chapala. As I wasn't working on a series at the time, I simply went out and sketched whatever caught my eye. After about two weeks I was looking through what I had done and saw that the most frequently drawn subjects were water fountains. So it was quite a simple decision to follow through with the fountain as my guiding motif. The upside was the opportunity to develop more complex ideas about composition and to create a narrative in these works orchestrated through the subject of the fountain.

Yes, fountains can take on an even grotesque identity in relation to their surroundings. I'm guessing that there are people who have been responsible for the design and placement of fountains who have often overestimated the element's importance in the urban landscape. My painting *The Large Fountain*, 2015, is a response to the grandiosity of a fountain I saw in Guadalajara. My narrative here is the fountain as spectacle. Another work, *The Fountain of Good and Evil*, 2015, is guided by the idea of good and evil to raise the question of what these designations mean, how these determinations are not only made, but how they have resurfaced in a major way in the discourse, even rhetoric, in contemporary society. The sculpture of the winged messenger or goddess on the fountains cap points her finger in an accusatory way, while the sculpted young men below are content in their continuous act of (water) urination.

**IH**

Another question is the distinction between art that illustrates, and art that registers. Both can represent things in and of the world. In exploring this, my thoughts snapped back to your series, in particular the *Earth/Mars* works and *Rise and Fall*. Some may consider these to be primarily illustrative. I don't think so, even if they do 'illustrate a something'. I think they equally, and perhaps more importantly, 'register' the external world beyond what we already know.

**GP**

I agree. There is a big difference between illustration in the conventional sense, and as you describe it, that which 'registers' the external. Both are tasked with representing something, but illustration often places self-imposed limits on the potential for exploration of the external, and also the exploration and exploitation of the artistic discipline and media. In the best works of art both of these capacities are working at a very high level.

You don't have to necessarily be able to produce drawings at the standard of Jean-Antoine Watteau to still produce drawings of interest and value. Similarly, you don't have to have the skill of Velázquez to produce a good painting. So there are many degrees of art in this sense that certainly complicate judgment and qualification, however, if you bear in mind the two principle capacities of art that I mentioned, then you are on a very good footing for making judgments about the quality of a work of art. To add to this I'll use terms from art scholarship: all works

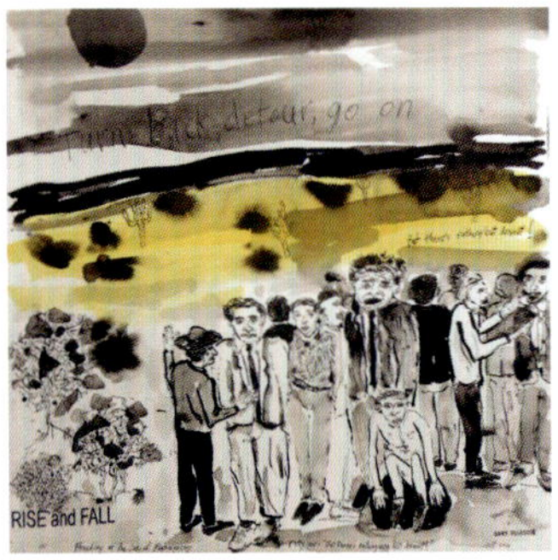
RISE and FALL
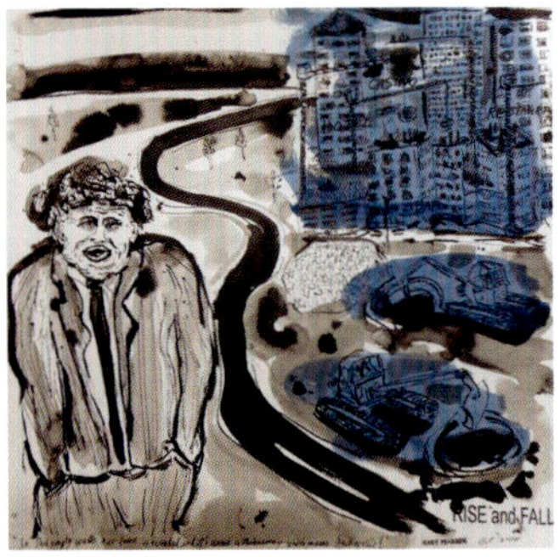
RISE and FALL
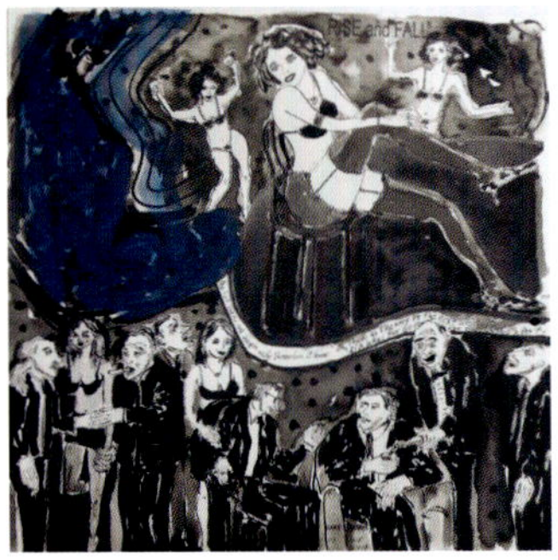
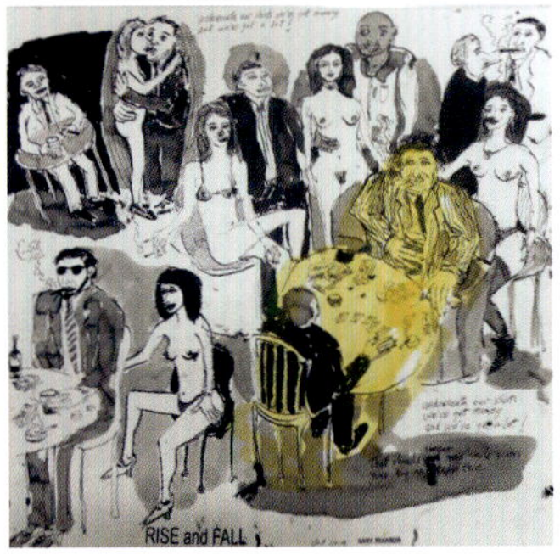
RISE and FALL
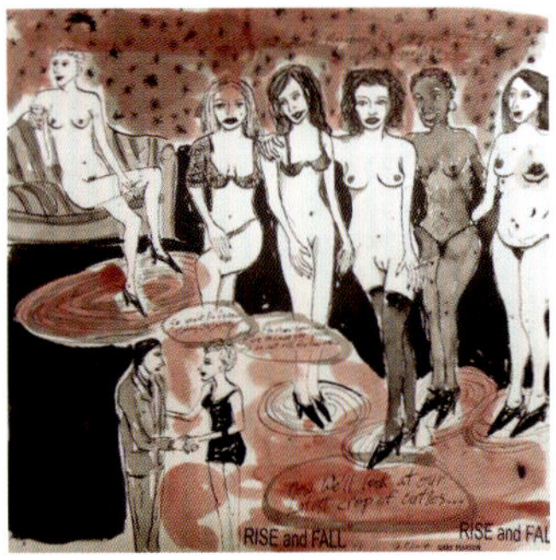
RISE and FALL
RISE and FALL
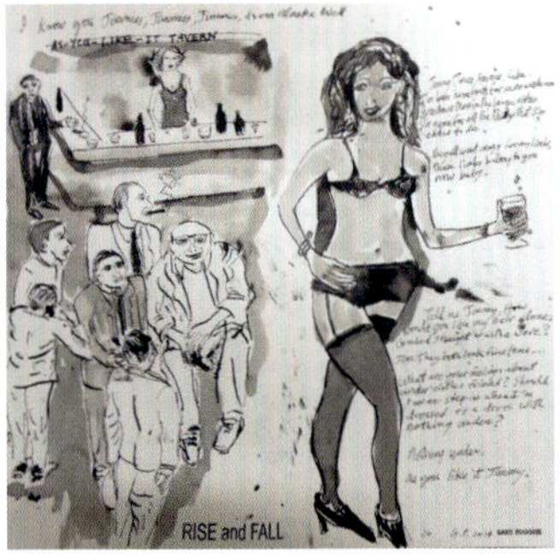
RISE and FALL
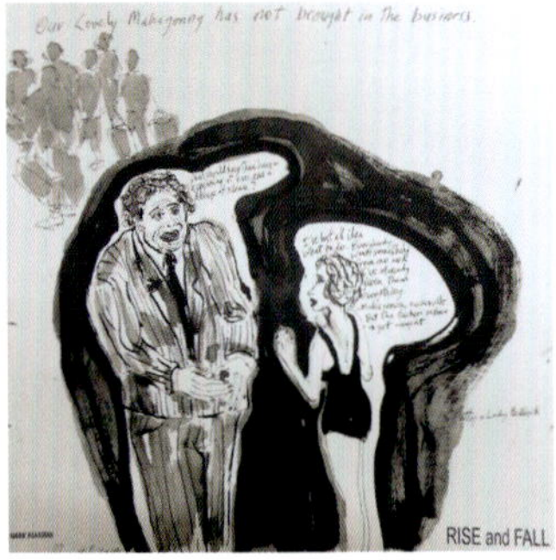
RISE and FALL
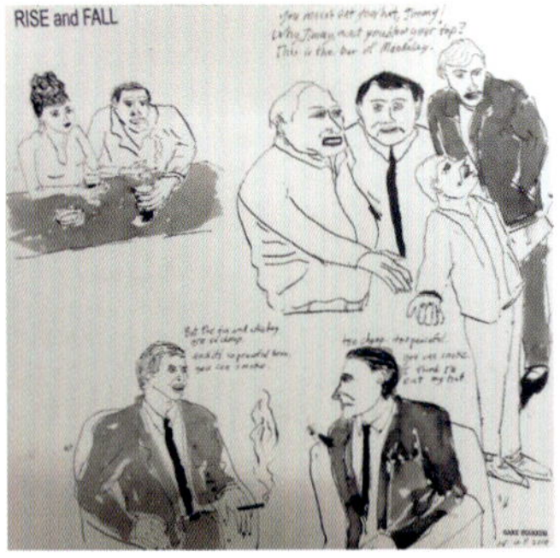
RISE and FALL
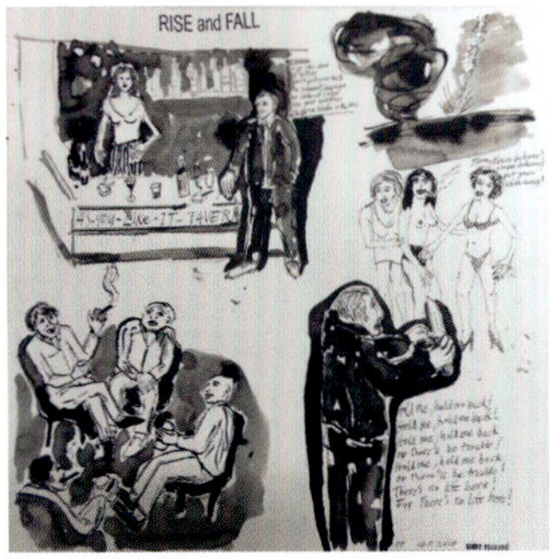
RISE and FALL
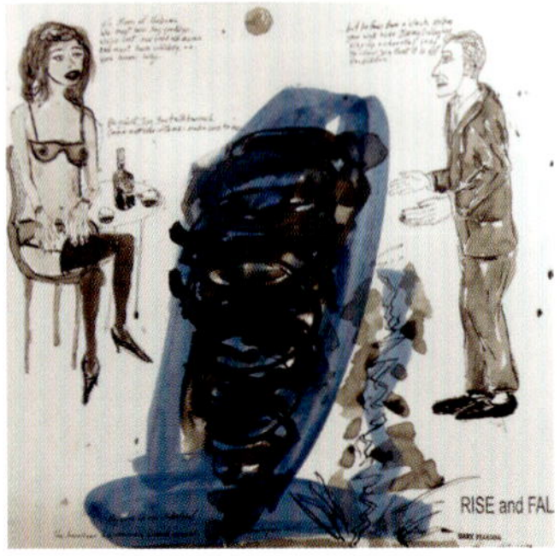

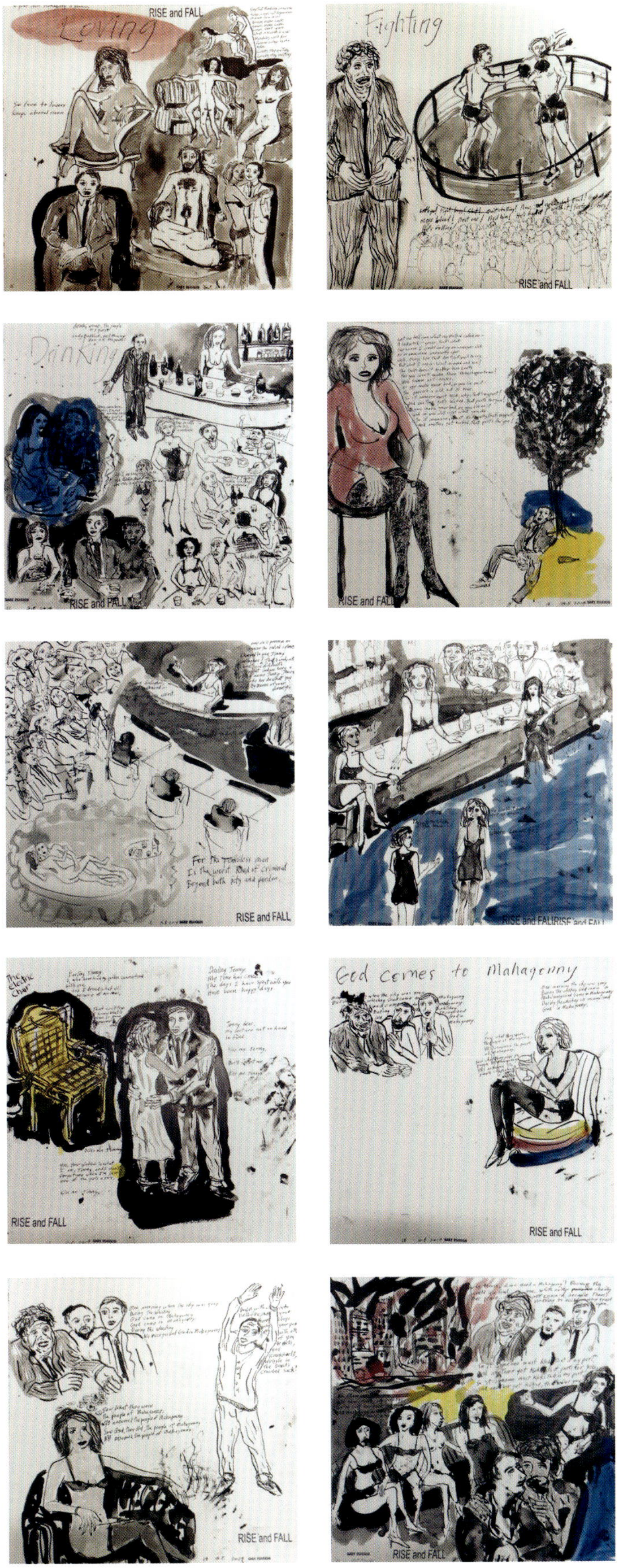

Loving
RISE and FALL
Fighting
RISE and FALL
RISE and FALL
RISE and FALL
For the penniless man
Is the worst kind of criminal
Beyond both pity and pardon.
RISE and FALL
The electric chair
RISE and FALL
God comes to Mahagonny
RISE and FALL
RISE and FALL
RISE and FALL

of art are comprised of two things: one is what is referred to as its *tenor*, which can be described as the work's formal framework, comparable to scaffolding or tent poles; the other is its *topic*, which is something that can be more complex and remote. They are interdependent and are major factors in establishing the works' meaning and quality.

For art that is primarily illustration, the artist most likely thought it was a simple matter of draping the topic over the tenor, as one would drape the tent over the tent poles. It's not that easy. While it's true that the iconography or form language (the tenor) is largely responsible for carrying and conveying the topic, they both must be subject to a rigorous thematic and counter-thematic exploration to reveal meanings that, as you describe, 'register' the external beyond mere depiction.

My *Rise and Fall* drawings do illustrate the principle episodes of Brecht's play, but I also gave myself creative licence to devise the iconography and its staging, the stylistic approach, selection of text lines, and selection of the media: ink, oil and rubber stamp. The drawings are intentionally messy and gritty, and the text sections are often dispersed in a captioned manner. This was done to correspond to my reading of the play, how I interpreted it, how I visualized it. It is hoped that this intervention has taken these 20 drawings beyond that of illustration per se.

It's really a matter of putting the effort, the extra effort, into getting to know your subject. If you feel you know your subject in advance of producing a painting or a drawing and are not willing to work at uncovering something you didn't know then, yes, there's a very good chance the work will end up as illustration.

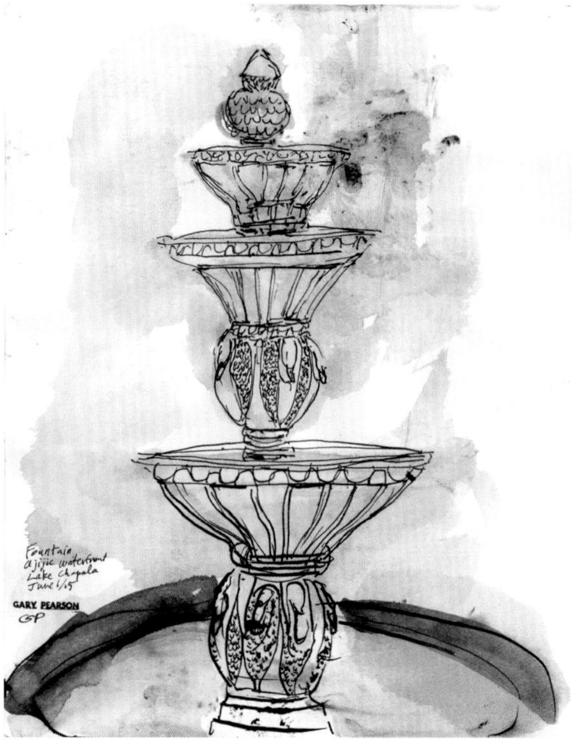




*Fountain at Lake Chapala Waterfront*, 2015

1 Cuddon, JA, *The Penguin Dictionary of Literary Terms & Literary Theory*, CE Preston ed, London: Penguin Books, 1999 revised edition, p 676.

2 Quotation displayed at the Munch Museum, Oslo, Norway, in 2010.

3 Quoted in Sally Banes, *Greenwich Village 1963: Avant-Garde Performance and the Effervescent Body*, Durham and London: Duke University Press, 1993, p 120.

4 Quoted in "Location and Actuality: Gary Pearson interviews Christos Dikeakos, Jeff Wall, and Ian Wallace", *Lake: A Journal of Arts and Environment*, issue 2, 2008, p 53.

5 Murch, Walter, *In The Blink of An Eye*, Los Angeles, CA: Silman-James Press, 1995, p 1.

6 Fry, Roger, "An Essay in Aesthetics", *Vision and Design*, New York: Dover Publications, 1998, pp 14–15; first published in *The New Quarterly*, April 1909.

7 Willett, John, "Short Description of a New Technique of Acting which Produces an Alienation Effect", *Brecht on Theatre, The Development of an Aesthetic*, John Willett ed and trans, New York, NY: Hill and Wang Publishers, 1992, p 138.

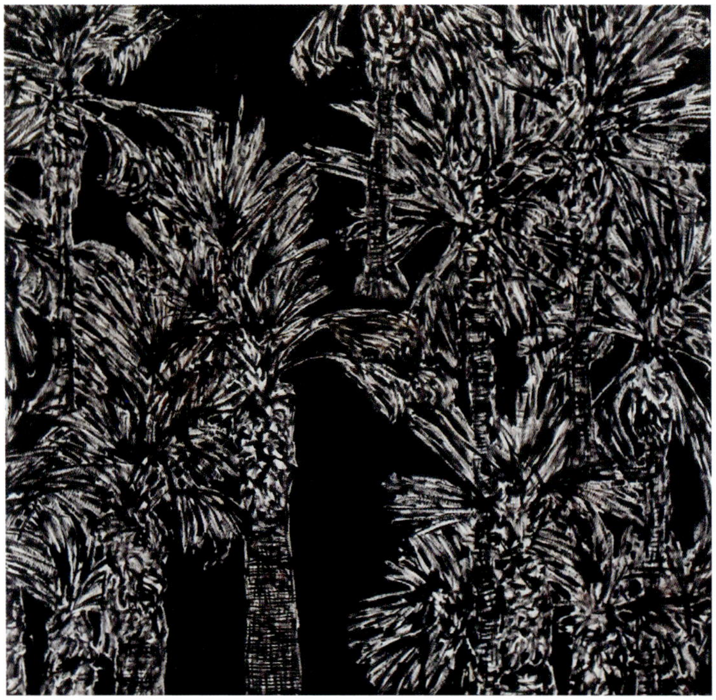

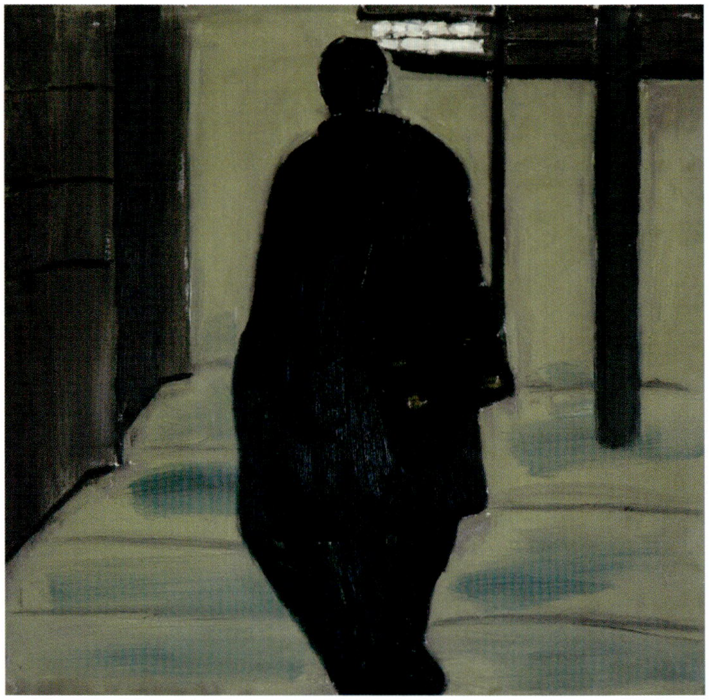

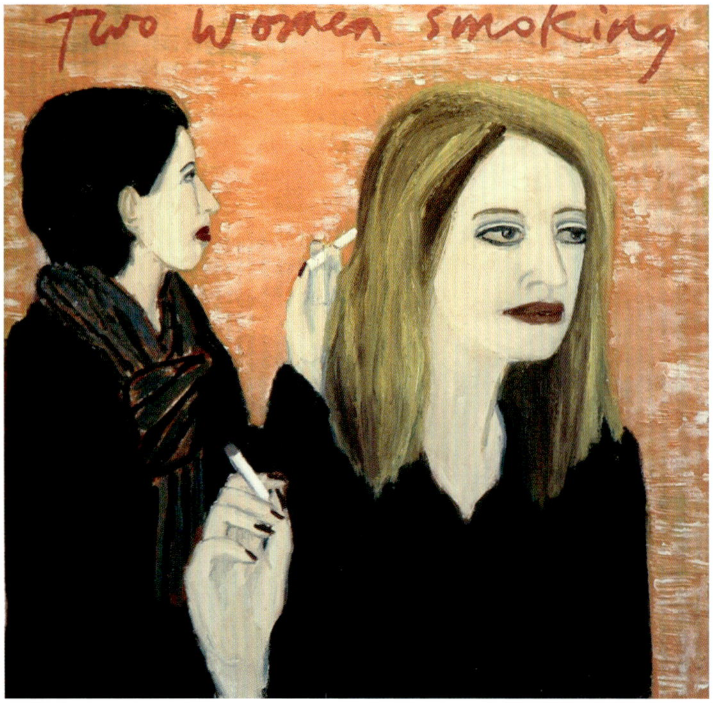


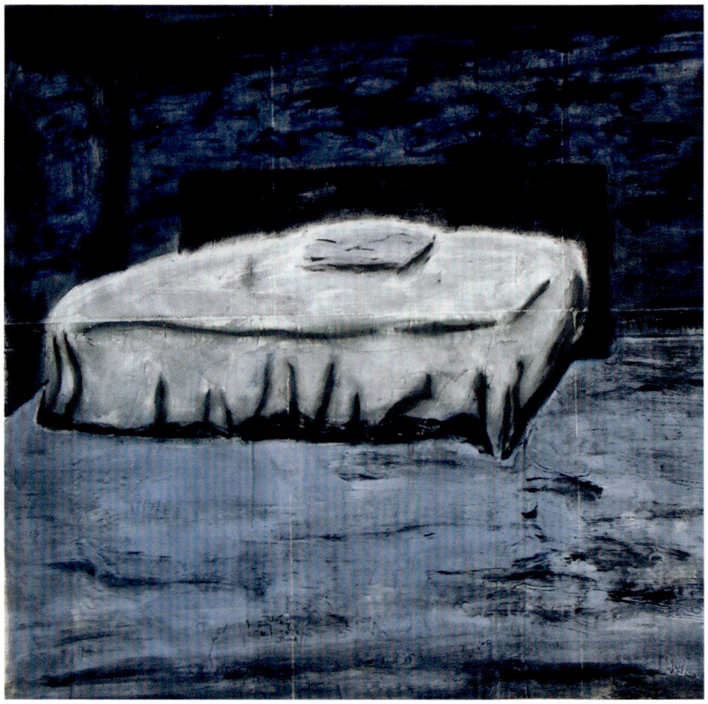

*Fernandina Palms*, 2004
*Somewhere*, 2008
*Two Women Smoking*, 2008
*Shepherd Street (at night)*, 2009

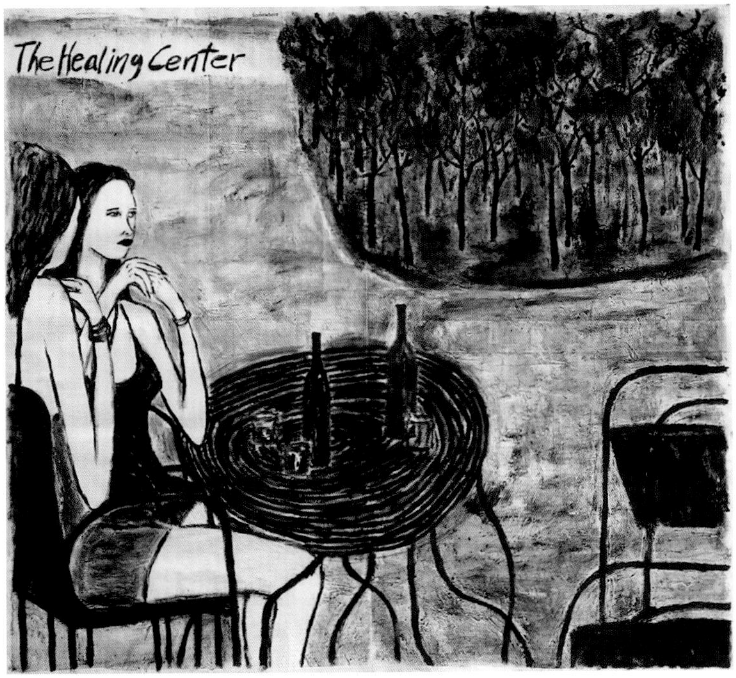


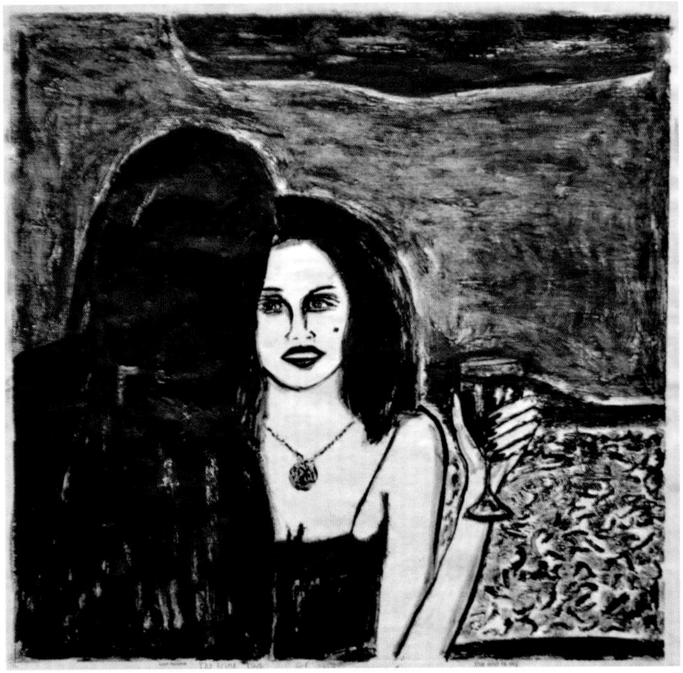

*The Healing Center (monochrome)*, 2009
*The Wine Bar*, 2007

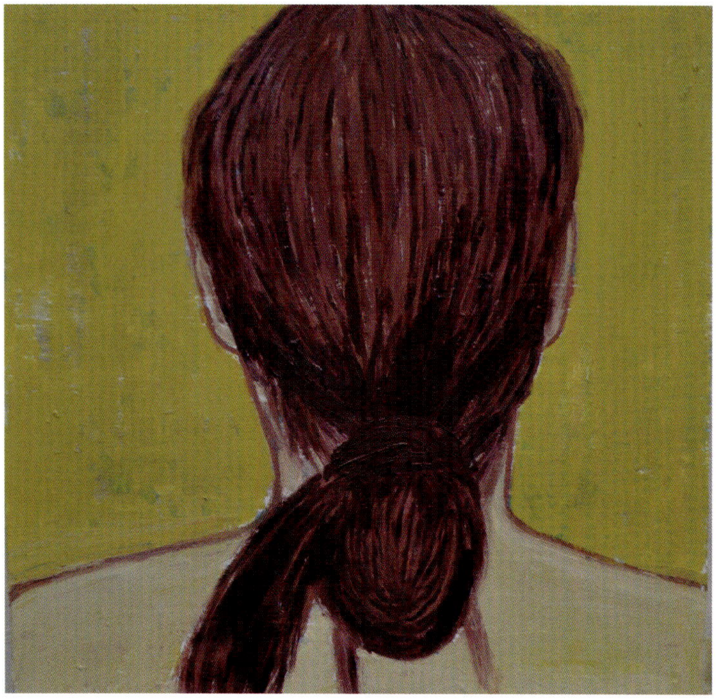

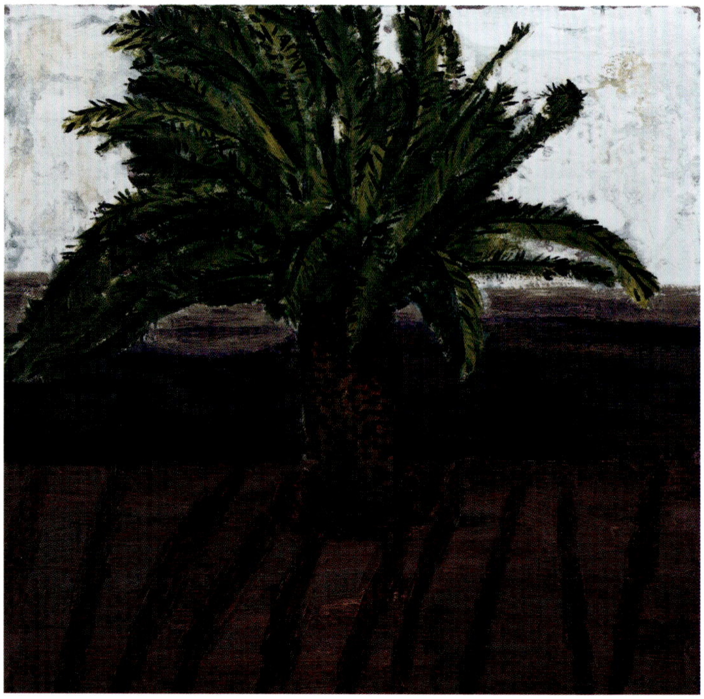

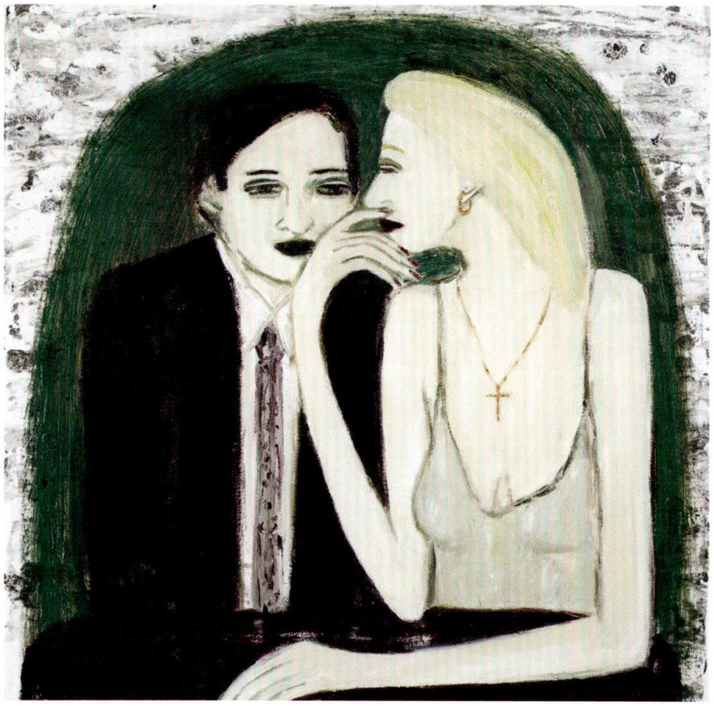

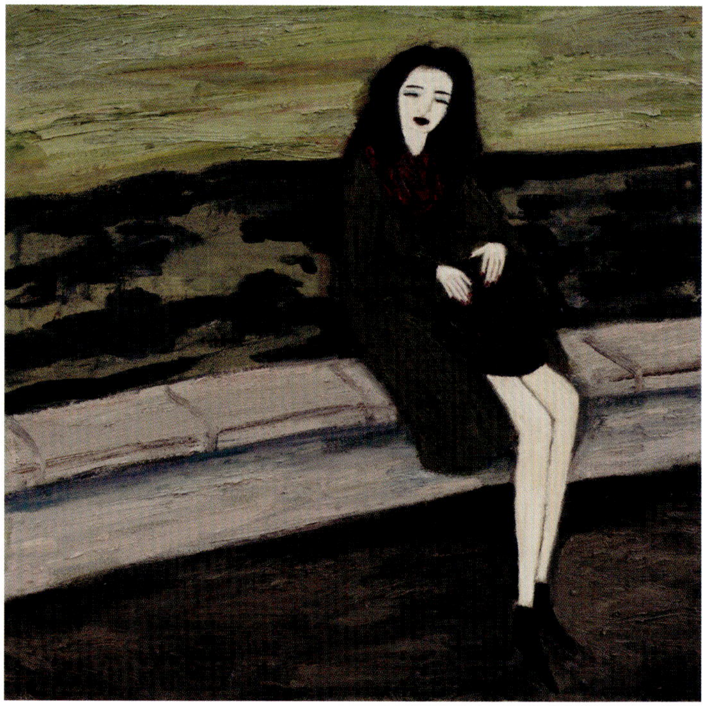

*Portrait of a Red-Haired Woman (back view)*, 2007
*Palm Tree*, 2008
*The Secret*, 2011
*The Green Coat*, 2014

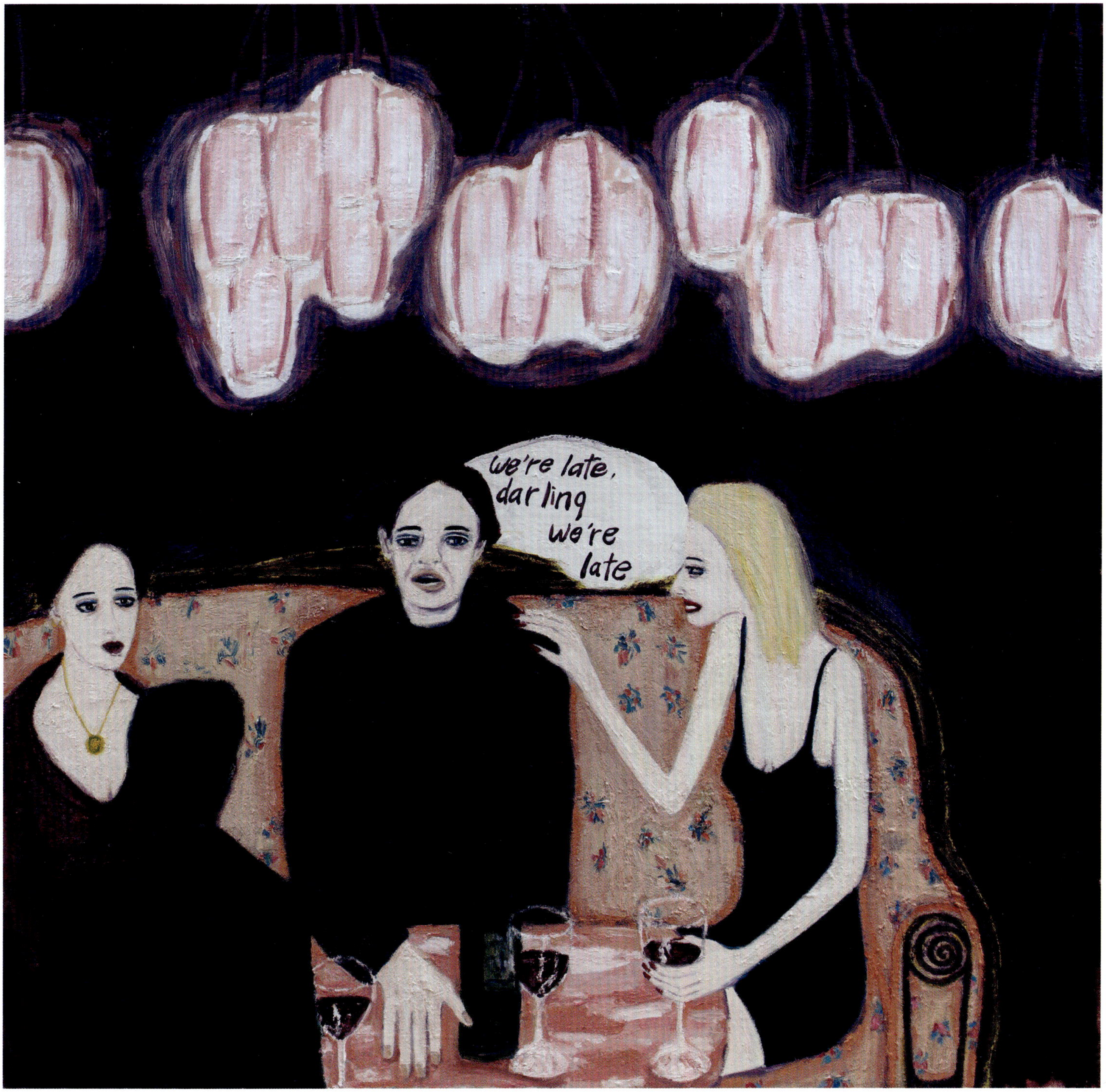


*Speak Low*, 2013

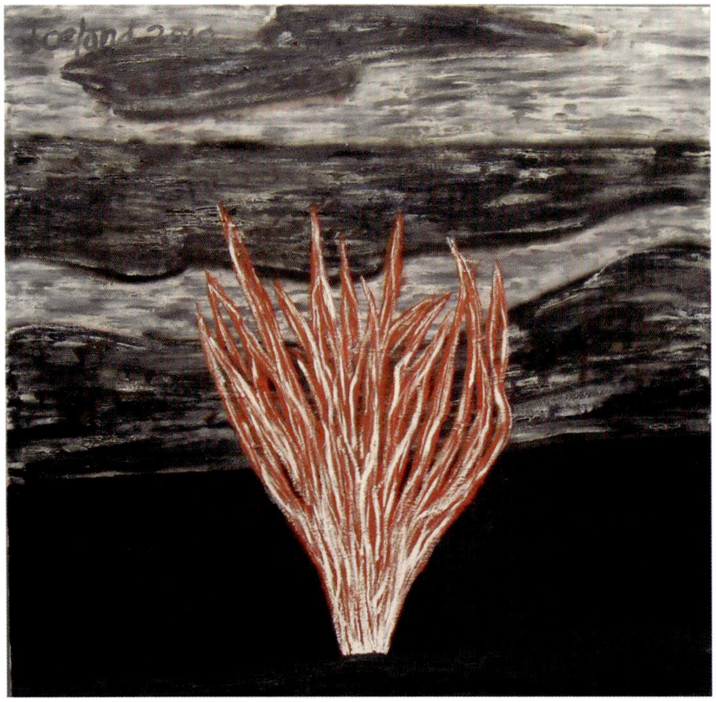

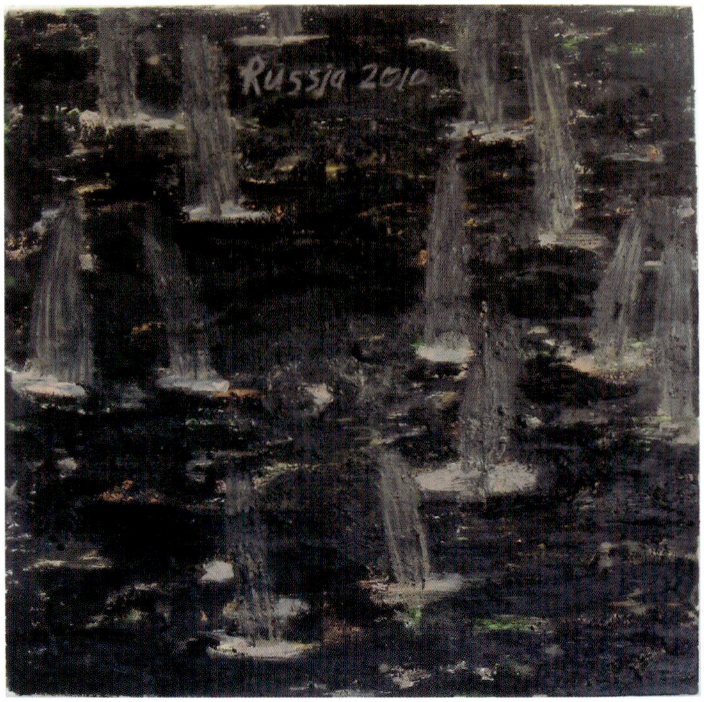

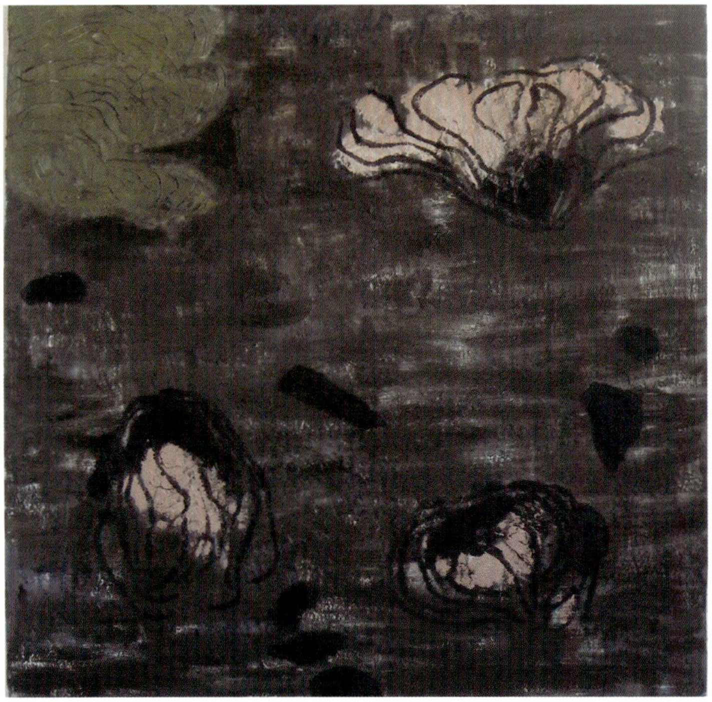
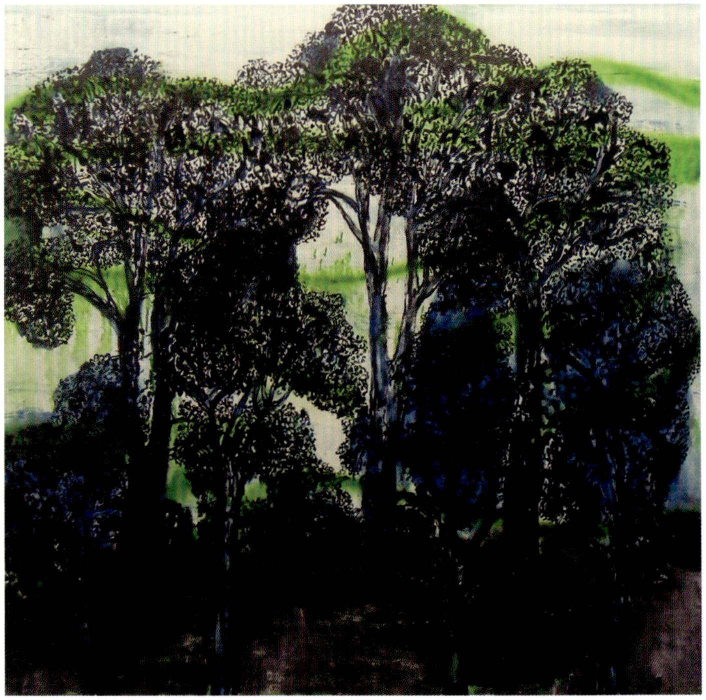

*Volcanic Ash Grounds Air Traffic in Northern Europe (Air)*, 2010
*Crippled by Drought, Russia Places Ban on Grain Exports (Fire)*, 2010
*With Little Fanfare, Well is Plugged with Cement (Water)*, 2010
*Earth*, 2010

The karaoke bar was located under a palm grove and tables and chairs were positioned in an informal arrangement nearby. Near the lane approach to the bar a middle-aged couple were sitting at a table holding hands. The sullen-faced bartender brought fresh drinks to their table. A grey-haired male patron who looked to be in his 60s walked up to the karaoke bar and grabbed the microphone and recorded music began to play. It was a love song. The man at the microphone voiced the lyrics in a faltering yet heartfelt lament. The middle-aged couple got up and danced. The song ended. They walked silently back to their table. A few people clapped. Wind rustled the palm fronds. Surf pounded on the shoreline rocks.

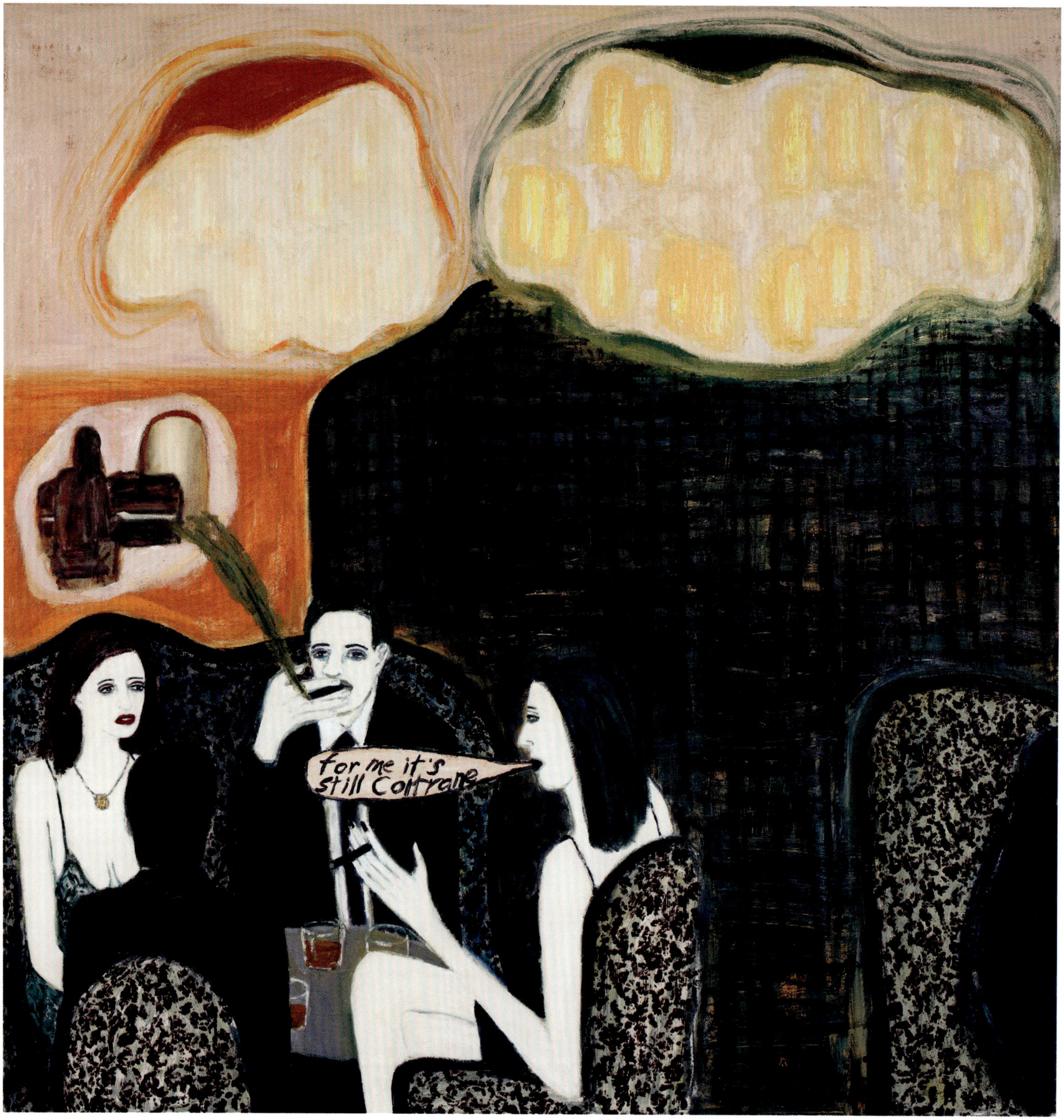




*Anna's Piano Bar and Smoking Room*, 2011

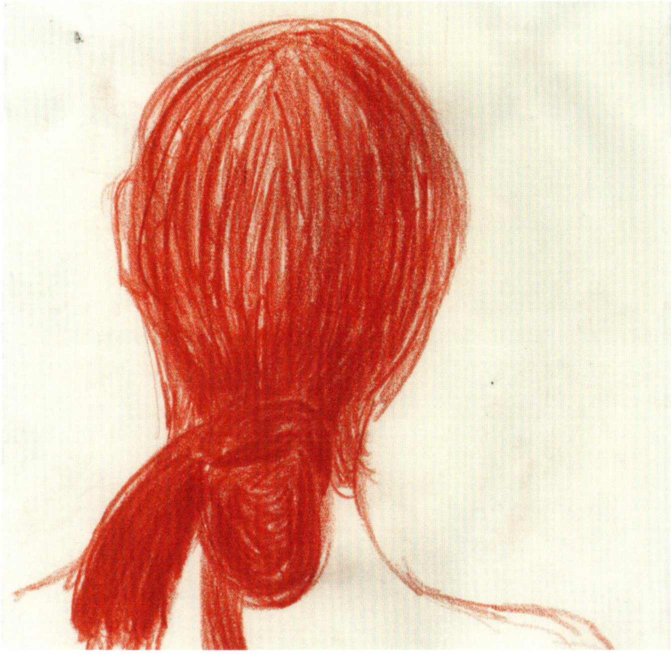

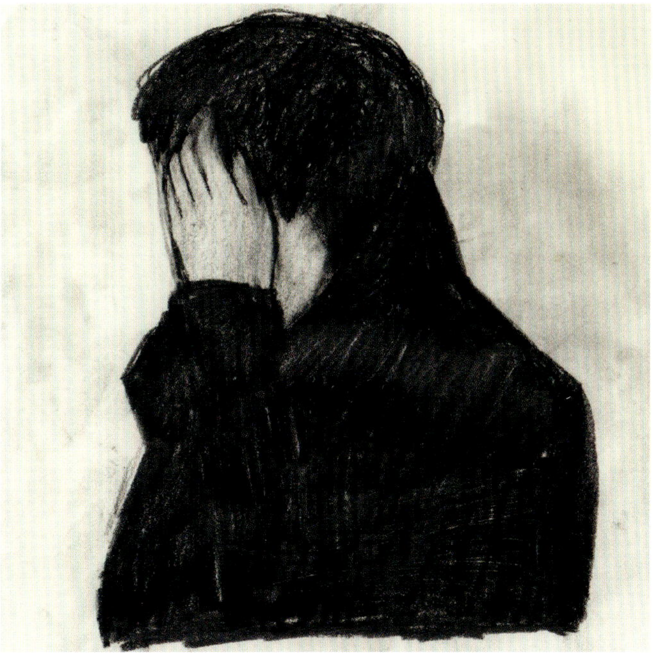

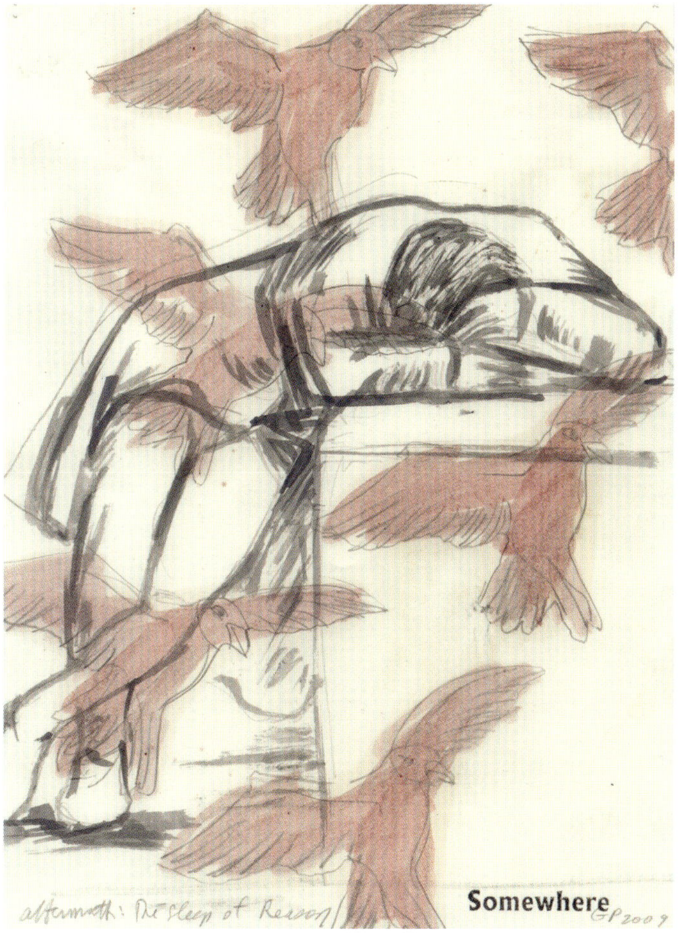



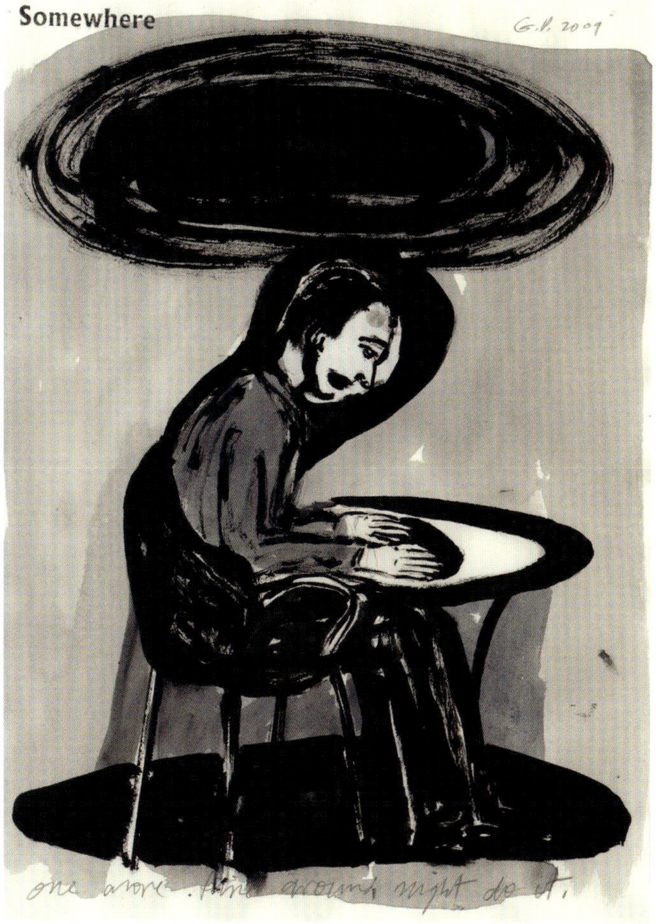



*Untitled (Portrait Sketch)*, 2009
*Man Covering His Face*, 2009
*Aftermath (The Sleep of Reason)*, 2009
*One More Time Around Might Do It*, 2009

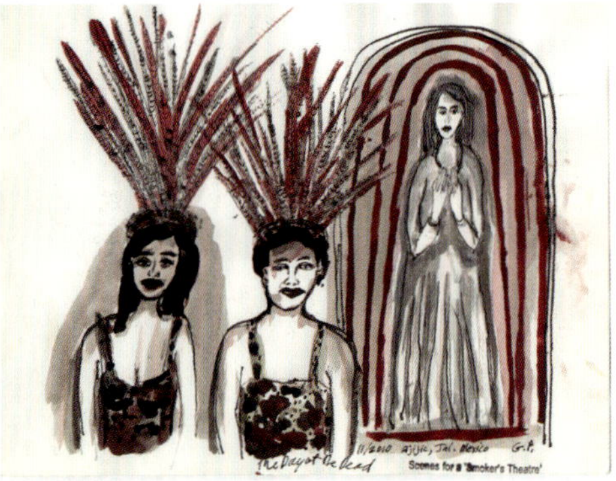

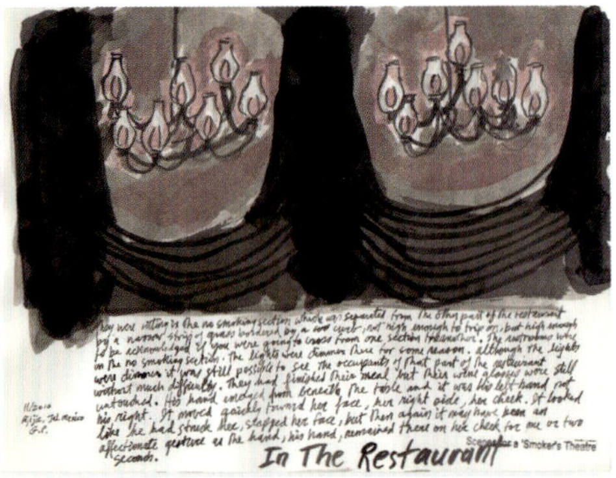

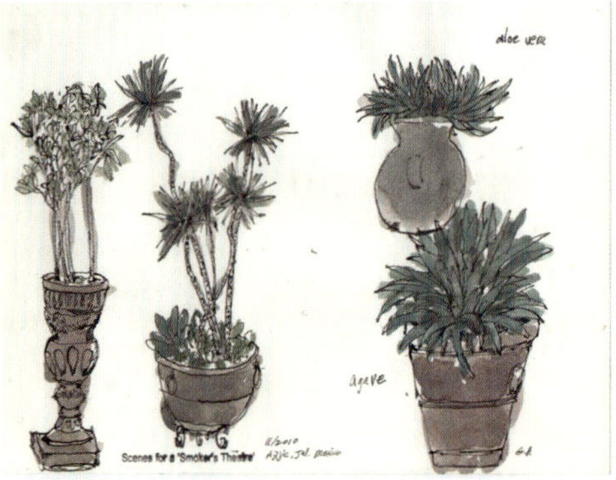

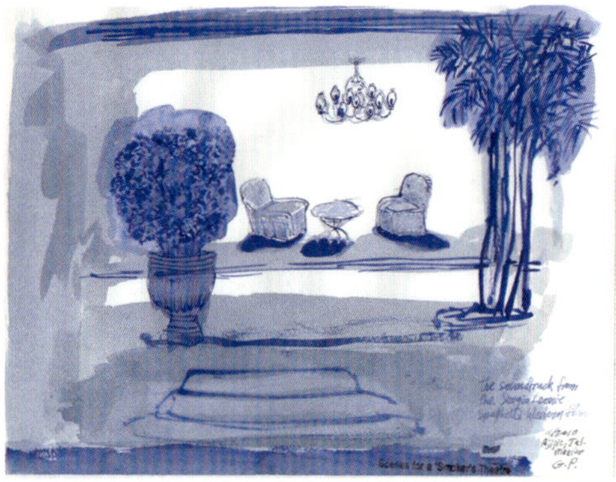

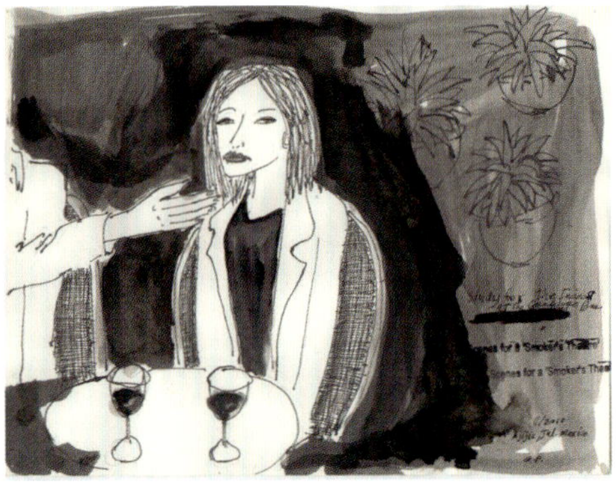

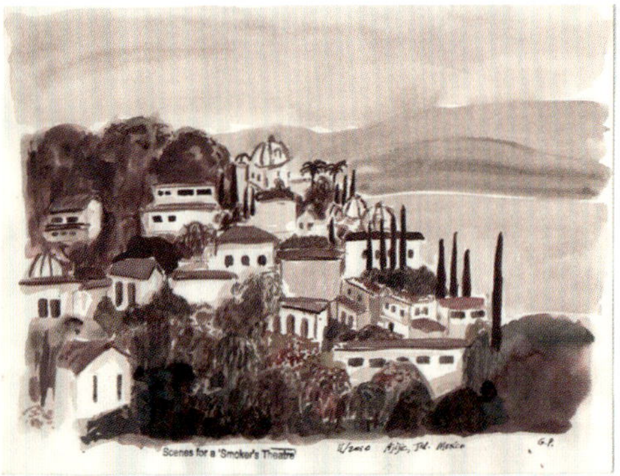

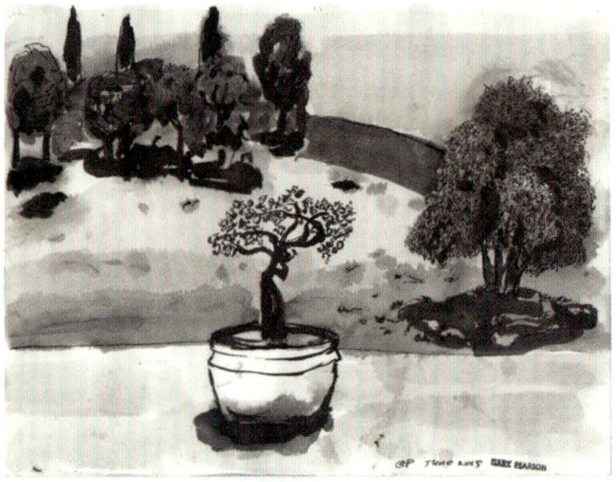
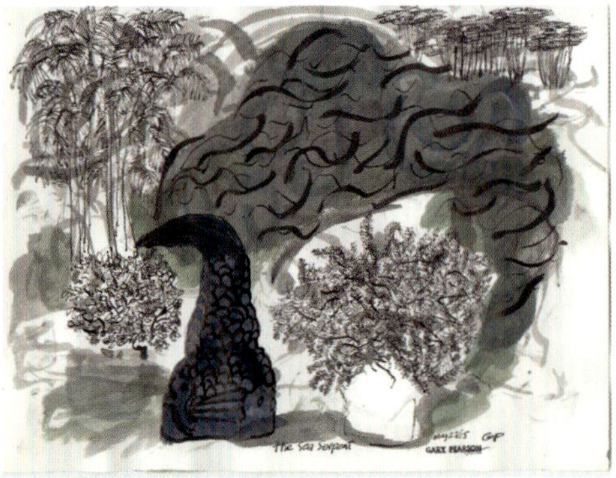

Various works and studies from 2010 and 2015

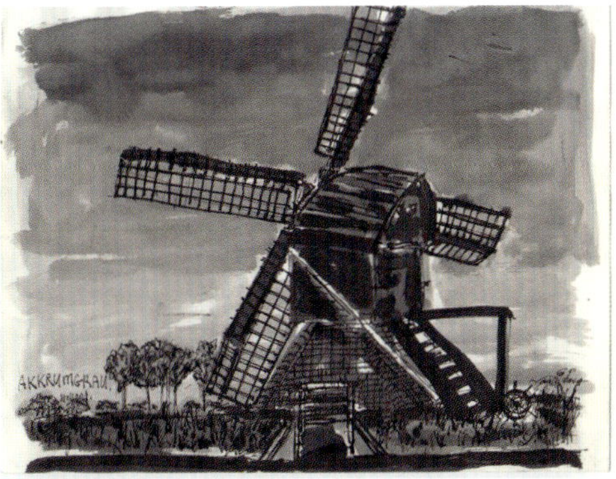
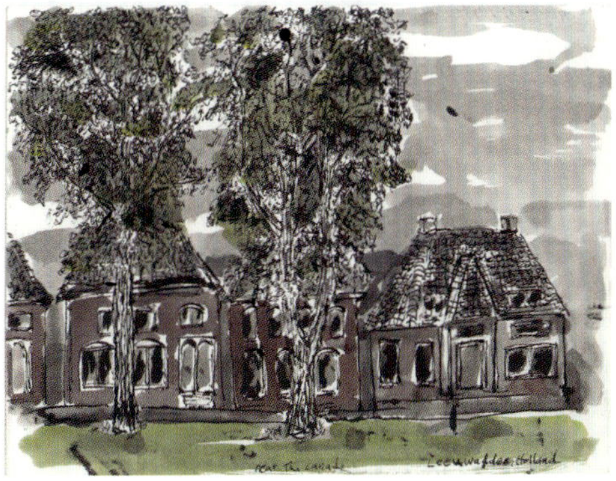
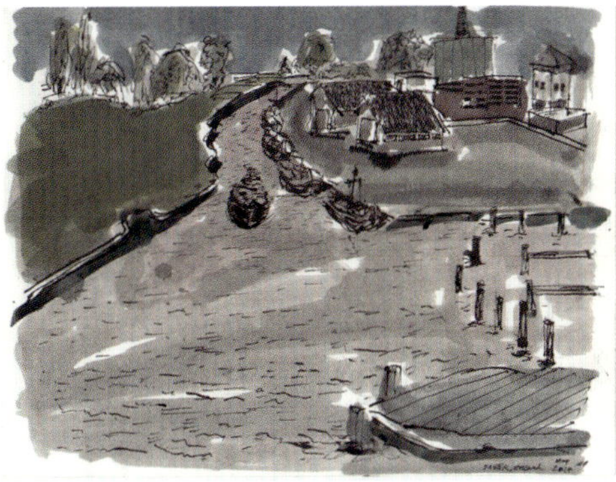
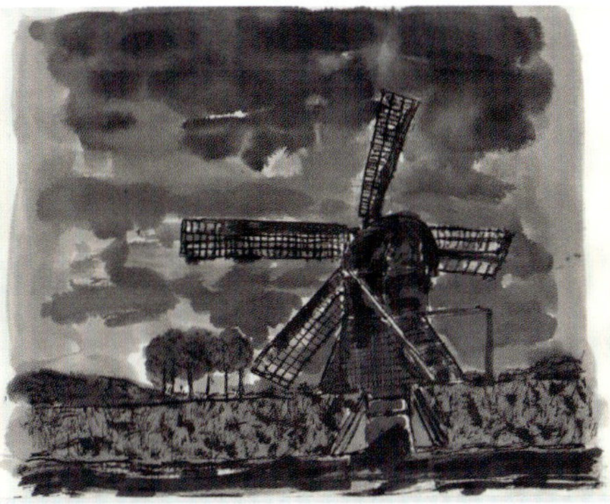
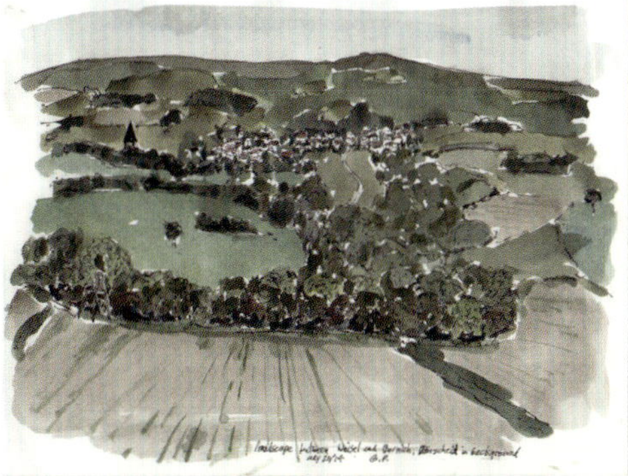
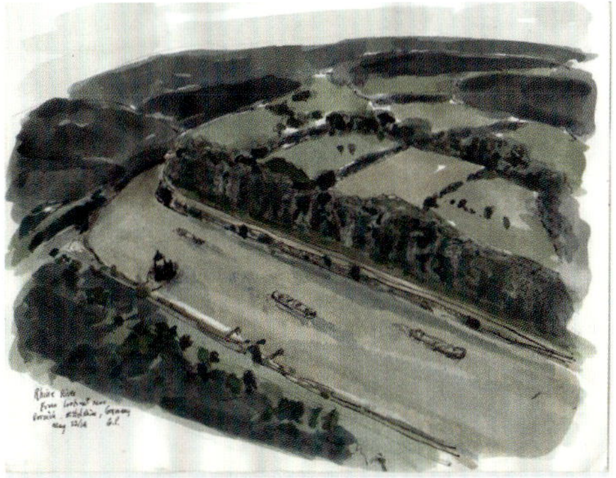
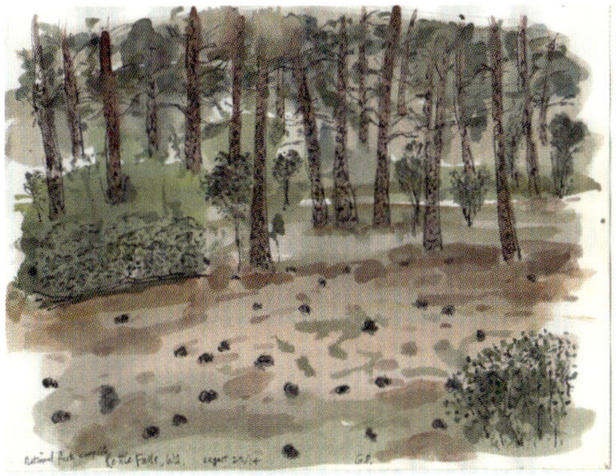
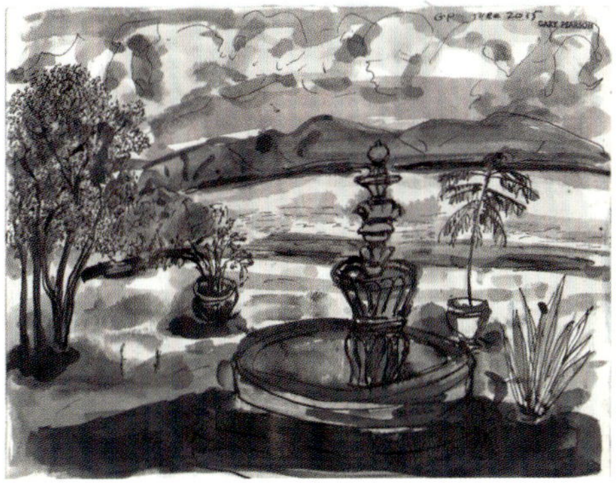



Various works and studies from 2014 to 2015

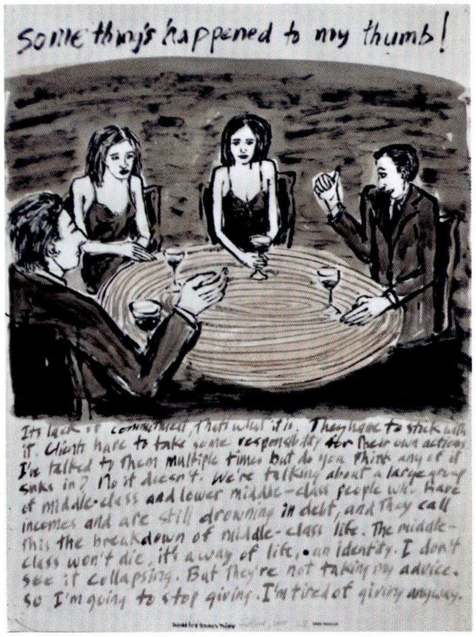


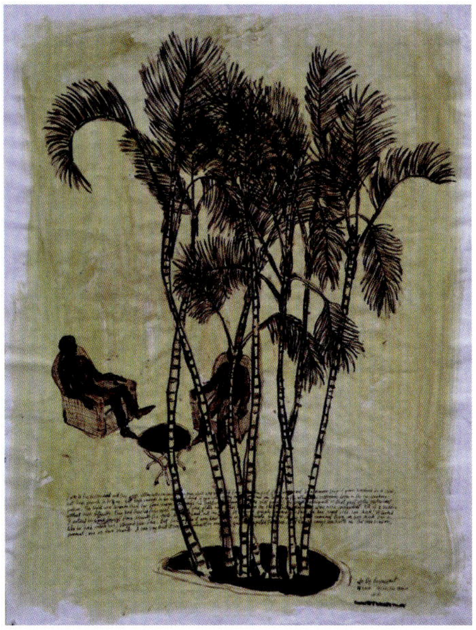

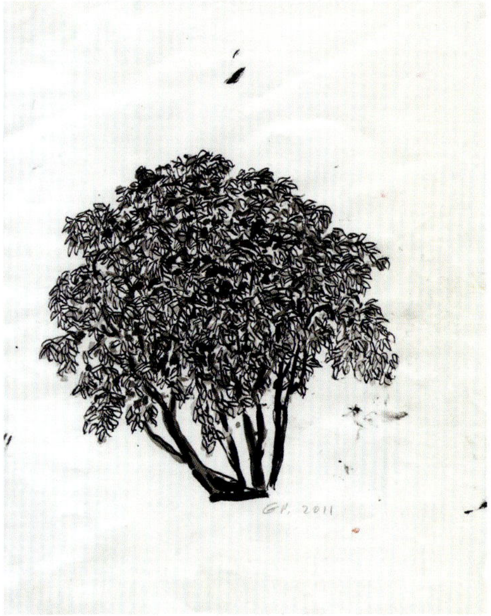


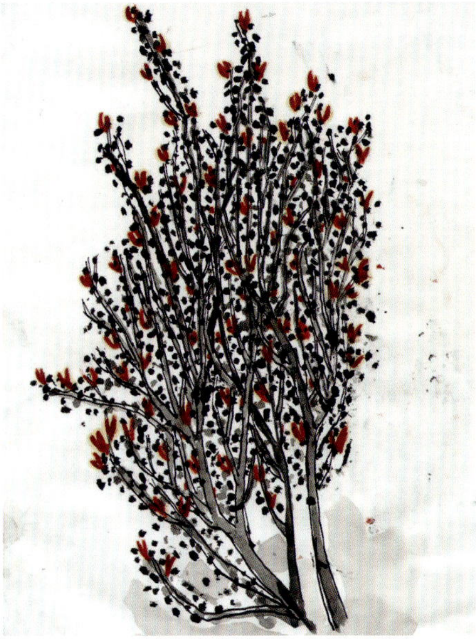

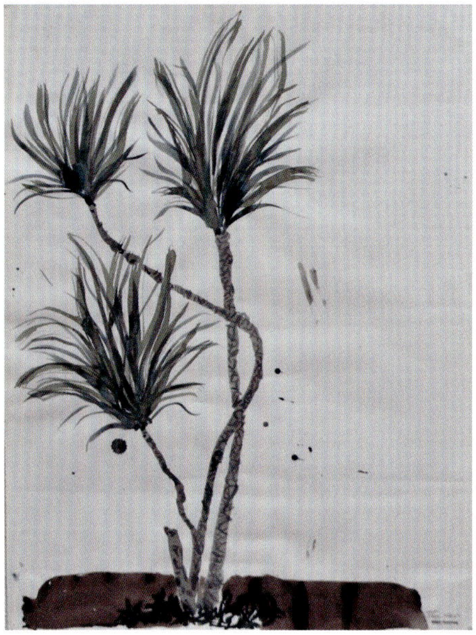

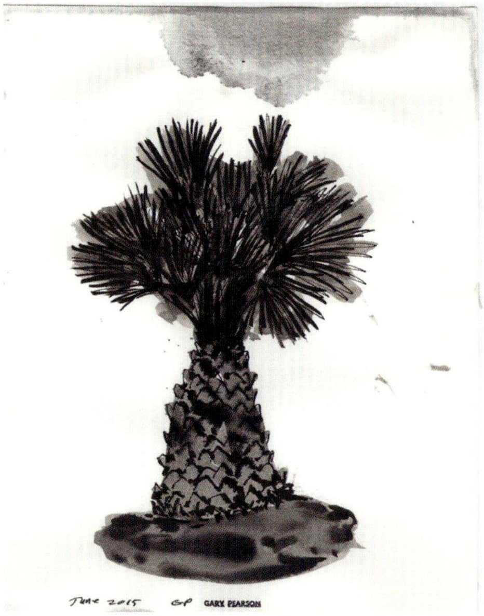


*Fatigue*, 2010
*In The Restaurant, Ajijic*, 2010
*Untitled (tree drawing)*, 2011
*Untitled*, 2011
*Palm*, 2015
*Palm Tree*, 2015

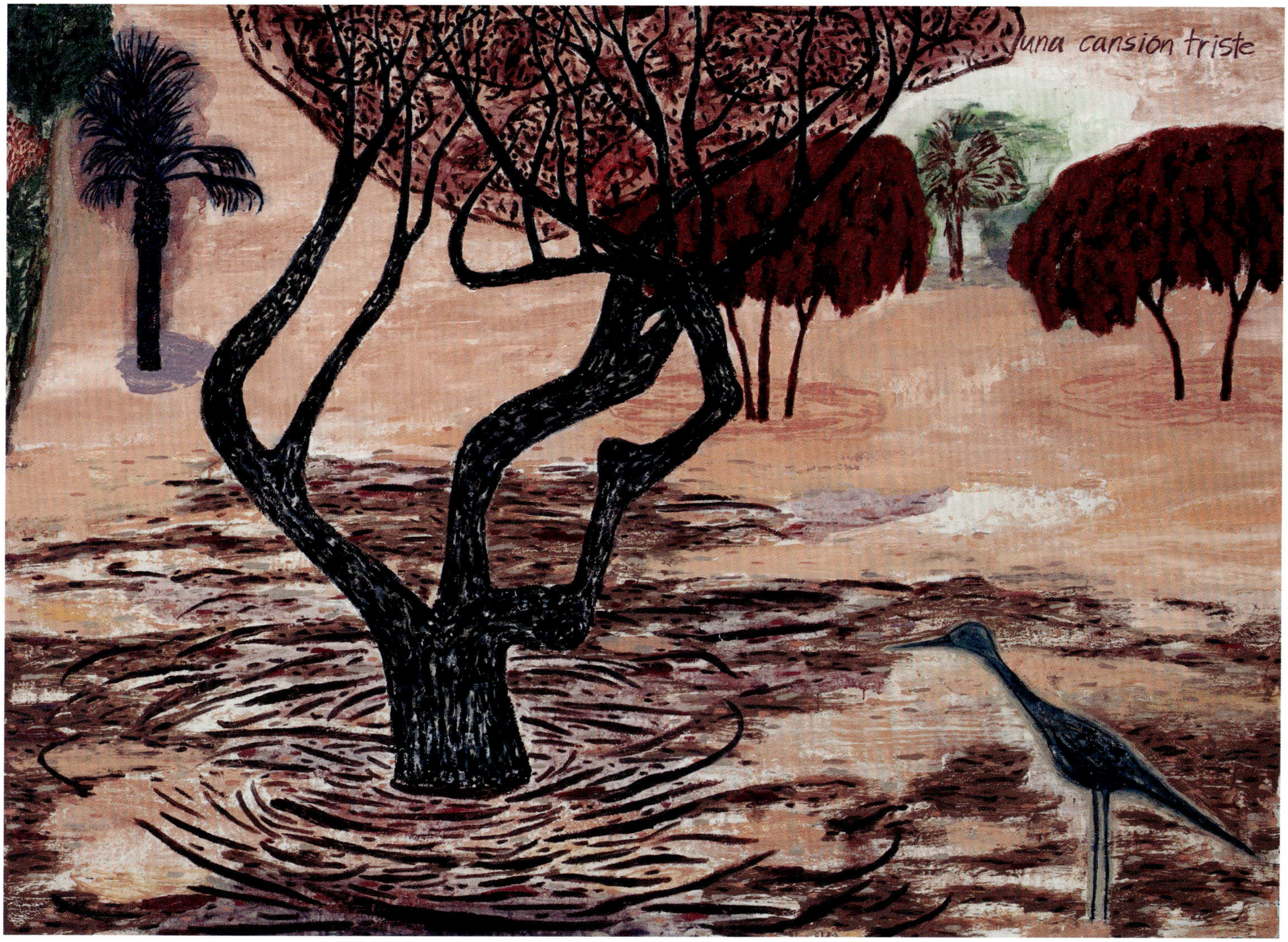




*Una Cansión Triste (A Sad Song)*, 2011

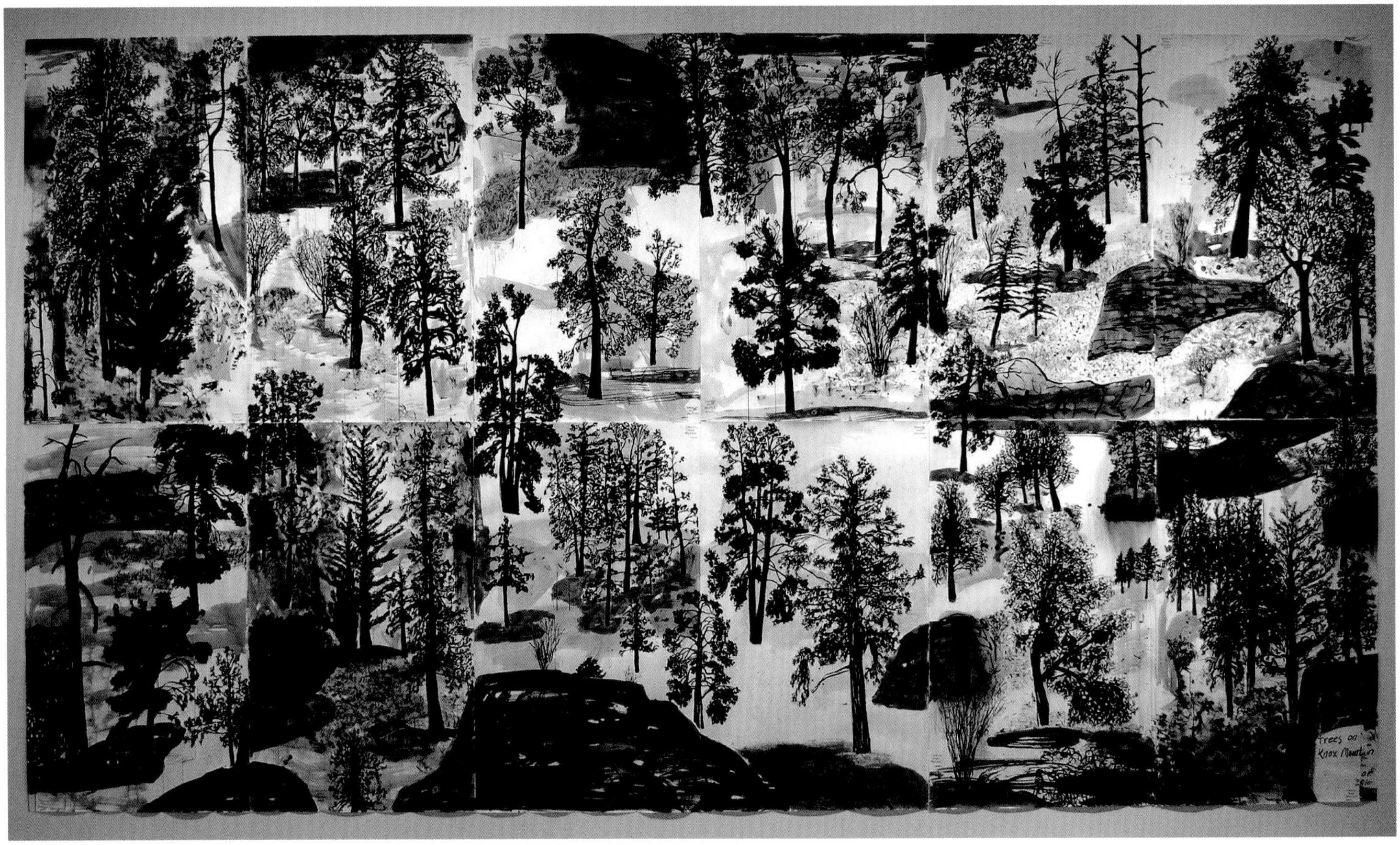

*Trees on Knox Mountain*, 2016

# Reflections on Gary Pearson's *Trees on Knox Mountain*

Aaron Peck

*I had to leave the country*
*Though there was some nice folk there*
*And now I don't know where I'm going*
*All I know is I'll hit the ground running*

Smog, "Hit the Ground Running"

One of the first things you notice about Gary Pearson's *Trees on Knox Mountain*, 2016, is its size. Consisting of 12 sheets of paper for a total of 3.6 by 6.4 metres, it is large. *Trees on Knox Mountain* is not a drawing exactly but a composite of drawings, placed next to one another, making one larger picture. Pearson composed his large-scale work so that there would be no single-point perspective. There is no foreground, middle ground or background. The viewer can approach any of the various sections of the drawing independently. In this way, the work has more in common with scrolls of classical Chinese painting than it does with much of the Western canon, except perhaps with David Hockney's recent Woldgate paintings. Pearson worked from over 150 photographs of trees and the surrounding Knox Mountain landscape to complete the drawing. Images of pines appear throughout it. Similarly to walking on a mountain, you can get lost in it. Exhibited at the Kelowna Art Gallery in 2016, *Trees on Knox Mountain* has since been broken down into six smaller units.

Ponderosa pines are the main variety of flora on Knox Mountain, but there are also fir trees, Saskatoon bushes, sagebrush and grass. When I look at *Trees on Knox Mountain*, I see something else as well. I see both a past and a place. Knox has a series of lookouts on roads and paths, all the way to its peak. In the summer, the dry grass hisses and rattles. Venturing off the pathways risks encountering rattlesnakes. As children in the Okanagan, we grew up aware of stories of rattlesnakes biting and killing young trailblazers, but these could have been more urban legend than fact. In reality, only two people have died from bites in the Okanagan since 1900.[1] Along with black widow spiders, rattlesnakes represented a kind of hidden threat, as well as a lingering sense that untameable nature lurked beneath the veneer of suburban development.

It is not visible, but I can sense it in *Trees on Knox Mountain*, which displays the terrain of that hillside, its aridity, as well as its stark and remarkable beauty. I understand why people move to the Okanagan, yet some of us, as the Smog song goes, had to leave. In 1999, the same year that song was released, I left for Vancouver to complete a degree in English literature and art history at the University of British Columbia that I had begun at Okanagan University College (OUC) in Kelowna. To my knowledge, I had never met Pearson. Yet, when in April of 2016 we lunched at one of my favourite Japanese restaurants in Vancouver to discuss the possibility of me writing this essay, he looked uncannily familiar.

Pearson is from a generation of Okanagan artists and writers I respect—people, such as John Lent, who moved to the valley as adults and managed to forge a creative life in its picturesque landscape inhabited by a population that was largely indifferent, even hostile, toward arts and culture. He is from that generation that, for professional or personal reasons, refused the provincialism of the place in a way that I, a child of it, could not.[2] And yet, all these years later, nothing signifies home to me more than the smell of pine resin in dry summer heat.

What years were the forest fires? In 1994, the Garnett fire burned the hills surrounding Penticton, where my grandparents lived. I had a basketball hoop set up in my parents' driveway. I played obsessively. I was never very good, never able to play pick-up with the jocks or make the cut for my high school team, never able to trash talk convincingly or, for that matter, to join the fierce order of virility that competitive sports ignites. I played alone. That summer, as Penticton burned, in Kelowna I practiced in my parents' driveway as ash sprinkled from a pumice-coloured sky. When we drove to visit my grandparents, the hills around the big "PENTICTON" sign were charred. To my eye, they still look that way. Earlier, in 1992, two teenagers playing with matches accidentally lit nearby Mount Boucherie on fire. From the window of a car, I glanced above the high school as we passed it on Highway 97 to check if a group of trees that I helped plant on Earth Day in 1989 had survived. It had not. In Vancouver in 2003, I watched on TV as Okanagan Mountain Park burned. I later discovered that a number of my friends' childhood homes were destroyed. To see a painting such as Pearson's *It's Burning!*, 2014, is to think of those fires.

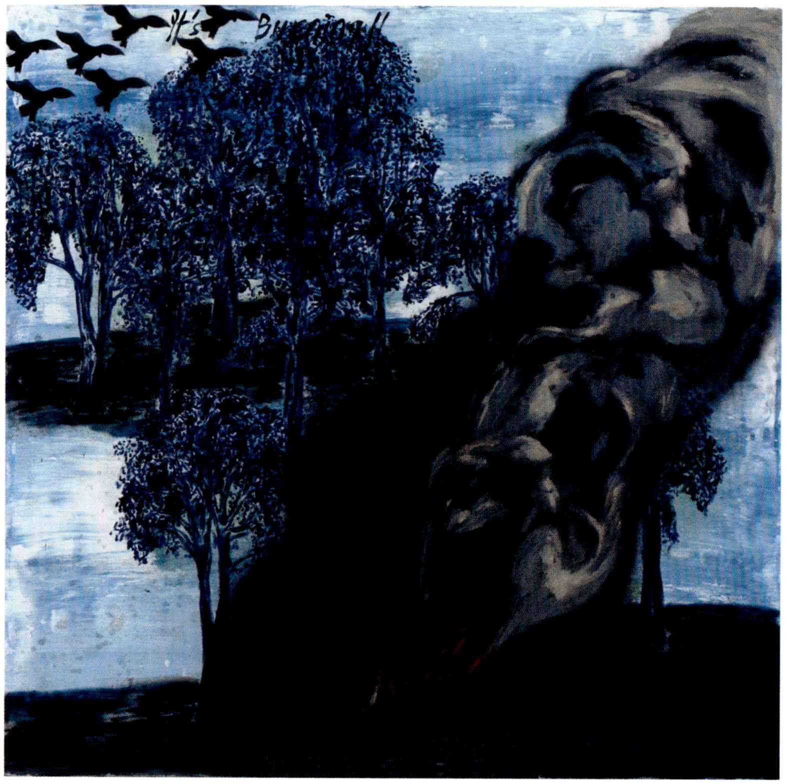

*It's Burning!*, 2013

I'm writing this essay in Brussels, where I currently live. It's early October, and the weather has shifted. I'm staring out of the window of my habitual cafe, Parlor Coffee Roasters on Chaussée de Charleroi, in the commune of St-Gilles. The light is typically northern. Brussels is at a latitude of 50°51'N, which makes it on par with Kamloops, BC, at 50°41'N. Yet Brussels shares nothing with any part of the BC interior. The trees here are different. Even the rain is. There's a series of parks south of the city that comprise the *forêt de Soignes*, which has the distinction of never having been anything other than a forest. No significant human development, except the odd chateau, has ever altered it. The *forêt de Soignes* is known for its carpet of bluebells in late April. But, to me, nature reserves like those feel commonplace, because I grew up among them. There is one in Kelowna's Mission neighbourhood, Woodhaven Nature Conservancy, where I gave a reading in the summer of 2014. When I was a child, we called it the Woodhaven Bird Sanctuary. It was only a ten-minute bike ride from the house I grew up in. The namesake of my elementary school, Bear Creek, runs through Woodhaven, near a 100-year-old horse stable. Aside from that, the area is mostly untouched, along with entire zones of BC, which remain on the historical and geographical edge of European destruction.

Pearson's work and life look toward Europe and European models. The stylistic influence of figurative avant-garde painters such as Giorgio de Chirico, Otto Dix and Georg Grosz, among others, is evident in his painting, while his writing and video work further expand his practice into contemporary media. In general though, he is drawn to German Expressionism. Somehow he transforms it into an Okanagan idiom. But what does that mean, an Okanagan idiom? That question is at the heart of this text, and what I see in Pearson's work. In person, the artist speaks with what I might call a 1980s Vancouver accent. He has the cadence and inflection of a number of people his age who, like him, spent time in Vancouver in the 80s. When I was a child, his kind of accent meant sophistication. He does not speak as though he is from the Okanagan (although I wonder if I do hear hints of the northern BC in his speech—he was, after all, raised in Prince George).[3] In any case, he doesn't have an Okanagan accent. I don't either, anymore, although I know how to put it on, often in the presence of old friends; it's automatic, and often out of my control. So what is it about Pearson's work that registers or responds to the Okanagan? I am convinced that it is more than the geographical happenstance of his residence. Of course, there are certain motifs (fire, smoke, arid landscapes), and there is also his colour palette of near-monochromes, at times matching the colours of the Okanagan winter. Even a painting such as *Condominium*, 2014, showing us the side of a large apartment block, seems to possess this—the size of the building, only a few stories higher than the tree, fits with the average height of buildings in Kelowna, which, as I was told as a child, conformed to zoning regulations and safety in case of earthquakes. Now that building technologies have improved and skyscrapers can allegedly withstand seismic threats, even on swampy ground, the height of most buildings in the Okanagan remains modest. I could imagine the structure depicted in *Condominium* around Harvey and Ethel, or anywhere further along Harvey, in Kelowna. When Gary depicts the contemporary world—not the world of an imaginary Europe—often the settings seem placed in Okanagan realities, even if they are, in fact, not.

Pearson's landscapes stand independent of their geography, but for someone who was shaped by a place his paintings also have a more complex context. For me, while there is no violence depicted in his work, its presence nevertheless can be felt. The eeriness of his paintings,

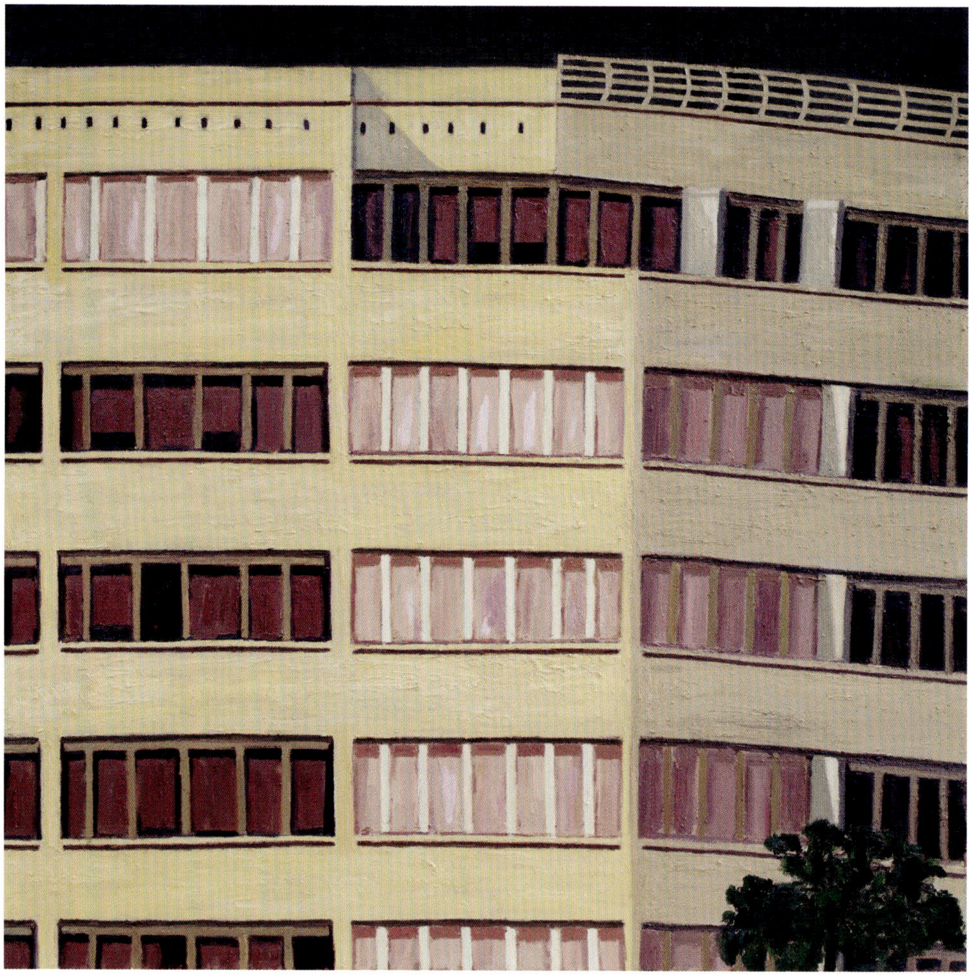

*Condominium*, 2013

the sense that something is lurking underneath, matches the subdued violence of BC—saturated in oil money from the 1990s onward, and in organized crime. Not to mention the devastation caused by the forestry industry. The Okanagan is not unique in this way. It's the reality of all of Western Canada—the colonial frontier mentality cultivated beneath a weak pretence of development and progress, situated on unceded First Nations land. This facade, which of course is reflected as much in early frontier architecture as well as in its contemporary buildings, has become part of the culture. Now and then, that facade is punctured. I remember the first time I witnessed random violence. It was during a heat wave in Kelowna in the mid-1990s. Bridge-bound traffic along Harvey had come to a standstill. The temperature was around 35°C. Horns were honking. And then a man got out of his car, walked to the car behind him, opened the door, grabbed the man in the other car, threw him to the ground and started kicking him into the curb; violence, like a forest fire, in conditions that made it both unexpected and obvious. Was it the heat, or was it what I saw? I almost threw up. We were near the beach. It could have been a scene from a Godard film.

Pearson's paintings suggest a place where the quality of life and outward beauty do not entirely hide its brutality. Welcome to Beautiful British Columbia, Super Natural. That sense of spiritual darkness bridges his European motifs to his Okanagan idiom. What is it about this shadow of Europe projected onto an occupied territory? A painting like his *Girl and Dog*, 2014, which reflects the influence of the dreamscapes of de Chirico, depicts an empty street in what appears to be a European city. The painting is based on a photograph he took in Leeuwarden, the Netherlands, in about 2012. With the way he has modified the image for this painting, we are no longer in photographic reality, we're in a dreamscape, or fantasy. We're in the Okanagan dreaming of Europe. The road appears unpaved with the traces of muddy wheel tracks, which implies that the painting has transported us into the past. A girl sits on a chair against a building that has a sign saying "café-bar", next to a bicycle. The bicycle places the painting within the early modern era, so maybe the late nineteenth century or early twentieth—the imagined world of early-twentieth-century avant-garde figurative painting? Near the girl, in the road, he depicts a dog lying on the ground. And that is all. It is an affecting painting because of what it leaves unrepresented. There is some kind of event or action, but it is unclear *what*. The dog on the street—is it sleeping or dead? If Pearson presented the photograph, the image would lose some of its power. It would be clear that the dog was resting with her master. As a painting, it is transformed into something else, something more suggestive, even sinister.

There are other elements, too. His tendency toward an early-twentieth-century German Expressionist aesthetic, perhaps the last significant moment in the avant-garde to emphasize figuration, has meant that Pearson employs both of that era's two great scenes: the cafe and the cabaret. They appear frequently in both Pearson's videos and paintings. I also recognize the motifs from another source, because the cafe, or coffee house, figured in my teenage years in the Okanagan. Place, such as the Bean Scene or Judge R Bean, were where bohemians, beatniks and other freaks and freethinkers gathered. There was a sense that spaces like these were gathering spaces of creativity. A friend of mine, also from the Okanagan, recently translated Patrick Modiano's *Dans le café de la jeunesse perdue* (as *In the Café of Lost Youth*). After rereading it recently, it occurs to me that the mid-twentieth-century Parisian underworld cafe culture as described by Modiano was a model for the one that existed in the Okanagan during my own lost youth, the kind of scenes that continually appear in Pearson's paintings.

The cafe symbolizes art, creativity and freedom. For example, in Kelowna in the 1990s, cafes were the only places you would encounter 'out' trans or queer people in public. Pearson's depictions of cafes remind me of those spaces. And here I am in one in Brussels! The decor and spirit are different, more an effect of changing aesthetics and cultural attitudes than geography (the Nordic style that replaced the homely 90s style of second-hand furniture and big café-au-lait bowls). No doubt Kelowna now has its third-wave places too, in an interchangeable *Kinfolk* magazine kind of way. Here or there, I could strike a figure that might appear in such a place, *n'importe ou*. It was in cafes throughout the Okanagan in the 1990s, with their ratty couches and coffee, that my friends would put on shows—gigs, we called them—of local bands with names like Maev Brennan, a nod to a local reporter (who appeared in Pearson's anthology of Okanagan artists, *The Creative Voice*), or the Metic. Now, as a kind of elevator music, indie rock plays at these cafes all over the world.

And yet, as with *Girl and Dog*, I grew up in the Okanagan dreaming of other places, other cafes, but I was unaware of what they looked like yet. When you're young, unless you have the luxury of travel, the landscape around you forms your sense of the world. Later, other images and landscapes take their place until something again dislodges them from memory—in my case, a sudden invitation to write an exhibition catalogue essay from an artist living in my childhood town. Do you ever really leave? Of course—and yet, of course not. Treks up Knox Mountain

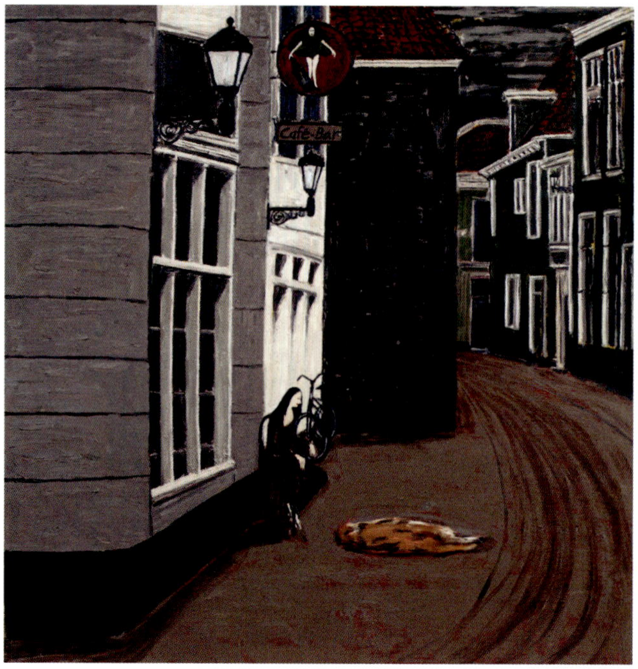



*Girl and Dog*, 2014

are among my first memories—the lookouts, our family Datsun, the pine trees and the sage brush; only later do you realize that other worlds exist too. I see that in Pearson's work. Those worlds are placed next to each other, like images in a slide projector tray.

Throughout the 1980s, my parents ran a craft store in Kelowna on Pandosy Street, just a block from the current Mosaic Books (I grew up with it at its old address, near the museum). I spent some of my early childhood in their store's backroom watching *Mr. Dressup*. A few years ago, I stopped by the old space. It was the first time I had been in Kelowna in ten years. We were passing through on our way to Vernon to visit a friend of mine. There, in front of the old storefront, I raced into the side alley and through the back parking lot, where I would play when I was little. Not long after the Regatta riots of 1986 and 1987, my parents sold the store. The morning after the first riot, we cleaned up the shards of broken glass and tallied whatever pottery and beads had been stolen.[4] The next year we watched news coverage on television the day before the second riot, of men holding hitchhiking signs: "Trying to Get to Kelowna Riot". The day after, again we cleaned up the mess. That year, 200 people were arrested, and, according to the Associated Press, "Damage was estimated at $500,000 Canadian, most of it in broken glass."[5] These memories are, of course, juxtaposed with more fond ones of the lake and hikes at Bertram Creek Park, Knox, or Woodhaven. Still, these circumstances make me look at Pearson's work differently. When I see his work, I see something of the place where I spent my childhood. I see something with a surface that hints at more—the threat of fire or organized crime, a rattlesnake in the crooks of a grass-covered pathway.

What leads a person here? What leads them away? Happenstance—that is to say, a teaching job—led Pearson to Kelowna. Necessity—that is to say, a university degree—led me to Vancouver. Then other things led me even further afield. If our lives are shaped by our will, our will, in turn, is governed by chance. At the time I left the Okanagan, I could only think of it the way James Joyce thought of Ireland—that in order to create art, or even really just to live, you had to put yourself in self-imposed exile; you had to leave. But, as I age, I realize that is untrue, that my initial 18-year-old reading of *Portrait of the Artist as a Young Man*, sitting on a porch in Peachland overlooking the valley, reflected the way a teenager thinks. Pearson, along with a handful of others, made an artistic and cultural life for themselves in Kelowna, and others continue to do so now. And in that way, he is very much a BC boy. As, in another way, am I. In considering his work, I also think about more than landscape or painting or video art. I confront a time that is no longer accessible, and what that time means to me, and how it reveals itself in the artist's work. Which led me to listen to Smog, returning me to the feeling of those aimless nights driving Highway 97 with the windows rolled down during the last full summer I spent in the valley, the scent of pine resin in the air. That time is gone. What of it? For me, it resurfaces in unexpected details in Pearson's work, such as those trees of Knox Mountain.

In the late summer or early fall of 1994, a friend and I walked down to Sarsons Beach. Reports claimed that the northern lights would be visible in subdued colours. We watched them for hours and talked. In retrospect, those hypnotic glimmerings, which on that evening rarely erupted into any colour at all, shared the same colour palette as Pearson's paintings. Downtown, we knew which bars the biker gangs owned; I often felt less safe on the block of Lawrence between Water and Abbott, where some of the strip clubs were, than I did when, in my mid-twenties, I lived in a pre-gentrified Harlem. In the Okanagan, I preferred the empty beach, where we observed the outer atmosphere flickering against the stars. If I close my eyes, I can still see it.

1 "Beware of rattlesnakes and their bite this season", *The Oliver Chronicle*, 24 May 2013, http://www.oliverchronicle.com/beware-of-rattlesnakes-and-their-bite-this-season/.

2 In 2005, OUC, with small campuses scattered throughout the valley, was dismantled. Its central campus was transformed into the "University of British Columbia—Okanagan." As such, the school I attended no longer exists. Pearson was among OUC's faculty who transferred to UBCO. If UBCO had been around in the 1990s, I wonder if I would have ever left the Okanagan.

3 The great BC writer and Okanagan boy George Bowering, on a number of occasions, has insisted to me that Elite Restaurant in Penticton, a classic diner that serves pies I like, is properly pronounced *Ee-lite*, not *eleet*. A few years ago when I asked the manager about the pronunciation of the restaurant, his nonchalant reply was, "Some of the older-timers call it that."

4 The leftover stock from that store still remains in the storage unit of my mother's Vancouver apartment. I even brought two pieces with me to Brussels—a cup for toothbrushes and a soap-dish. The other day, while I was cleaning, the dish cracked. Within hours, I had it tentatively together again, glued with Epoxy.

5 "Nearly 200 Arrested in Regatta Violence", *Associated Press*, 27 May 1987, http://www.apnewsarchive.com/1987/Nearly-200-Arrested-in-Regatta-Violence/id-f385167aa2e912221dab7ab925a96c88, accessed 20 February 2017.

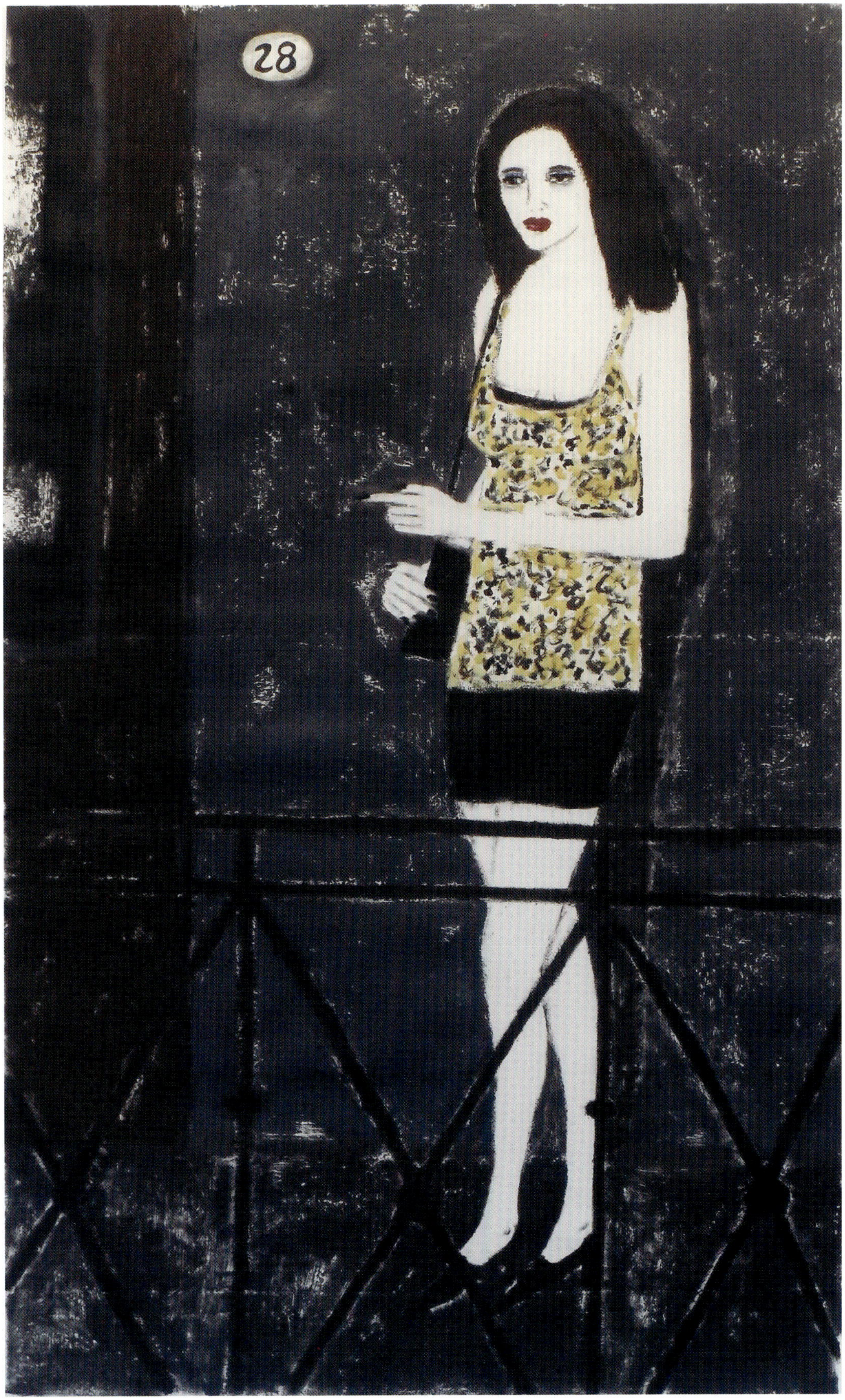




*No. 28 Carrer de Ferran*, 2013

He was in a hat shop in Granada, Spain, trying on an Andalusian beret, which looks very close to the kind of beret Rembrandt wore in many of his self-portraits. The man was about 60 years old, German, with grey, somewhat greasy hair that fell straight to his shoulders. His wife complimented him on his appearance as he stood in front of the mirror adjusting the angle of the hat's incline. He openly complained about the €50 price tag but both the clerk and the man's wife ignored him.

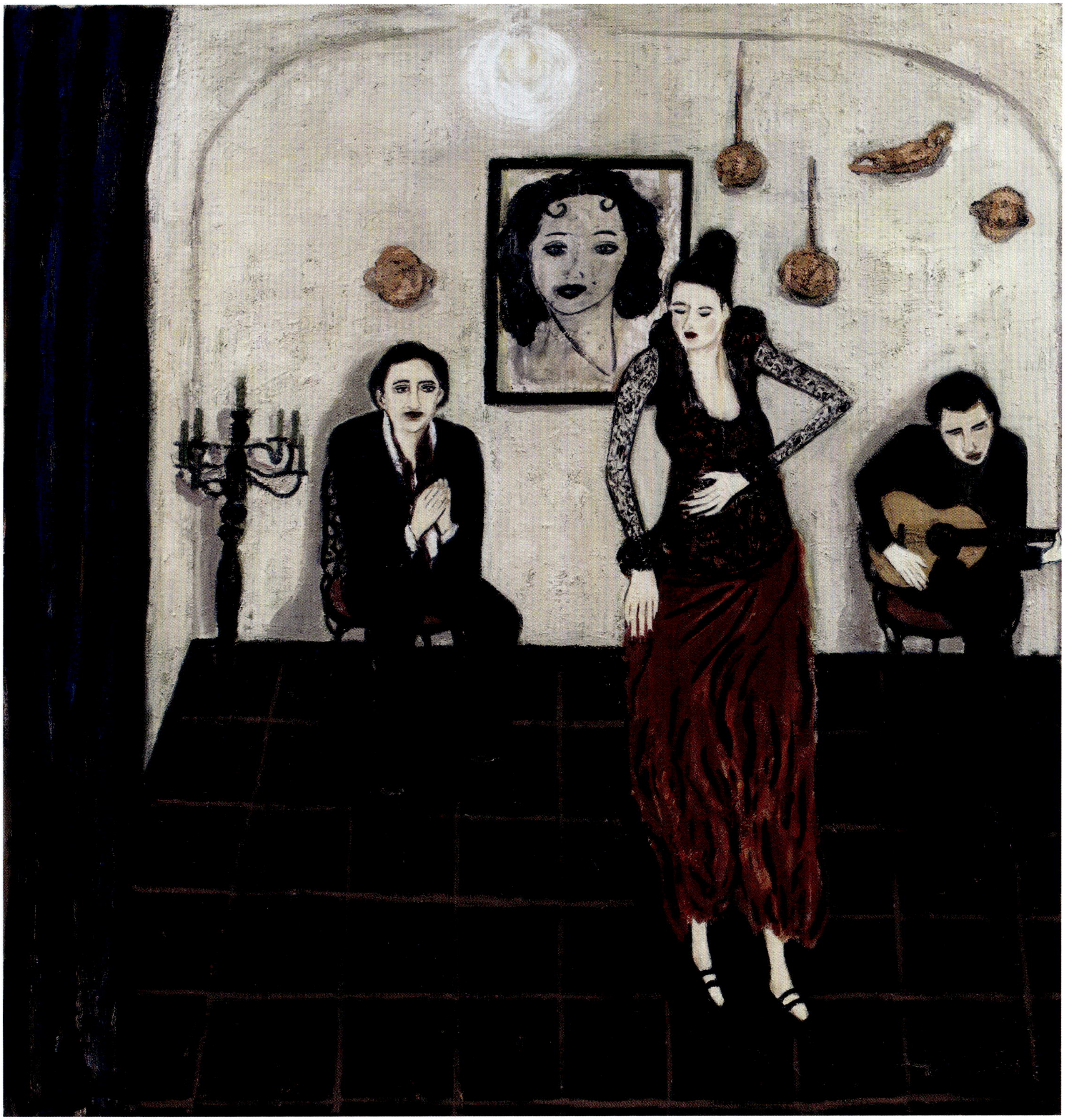



*The Flamenco Dancer*, 2014

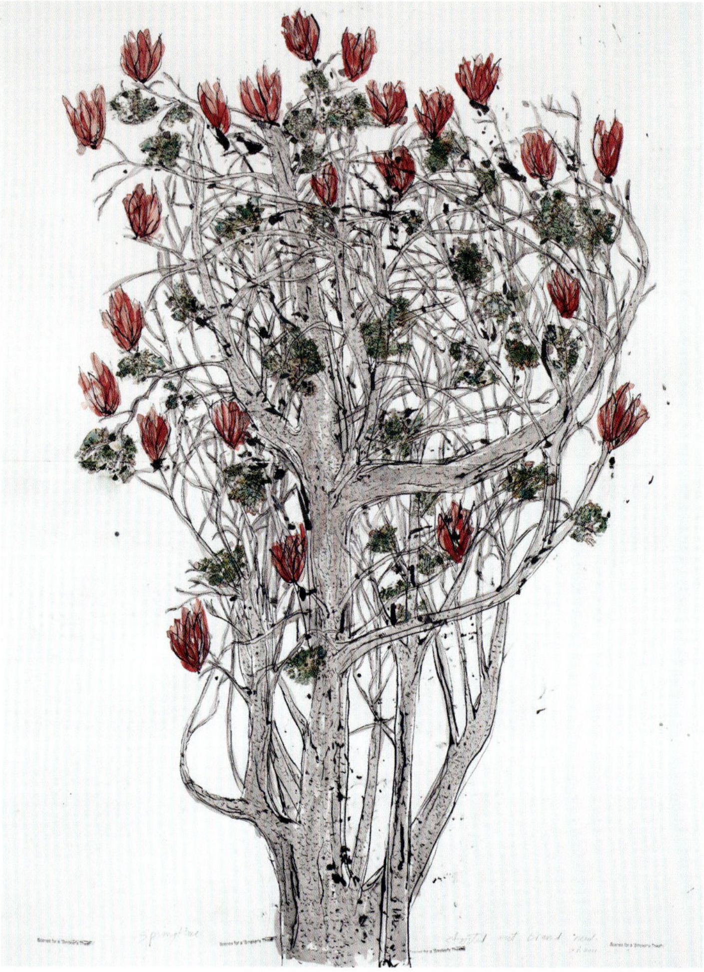

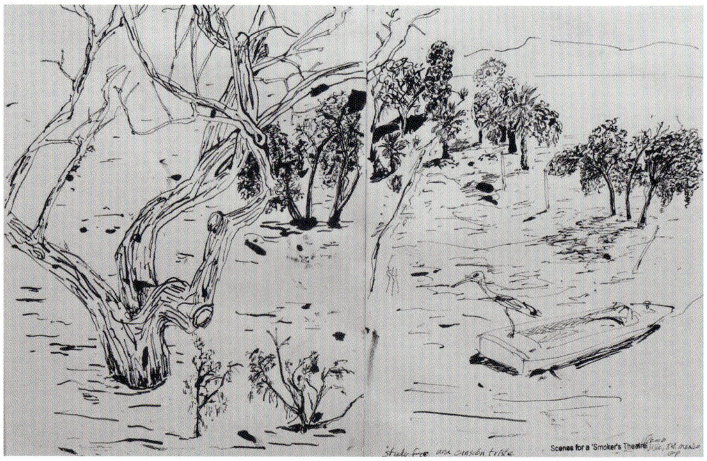


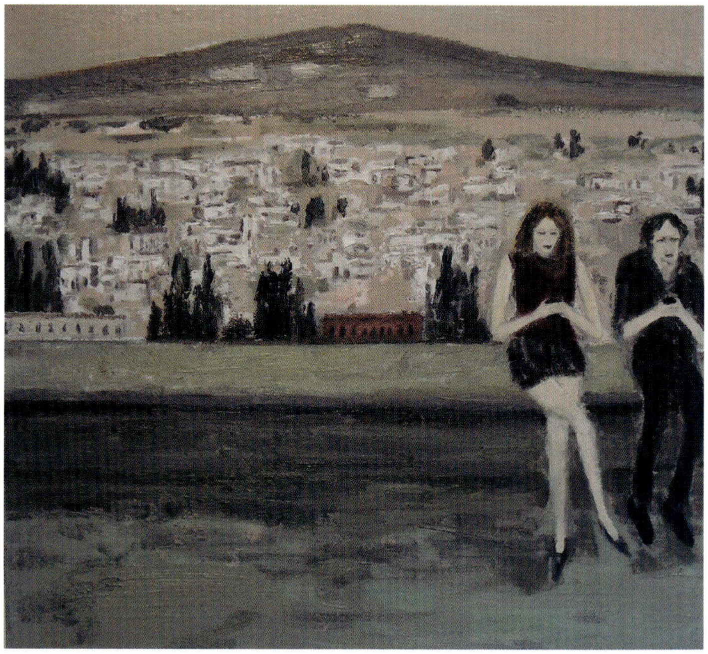

*Springtime Started Out Brand New*, 2010
*Study for Una Cansión Triste*, 2010
*The Conversation*, 2015

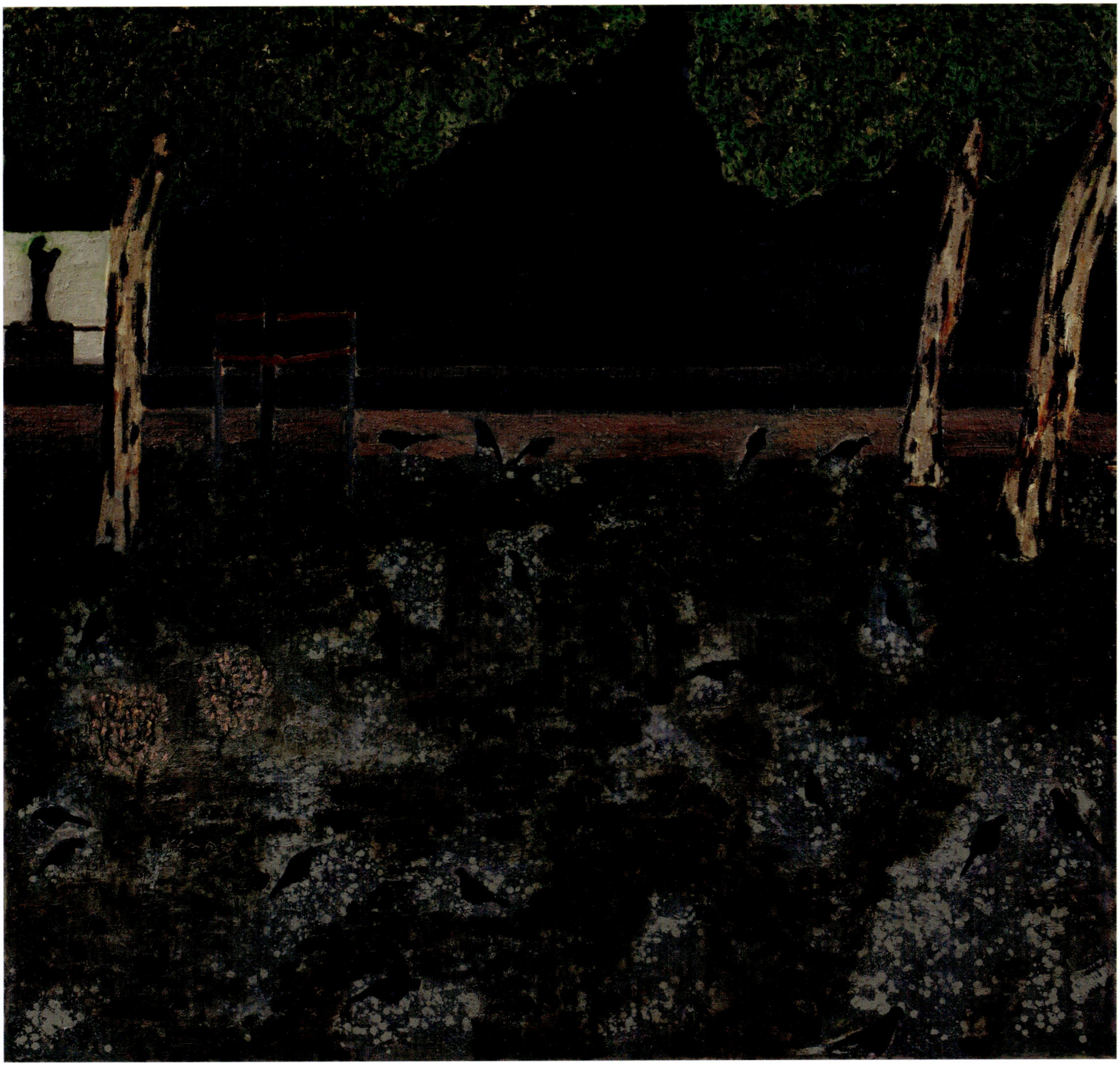

*Mother and Child*, 2014

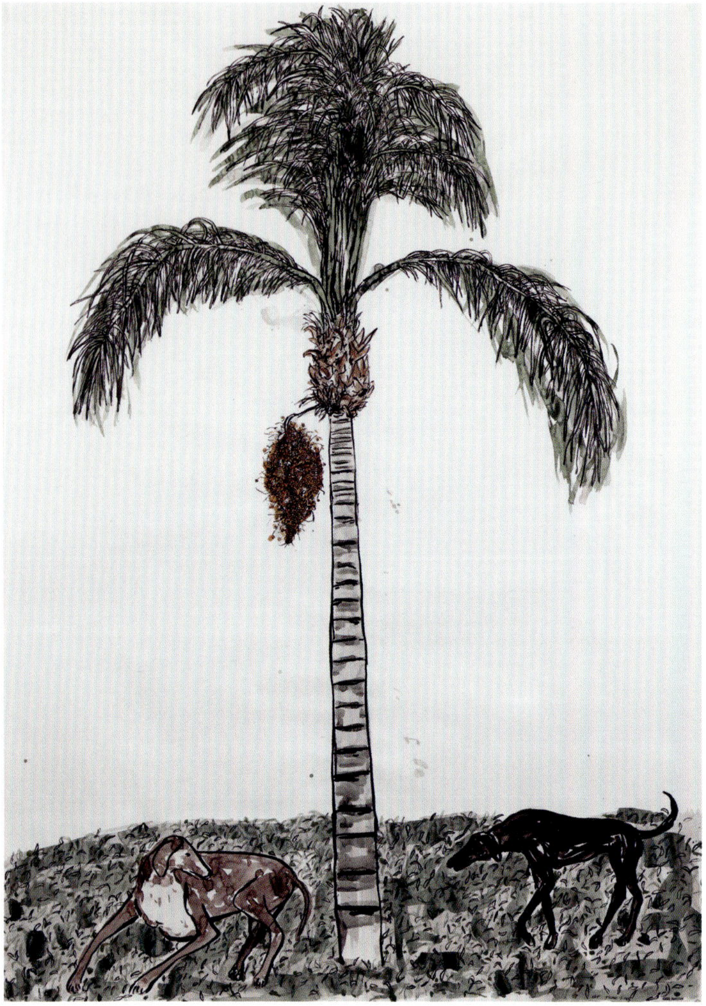

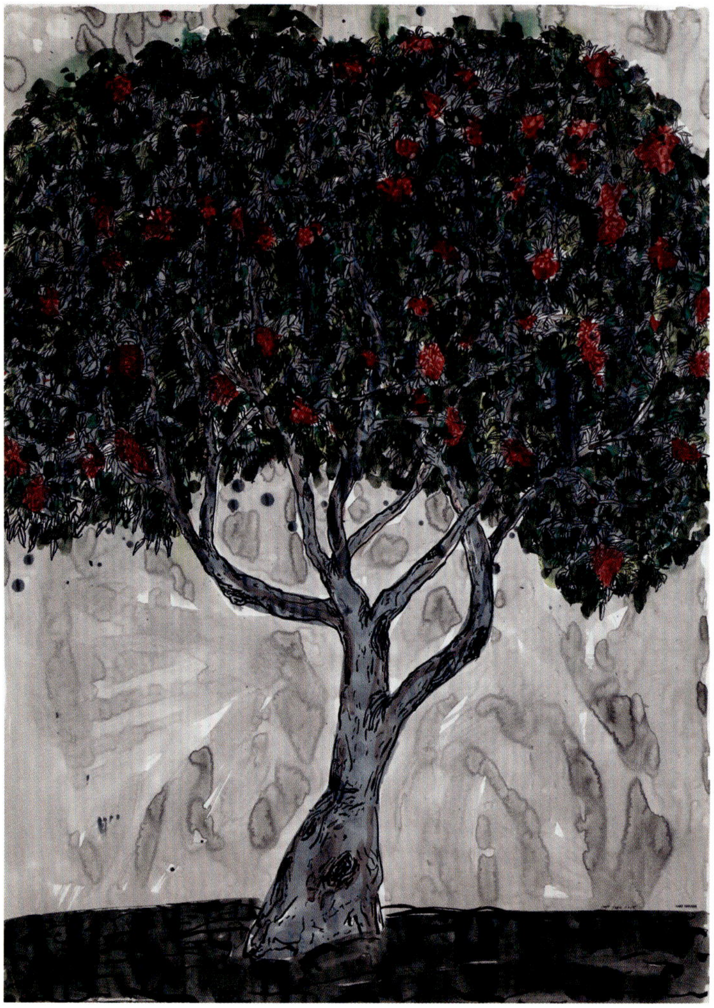

*Untitled (dogs)*, 2015
*Untitled*, 2015

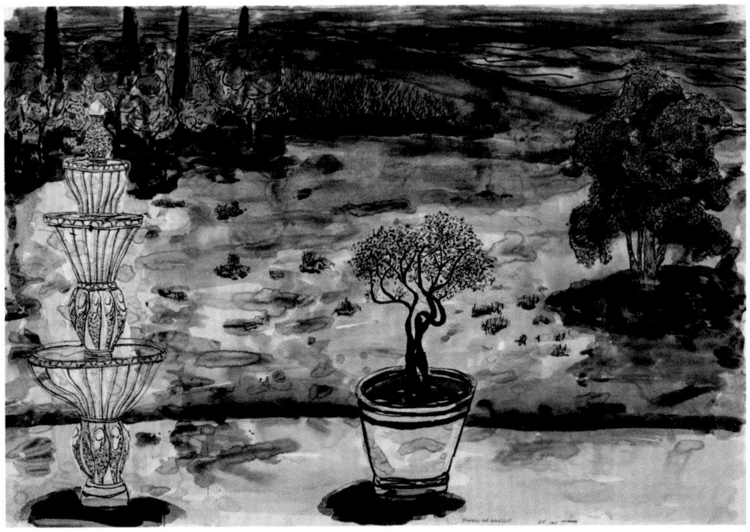

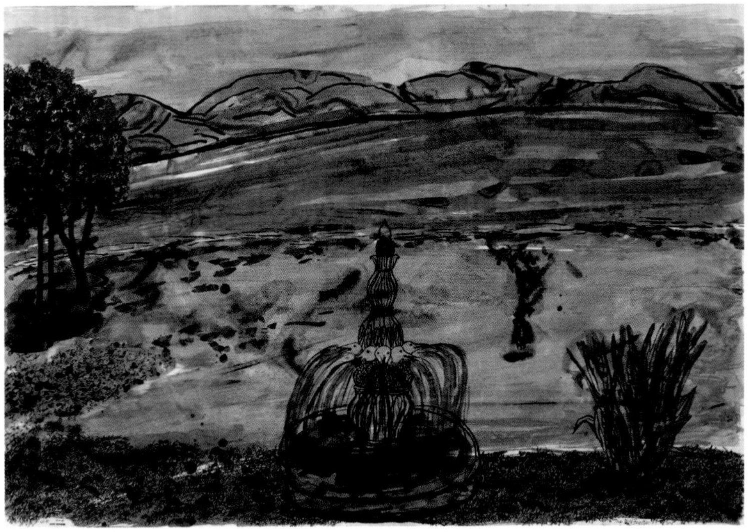

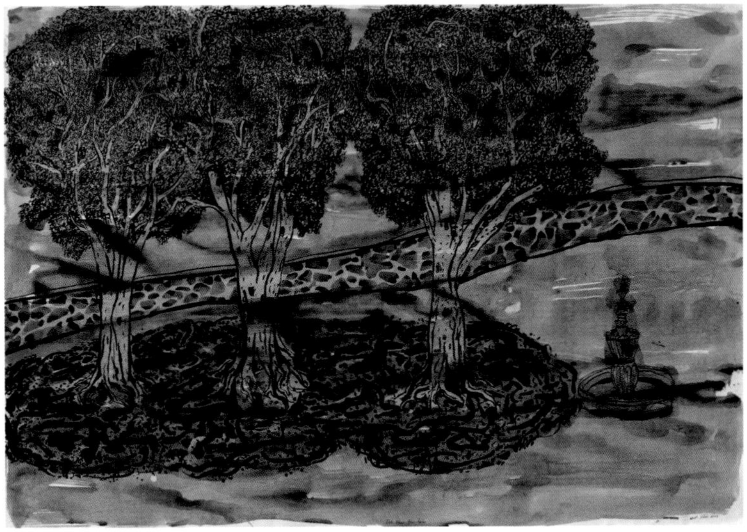

*Fountain and Potted Plant*, 2015
*The Bird Fountain (paper work)*, 2015
*The Blue Fountain*, 2015

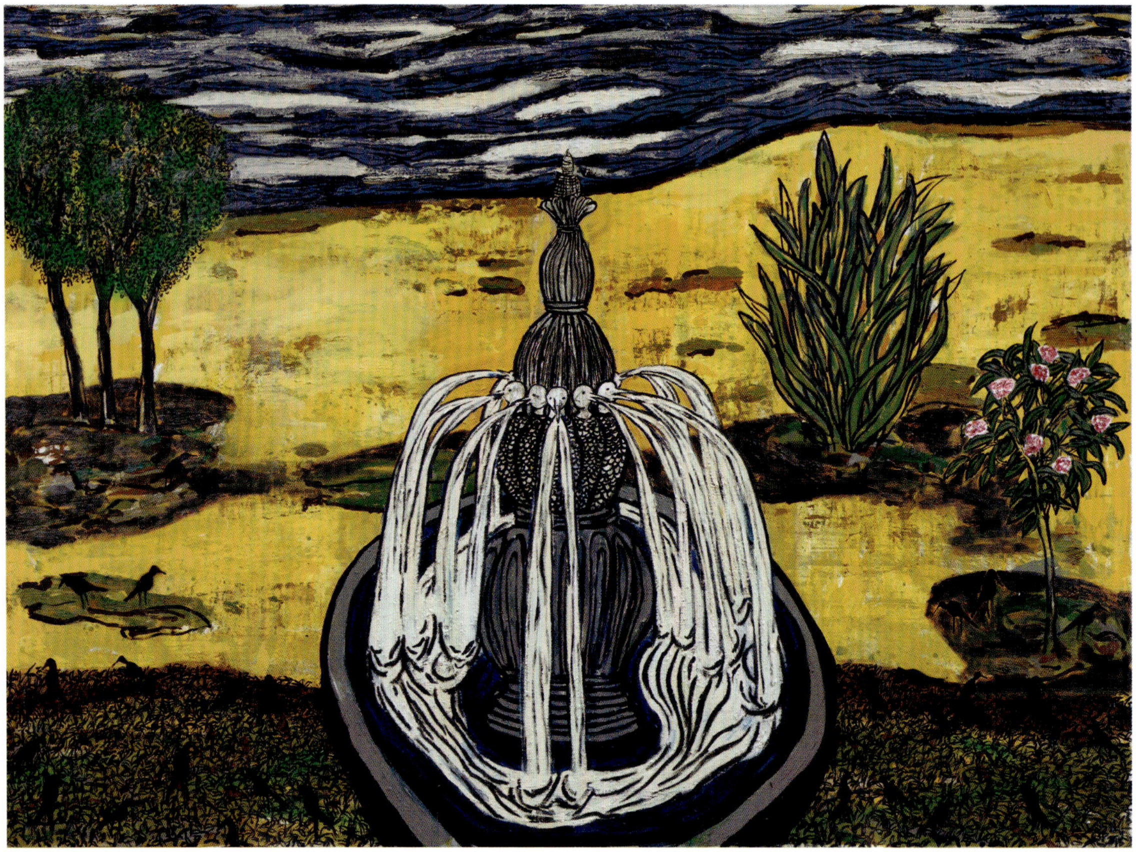

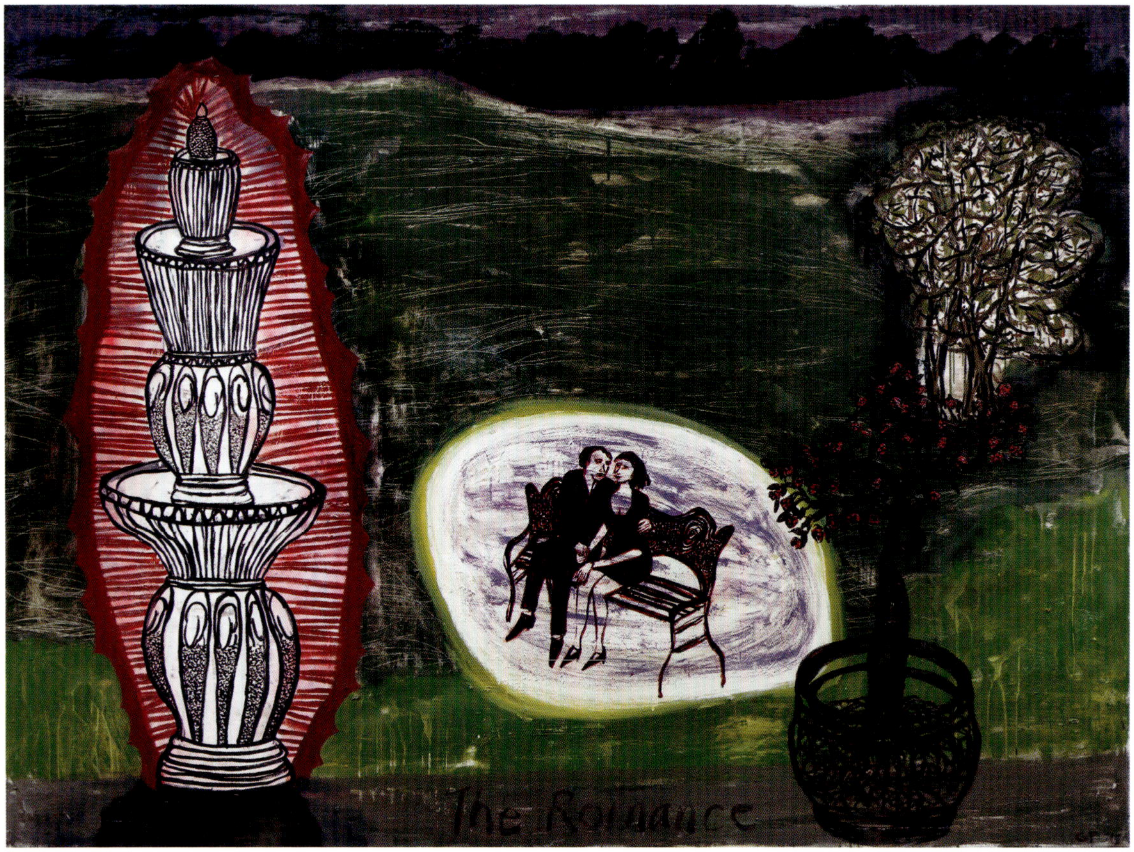




*The Bird Fountain*, 2015
*The Romance*, 2015

A woman in her late forties sits on a stool at a raised bar-room table. She has a drink in front of her. She drags obsessively but dispassionately on her cigarette. She only pauses to exhale, and never puts the cigarette down or shakes off the ash. The cigarette is always between two fingers and almost always in her mouth. As each cigarette burns down, another one is lit from the hot ash. She does not take a drink from her cocktail.

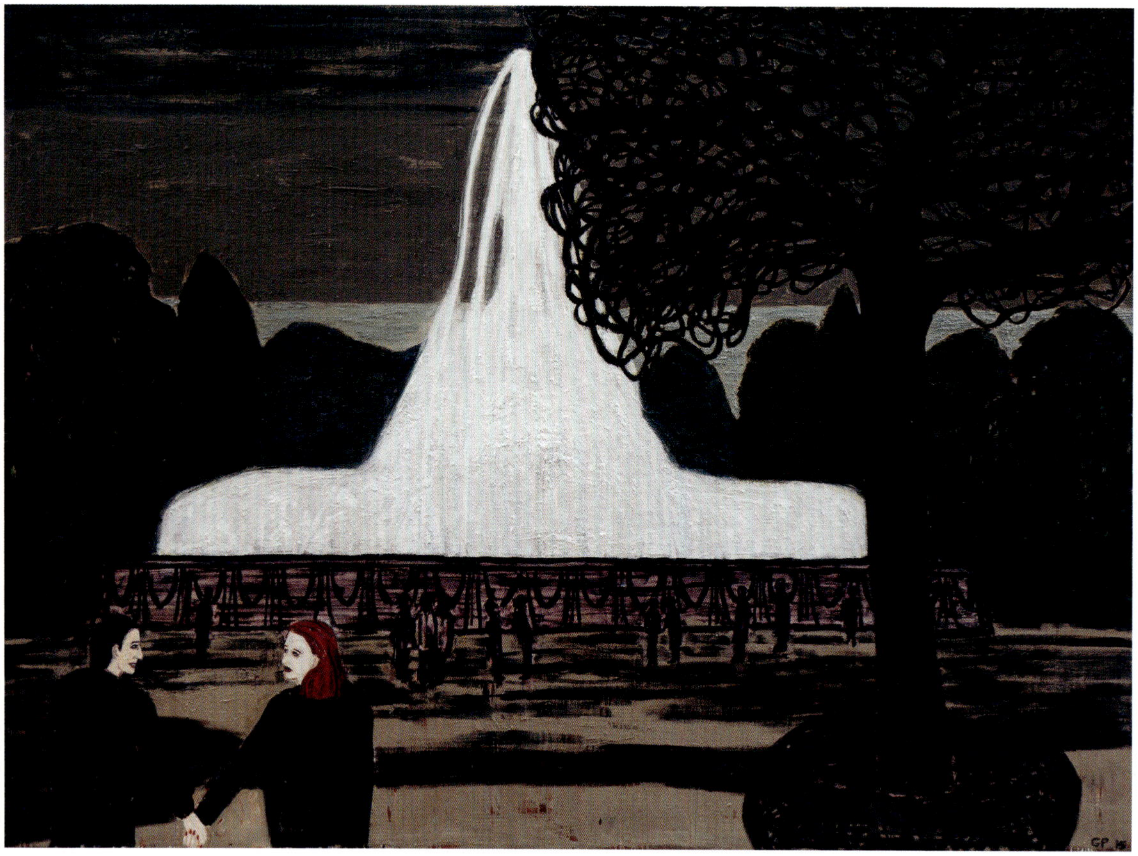

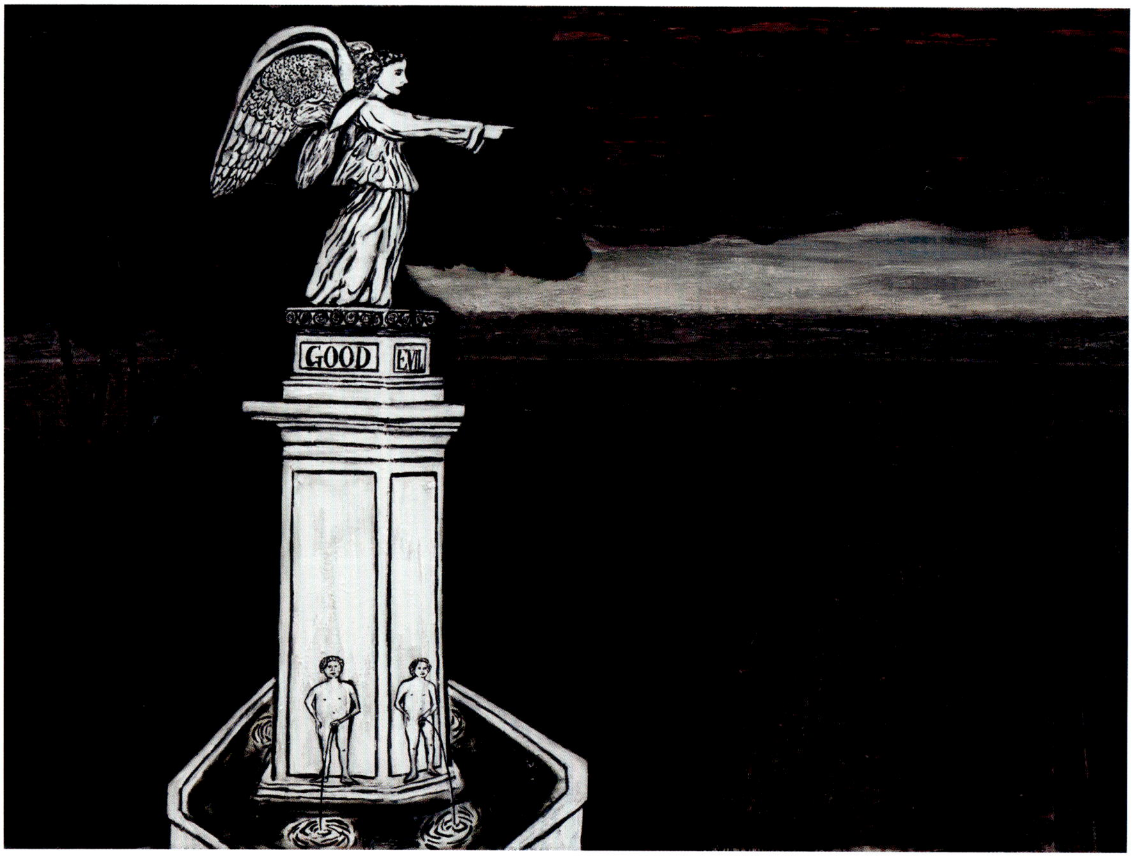


*The Large Fountain*, 2015
*The Fountain of Good and Evil*, 2015

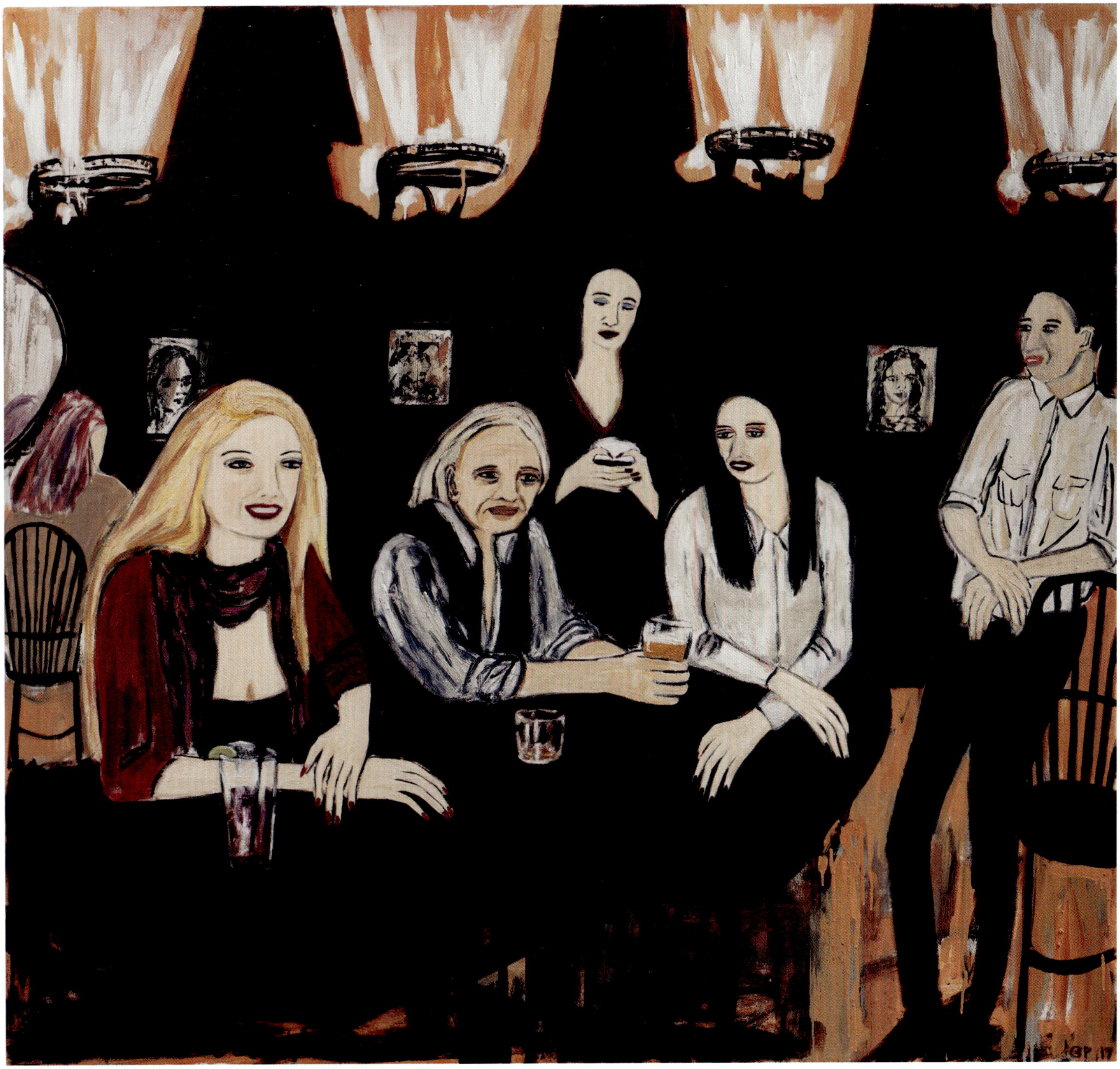

*Honky Tonk*, 2017

I won't go out there anymore. I'm embarrassed to leave the house. You know what she's doing when her boyfriend comes over. He comes in for a couple of minutes and then they go outside.

The neighbours have been talking. It's embarrassing and immoral. They don't even stay in the garage. They're doing it in broad daylight on the sidewalk, on the street!

What's become of young people today? My God, where did we go wrong!

## Chronology

**1951**

Gary Pearson is born in Melfort, Saskatchewan. Both of his parents, Ellen and Birger, are children of Swedish immigrants. The family moves to Prince George, BC, the next year. Birger Pearson works as a tree faller, and later as a sawmill worker. The neighbourhood in which they live is on the outskirts of Prince George and is populated mostly by Métis and Cree families from Alberta, and immigrants from Sweden, Germany, the Ukraine and Poland. The Pearson house is a Saturday evening gathering place for music and dancing. Pearson's father plays the accordion and harmonica, and other musicians from the neighbourhood include a fiddle player, guitarist and spoons; with music consisting of polkas, Swedish *schottis*, waltzes and old-time country. As a child Gary Pearson is an avid reader and drawer, which his parents support through the purchase of books from the Scholastic Book Club of Canada. When he is about ten years old he enrols in a three-year correspondence cartooning course through the Famous Artists School, out of Westport, CT.

**1960s**

As with most teenagers at the time, the artist is immersed in popular music and culture, and when The British Invasion hit the airwaves and record stores in 1963, it is a transforming experience. Although there is little opportunity to experience visual art in Prince George, the artist is a frequent user of the public library, where monographs of famous painters such as Vincent van Gogh and Henri de Toulouse-Lautrec line the shelves. His discovery of Jack Shadbolt's 1968 publication, *In Search of Form*, at the library is key. This book provides important artistic inspiration and motivation. It becomes a personal course book, a philosophical guide to creativity and an introduction to contemporary art.

Although Pearson draws a great deal, at this time he self-identifies as a writer. He both reads and writes poetry, and creates journal entries in his notebooks.

Born with a pronounced wanderlust, the artist is almost always 'on the road', hitch-hiking to Vancouver, the Okanagan, the Kootenays, Washington, Oregon and California.

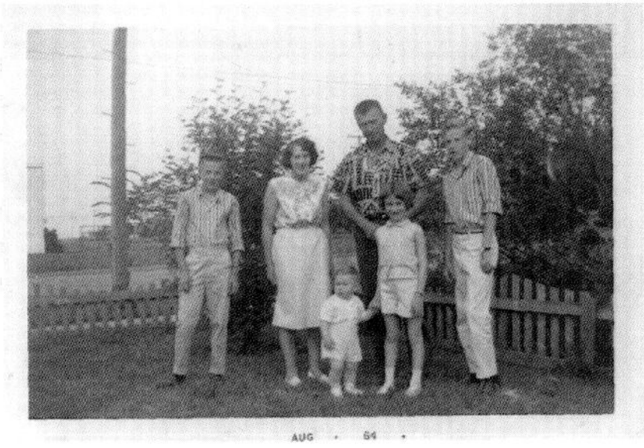

The Pearson family in Prince George, BC, 1964. The artist is at the far left.

**1970s**

In the early 70s Pearson enrols in a creative writing class taught by Barry McKinnon at the College of New Caledonia in Prince George. Pearson is stimulated by the contact with other young writers and the ideas in McKinnon's classes. He reads Dylan Thomas, Ezra Pound, Charles Baudelaire, Sylvia Plath, Charles Bukowski and Robert Creeley, and attends readings by McKinnon's visiting writers, including Al Purdy, bpNichol and Patrick Lane.

Pearson supports himself by working in the concrete curb and gutter industry, continuing to write and draw. In 1975 Pearson makes his first trip to Europe, travelling with his girlfriend, Dagmar Doering,

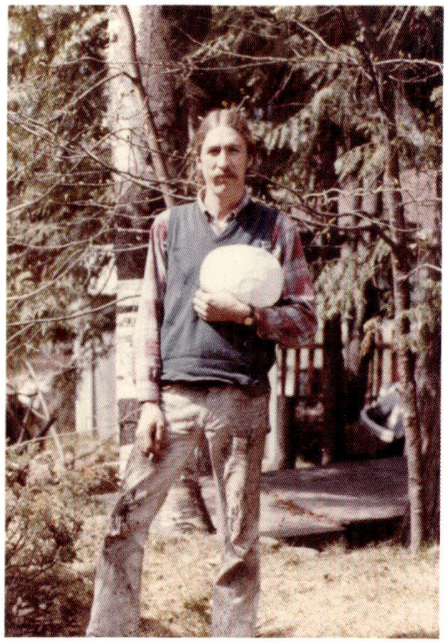
The artist in Nelson, BC, circa 1977.

who later becomes his wife. He visits the major art museums in Madrid, Barcelona, Berlin, Munich and London.

In 1976 he enrols in the Kootenay School of Art in Nelson, BC, where he studies foundation painting, drawing and anatomy, and creative writing at Notre Dame University, also in Nelson.

In 1977 he and Dagmar both transfer to the University of Victoria where he continues his studies in the BFA program. The course book for Professor Roland Brenner's second-year sculpture class is *Passages in Modern Sculpture* by Rosalind E Krauss, which serves to fill gaps in Pearson's knowledge of the history and discourse of twentieth-century avant-garde sculpture. His painting as an undergraduate is influenced by Pop art and the expressionist tradition, and his sculpture by modernist sculptors such as David Smith and Anthony Caro. In the latter part of his degree program Pearson is looking closely at the work of Edward Kienholz, particularly his *Volksempfänger* series.

**1980**

Pearson graduates with a Bachelor of Fine Arts from the University of Victoria, and he and Dagmar get married. They go on a road trip for an impromptu visit to the home of Edward Kienholz in Hope, Idaho. Upon their arrival, they are warmly greeted by Kienholz, and invited to join him, Nancy Reddin Kienholz and their extended family for brunch, which is already underway. Later Kienholz takes them for a tour of his studio, where the featured piece is a nearly completed *Sollie 17*, 1979–1980, widely considered to be the centrepiece of the artist's *Spokane* series, 1979–1983. Following this, Keinholz tours them through the Faith and Charity in Hope Gallery, adjacent to his studio, which is featuring a temporary exhibition of Alberto Giacometti's small sculptures and drawings.

The Prince George Art Gallery (later renamed the Two Rivers Art Gallery) invites the artist to have his first solo exhibition, and gives him the upstairs studio space to work in for six months. He creates a number of large-format drawings for the exhibition Recent Drawings, which opens on 5 January 1981.

**1981**

The artist enrols in the MA degree program at the University of Saskatchewan, in Saskatoon, where Otto Rogers becomes his thesis supervisor. With the financial support of the Saskatchewan Arts Board, he takes his first trip to New York, where he visits museums and private galleries in Manhattan. Pearson's graduate studio work is mainly in drawing. He meets the American art critic Clement Greenberg when he is a visiting scholar at the University. Pearson teaches as a sessional lecturer in drawing for two years in North Battleford, SK.

**1983**

Pearson graduates with a MA from the University of Saskatchewan. His thesis title is *Form in Repetition: A View of Non-hierarchical*

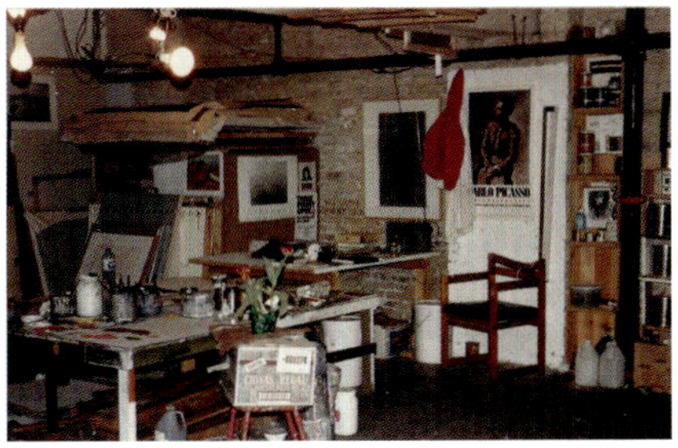

Pearson's Hamilton Street Studio, Yaletown, Vancouver, BC, where he worked from 1984 to 1989. The space was shared by artists Robert Linsley, Ellen Ramsey and Kati Campbell.

*Composition in Art*, which is an examination of Carl Andre's *Twelfth Copper Corner*, 1975, and Richard Serra's *Casting*, 1969.

Pearson moves to Kamloops, BC, where he teaches at Cariboo College (now Thompson Rivers University) on a one-year term sabbatical replacement in Two-Dimensional Foundation and Art History.

He is included in the Cleveland (UK) 6th International Drawing Biennale, Middlesbrough Art Gallery, Middlesbrough, UK, which includes featured artist Eduardo Paolozzi. A catalogue is produced, with an essay by John Elderfield.

**1984**

Pearson and his wife relocate to Vancouver and rent an apartment in the West End. He finds a studio on Hamilton Street, in Yaletown, where he begins a series of abstract paintings and mixed-material assemblage sculptures. The Hamilton Street studios occupy a full floor of the building, and are shared by Pearson among the artists Robert Linsley, Ellen Ramsey and Kati Campbell.

**1985**

Pearson is hired for part-time teaching in the Extension Division of Emily Carr College (now University) of Art + Design until 1989. He has a solo exhibition of paintings curated by Grant Baker, at the AMS Gallery, University of British Columbia, and is a participant at the Emma Lake Artists' Workshop, in northern Saskatchewan. New York-based art critic Karen Wilkin, and painter Maryann Harman (from New York/Virginia) are the featured guest participants.

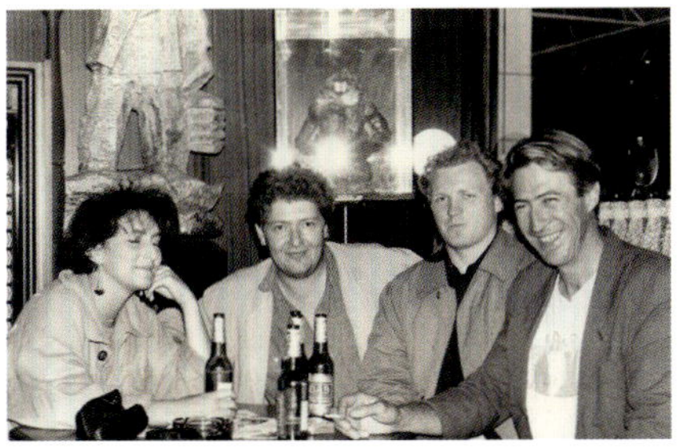

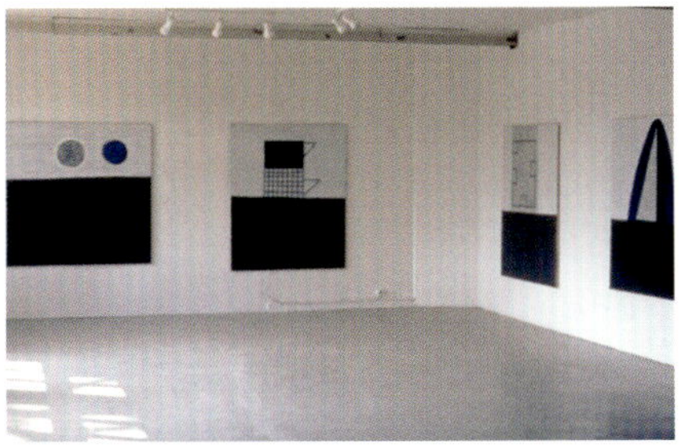

Gary Pearson at La Paloma Bar, Reeperbahn in Hamburg's St. Pauli district, 1988.
From left to right: Fiona Mowatt, Jürgen Brockmann, Phillip McCrum and Gary Pearson.

Installation view: Vancouver – Hamburg, 1988, KX Kunst auf Kampnagel, Hamburg.

**1986**

The artist has a solo exhibition of paintings at the Or Gallery, Vancouver, and is included in the exhibition *Vancouver Young Artists* at the Simon Fraser University Gallery, in Burnaby, BC.

**1987**

Pearson participates in Artropolis: An Exhibition of Contemporary British Columbia Art in Vancouver. He curates Abstraction/Drawing: Ann Kipling, David MacWilliam, John Scott for the Or Gallery. In preparation for this, he visits John Scott at his Toronto studio. Scott produces a work titled *Rorschach Totem Pole* specifically for the show. The exhibition, which is accompanied by an illustrated catalogue with an essay by Pearson, is well received and garners positive reviews from Douglas Coupland, writing for the *WestEnder*, Vancouver, and Robin Laurence in *Vanguard*.

He uses the welding equipment at his contractor employer's shop/yard on the New Westminster waterfront to produce welded steel and cast concrete sculptures, which he exhibits in 1989 at Western Front, Vancouver.

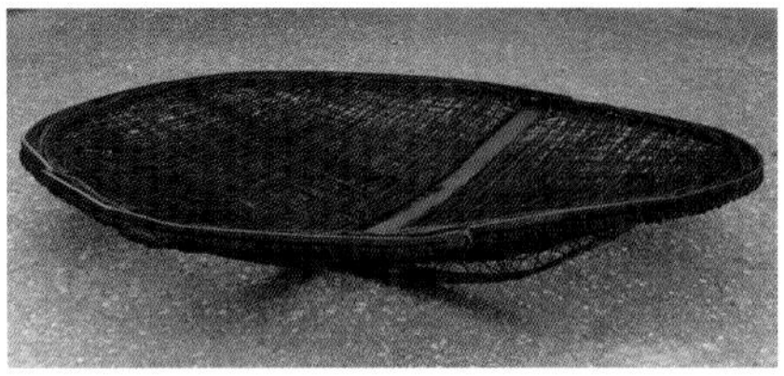

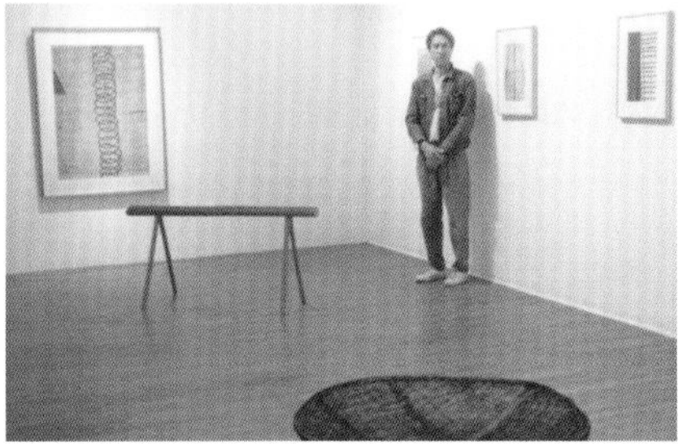

Pearson, *Untitled*, 1989, steel, wire, 120 cm diameter, 20 cm deep. Included in Drawing and Sculpture, 1989 at the Western Front, Vancouver, BC.

Gary Pearson at his solo exhibition at Western Front, Vancouver, BC, 1989.

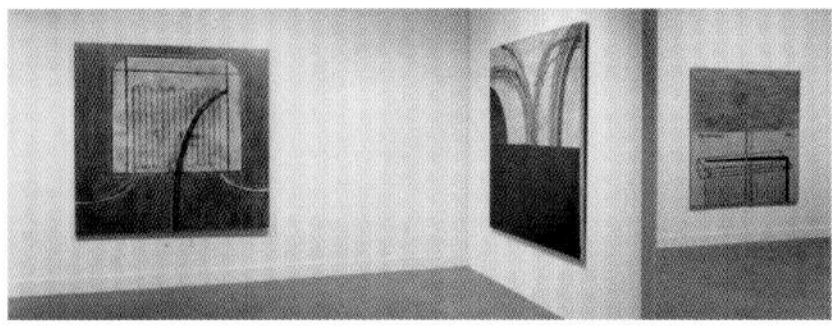

Installation view: Disjuncture: As a Syntax, 1990, Charles H Scott Gallery, Vancouver, BC. From left to right: *Circulation Chamber*, 1989; *The Original Crisis*, 1990; *Die Verbindung*, 1990.

**1988**

Pearson meets a group of Hamburg artists who are in Vancouver for an exhibition at Pitt International Gallery, which results in an exchange-exhibition, co-curated by Pearson with Zoe Lambert (based in Vancouver), Jürgen Brockmann and Hopek Quirin (both based in Hamburg). The exhibition Vancouver/Hamburg, takes place at KX Kunst auf Kampnagel, Hamburg. Brockmann and Pearson remain in touch and jointly organize and participate together in several projects and exhibitions.

**1989**

Pearson has a solo exhibition, Gary Pearson: Drawing and Sculpture, curated by Annette Hurtig at Western Front, Vancouver.

**1990**

Together with artists Jennifer Gordon and Kathleen McFall, Pearson is included in a group exhibition titled Disjuncture: As a Syntax, at the Charles H Scott Gallery in Vancouver.

The artist is included in Selections 49, at The Drawing Center, New York, and travels there for the opening.

Pearson is awarded a one-year artist residency in the International Studio Program, at the institute for contemporary art MoMA PS1, Long Island City, New York. He starts there on 1 July and lives in the large studio space, which has windows facing the East River and mid-town Manhattan. Across the hall is Jayce Salloum, the other Canadian artist for that year. The curators in residence are Ryszard Wasko, from Poland and Zdenka Gabalova, from the Czech Republic. The artist meets fellow residents Andreas Ginkel, Cornelia Schleime, Brad Buckley, Via Lewandowsky, Jos Vulto and other artists at PS1, which begins some long-term friendships and collaborations. He produces his *Paradise* series of paintings and drawings, his large *Arthur Rimbaud in New York* painting and writes poetry, including the long poem and performance piece *The Orient Express*, with original music composed by Andreas Ginkel.

**1991**

In February Pearson flies from New York for a solo exhibition, The Geometrics of Conjecture, guest curated by Robin Laurence for the Kelowna Art Gallery.

He travels to Philadelphia to see the Francesco Clemente: Three Worlds exhibition, both the Arensberg collection of Brancusi sculptures and the Duchamp works at the Philadelphia Museum of Art, and to Merion, PA, to see the Barnes Foundation collection. He continues work at the PS1 studio, makes visits to museums and galleries and meets and establishes friendships with many artists in New York.

He exhibits in Art in British Columbia at the Vancouver Art Gallery, and in a group show at S. Bitter-Larkin Gallery in New York.

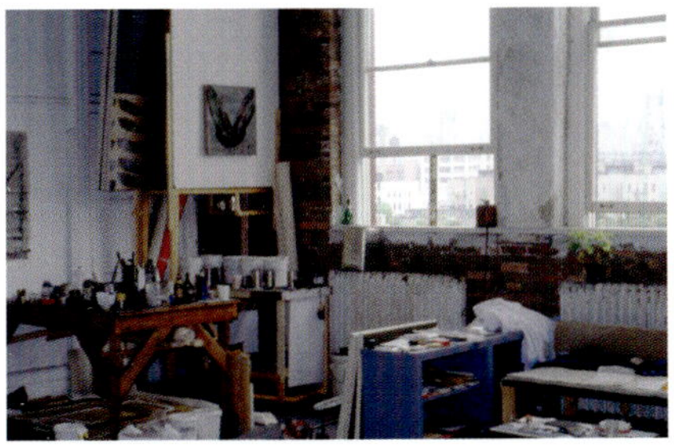

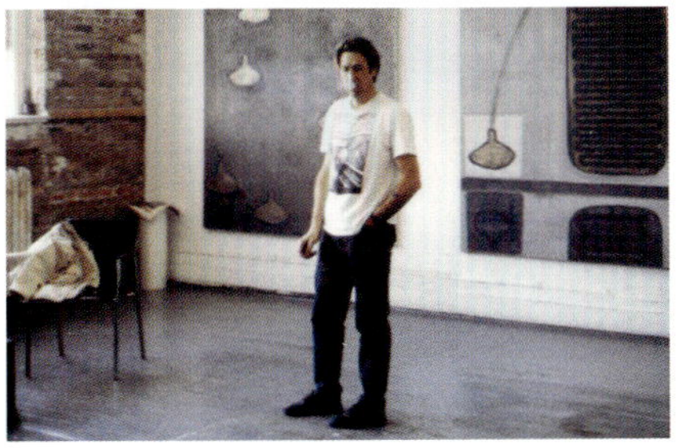

Gary Pearson's studio at PS1, New York, 1991.

Gary Pearson in his studio at PS1, New York, 1991.

He receives a Canada Council for the Arts B grant, and along with Persimmon Blackbridge is awarded the prestigious Jack and Doris Shadbolt VIVA Award (Vancouver Institute of Visual Arts), for 1991.

After completing his year-long PS1 residency he moves to Kelowna to begin a position as Professor of Drawing and Painting, at Okanagan University College, (now UBC Okanagan) in Kelowna, BC.

**1992**

Pearson and his wife purchase a house overlooking Okanagan Lake in the Poplar Point neighbourhood of Kelowna. Together with a few former PS1 artists he participates in group installation project titled Drift at Farsund Kommune, Lista, Norway, which is organized by Norwegian artists Solfrid Mortensen and Alfred Vaagsvold. Pearson spends three weeks in Lista, then travels to Oslo and Berlin. Ryszard Wasko invites him to come by train from Berlin to The Artists' Museum in Łódź, Poland. Pearson spends a week in Łódź then travels to Hamburg, before coming home. He writes the long poem: *By Train: Berlin* – Łódź.

Pearson has a solo exhibition titled New Drawings at the Davidson Gallery, in Seattle, Washington, and a solo exhibition titled Second Order: Paradise, at the Patrick Doheny Gallery in Vancouver. This second show is accompanied by a catalogue with a short essay by Karen Wilkin, and an interview with the artist by Eileen Truscott (then an instructor in art history at Okanagan University College in Kelowna).

Using a cello, voice and four boom-box tape playback recorders Pearson stages a public performance of his work *performance zone|zone performance* at Okanagan University College Theatre, Kelowna.

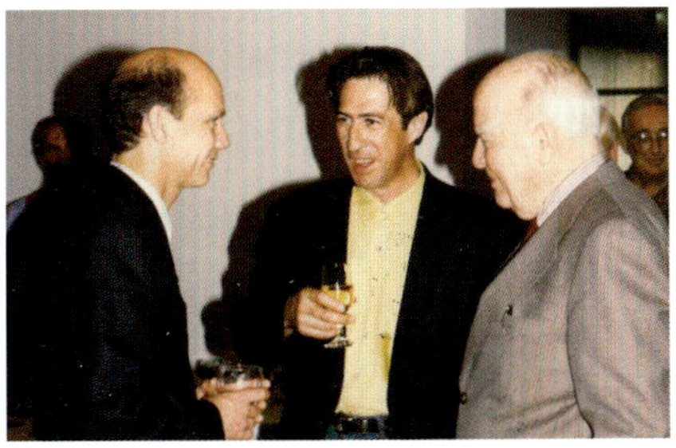

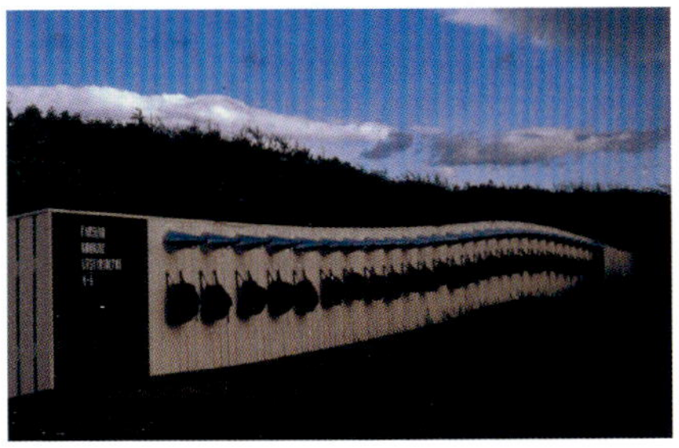

Gary Pearson at the VIVA Award ceremony held at Emily Carr College of Art + Design, Vancouver, BC, on 29 May 1991. From left to right: Greg Bellerby, Gary Pearson and Jack Shadbolt.

Pearson, *Farsund Community Equipment Depot A-AAA*, 1992, 18 megaphones, 28 rucksacks, rocks, painted sign, 1.6 × 23 m, Lista Fyr, Norway.

**1993**

Pearson builds a stand-alone studio near his house.

He is invited to participate in a group exhibition, Construction in Process IV (My Home is Your Home), at the Artists' Museum in Lodz, Poland. The Polish artist Ryszard Wasko supports Pearson's request that Jürgen Brockmann and the band The Notorious Heffel Brothers also be invited. The Heffels perform at numerous venues around the city, and the artist joins them for a performance-reading of his poem *By Train: Berlin – Lodz*, at Klub Szafa on 4 October. This poem is then published the following year in a special double edition of *New Observations* (issue 102, Suzy Sureck ed) that documents the exhibition.

Pearson has a solo exhibition New Paperworks at Westwerk in Hamburg, and is in the group exhibition Hamburger Künstler, guest-curated by Jürgen Brockmann for Kunstlerforum in Bonn, Germany. The artist gives a public performance-reading of *By Train: Berlin – Lodz* on 5 April, at the Clock Tower Theatre, in Kamloops, BC.

**1994**

Pearson participates in Critique Fax, curated by Brad Buckley, at First Draft in Sydney, Australia (which travels the following year to ICA

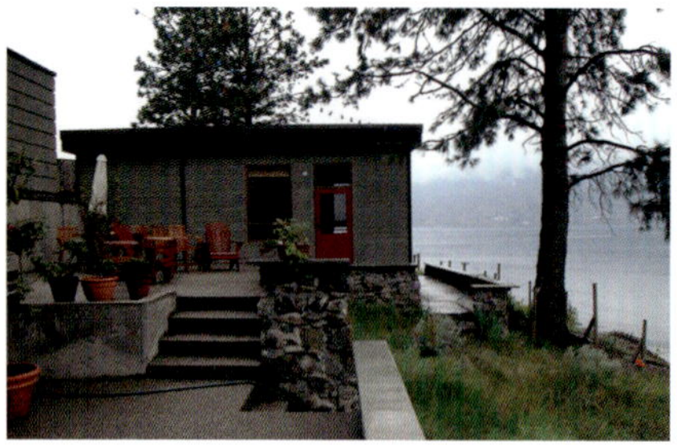

Exterior view of the artist's studio in Kelowna, BC, constructed in 1993.

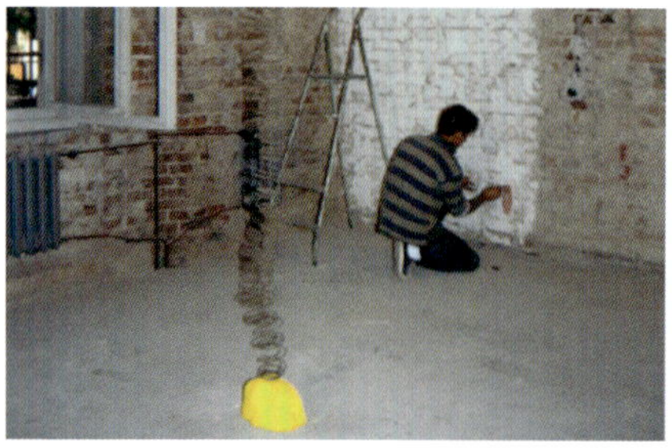

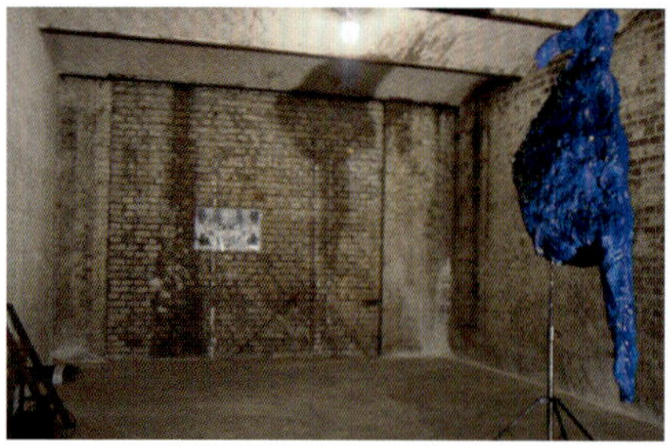

Pearson, *Zünder*, 1993, site specific installation, the Artists' Museum in Lodz, Poland.

Pearson, *Spectacle*, 1995, installation with photocopied text, audio tape, chair, painted plaster object, tripod stand. Exhibited in Posit Poznan, Miedzynarodowe Centrum Sztuki, Poznan, Poland.

Brisbane, and PICA Perth). The artist joins the Catriona Jeffries Gallery in Vancouver. Between 1994 and 1998 he has two solo exhibitions and is in two group shows there.

**1995**

The artist curates and participates in a group show titled Posit Poznan at the International Artists' Centre in Poznan, Poland (the other artists are Canadians Jack Jeffrey and Lee Goreas). The artists spend three weeks at the Artists' Centre creating work for and installing the exhibition. The show is accompanied by an illustrated catalogue, including artist dialogues published in both English and Polish. Pearson then travels by train to Venice to see the Biennale, and then to Hamburg.

Pearson is co-curator, along with his wife, Dagmar Pearson, of Greg Murdock: On Paper, at the Kelowna Art Gallery. He participates in Lie to Me, a poetry reading with writers John Lent and Allison Sivak, at Okanagan University College, Kelowna. He stages a solo performance-poetry reading at the Mind Grind Cafe, Kelowna, and a performance-reading of *Mirage and Spectacle* at Gallery A, Kelowna.

**1996**

Pearson is included in a group exhibition titled Aesthetic (Anti) Aesthetic at the Catriona Jeffries Gallery, Vancouver.

He acts as independent producer, director and scriptwriter for an eleven-part, half-hour-long arts television documentary series featuring interviews with Okanagan-based artists, writers and musicians, titled *Fran's CULTure Showcase*. Broadcast sponsor is Shaw Cable, and the series airs on Shaw Cable in 1996 and 1997 in the Thompson/Okanagan, Central Interior, and Vancouver Island areas of BC.

**1997**

Pearson produces an independent video titled *By Train: Berlin – Lodz, A Poetry Documentation*. It is shot in Seattle in black and white and is 11 minutes 13 seconds.

He records *All in Green* on audio cassette with The Notorious Heffel Bros at White Noise Studios, Hamburg. Pearson's tracks are *Paradise* and *The Orient Express*.

The artist is guest curator of a group exhibition titled Hotel on Fire, for the Kelowna Art Gallery. The show includes five artists: Geneviève Cadieux, Ken Lum, Via Lewandowsky, Brad Buckley and Jenny Watson. The catalogue has an essay by Pearson, as well a text by the German writer Dr Michael Haerdter and poetry by Jürgen Brockmann.

**1998**

Pearson goes for a three-month studio residency at Künstlerhaus Bethanien in Berlin. He works on various oil on paper works, including the large oil on paper *Two of Everything*. He also shoots videotape in the Kreuzberg area of Berlin, which he later edits for his video *Heinrichplatz*

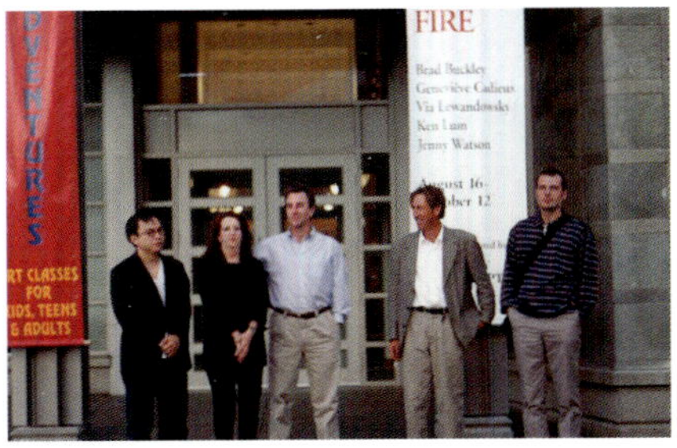


Opening day for the *Hotel on Fire* exhibition, curated by Gary Pearson, Kelowna Art Gallery, Kelowna, BC, February 1997.

From left to right: Ken Lum, Jenny Watson, Brad Buckley, Gary Pearson and Via Lewandowsky.

*in Berlin Kreuzberg*. Pearson does journal writing throughout his residency, most of which influences his series titled *The Night of the Diana Krall Concert, April 19th, 1998* (referred to hereafter as the *Diana Krall* series) and his video *Berlin Jazz Story*. He also works in Berlin's Drückwerkstadt print studios, producing lithographs, engravings and monoprints. At the end of the residency, Pearson has an exhibition of his work titled Two of Everything: Artist-in-Residence Studio.

Pearson writes a book titled *The Creative Voice: Art and Life in the Okanagan*, which is an anthology of 35 interviews with artists, writers, musicians and filmmakers in the Okanagan (published by Caitlin Press).

He also does set design for the music video *Pushing the Limits* by the John Noren Band, and curates Jürgen Brockmann – Works on Paper for the Goethe-Institut, Vancouver.

**2000**

The artist participates in a group show titled Colouring the West: A Century of Painting in BC, at the Vancouver Art Gallery.

Pearson acts as director, scriptwriter and co-producer (with Denis Abrahamsen) of a video titled *Berlin Jazz Story*. It is shot in Kelowna and features original music by Guenter Schulz, and voice-over narration by Kelowna resident John Coghlan. It premieres at Sturgeon Hall, Kelowna, BC, on 16 October.

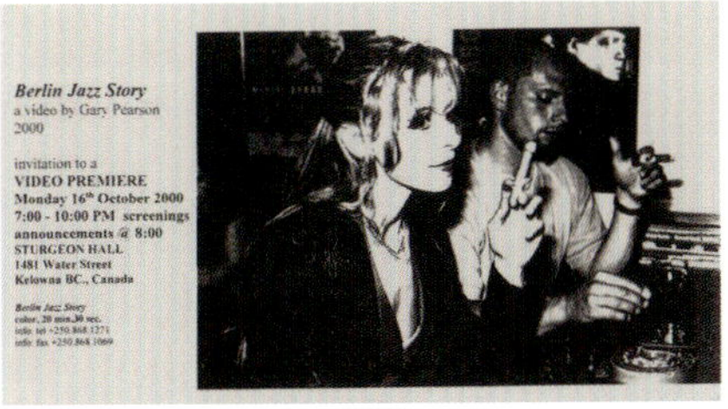


Invitation to the premiere of *Berlin Jazz Story*, a video by Gary Pearson, 2000.

**2002**

The artist acts as director, project manager, co-producer, and co-script and story writer (with Dr Jenny Tucker) on a video documentary titled *So Good So Far: the way forward* (colour, 26 minutes). It is filmed on location in both Ghana and Canada, and investigates the roles and working conditions of rural nursing and health care in Northern Ghana. Pearson and Tucker do both a research trip and a filming trip to Ghana (the crew is Kelowna-based, and includes artist Stephen Foster, media technician Michael Berger, and musician/photographer Guenther Schulz). The documentary premieres 31 May at the Alternator Centre for Contemporary Art in Kelowna, and its broadcast premiere is on 9 June on CHBC Television in Kelowna, BC.

Pearson is included in the exhibition 25th Anniversary Selections at The Drawing Center, New York.

He begins writing exhibition reviews for the art magazines *Border Crossings* and *Sculpture*.

**2003**

The artist has a solo exhibition titled Gary Pearson: One Way Ticket, at the Kelowna Art Gallery. It is accompanied by a catalogue with essays by curator Linda Sawchyn, as well as Michael Turner and Karen Wilkin. The show later tours to the Mendel Art Gallery, Saskatoon, the Two Rivers Art Gallery, Prince George and the The Robert McLaughlin Gallery, Oshawa, Ontario.

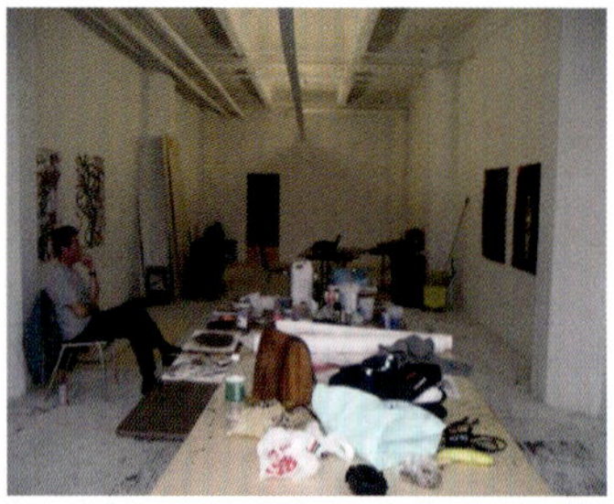

The artist's studio at the Triangle Residency Program, DUMBO, Brooklyn, March 2004.

**2004**

Pearson receives a six-month sabbatical leave from UBC Okanagan. He makes a road trip with his wife and their dog Tia in their VW Westfalia along the coastline of Washington, Oregon, and California. They then go through Arizona, New Mexico, Texas, Louisiana, Alabama and into Florida, before heading up the east coast to New York. He receives travel grants for this trip from the British Columbia Arts Council, and the Canada Council for the Arts. Pearson then has residencies at Triangle Studio in the DUMBO section of Brooklyn, NY, and in Pouch Cove, NL.

While on the road, Pearson works on small studies and sketches. During the two residencies he completes large oil-on-paper works based on these studies. He refers to these as his *Road Trip* series, but they are also closely connected to his *Greenville* series that was inspired by the music of Lucinda Williams.

Once back in Kelowna he begins writing monthly art reviews and articles on cultural topics for *Off-Centre Magazine* (Kelowna, BC) from September 2004 to November 2006.

**2005**

Pearson receives a Social Sciences and Humanities Research Council of Canada (SSHRC) ASU Research Grant to travel for a two-month-long residency at the University of Sydney, Sydney College of the Arts, in Australia. While there he begins his ongoing *Short Fictions* text pieces, and does many sketches, as well as large oil-on-paper paintings. He concludes the residency with a solo exhibition titled Oblique Stories, in the SCA Galleries I & II. An illustrated catalogue is produced with a foreword by the gallery's manager Kate Major, and a direct address text by the artist. While in Australia, Pearson travels to Brisbane to visit artist Jenny Watson and curator Ihor Holubizky.

He joins the Elissa Cristall Gallery in Vancouver, where he has a solo exhibition in October, titled I'm going back to Greenville.

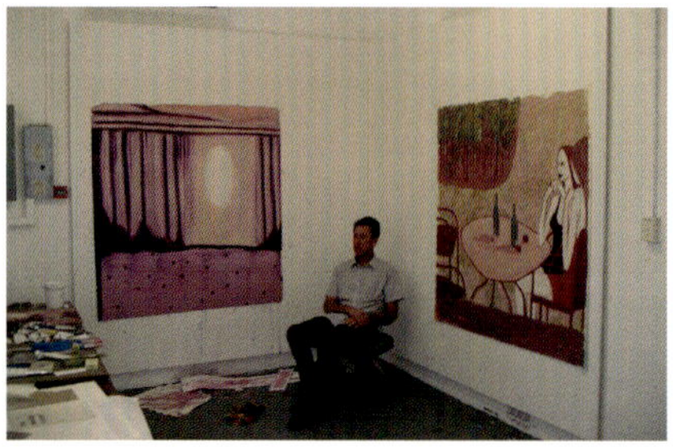

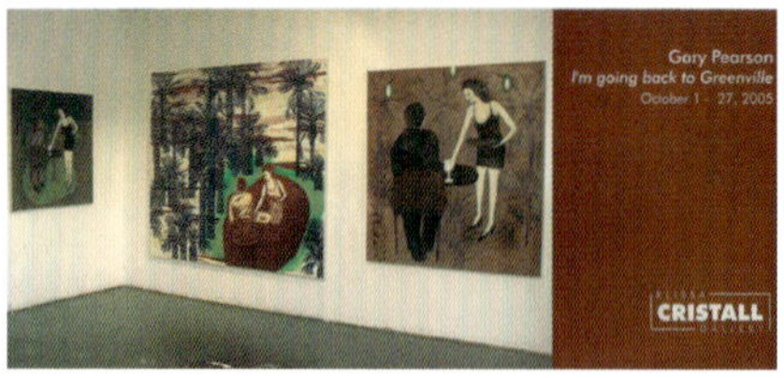


The artist's studio at the Sydney College of Art, University of Sydney, during his residency, August and September 2005. From left to right: *Come Back Later* (work on paper), 2005; *The Healing Center*, 2005.

Exhibition announcement for Pearson's solo show I'm going back to Greenville at the Elissa Cristall Gallery, Vancouver, BC, 2005.

**2006**

Pearson is included in the group exhibition Paint, curated by Neil Campbell, for the Vancouver Art Gallery. He has a solo show curated by Lisa Baldissera titled High Early, LAB Project, at the Art Gallery of Greater Victoria, and a solo exhibition titled The Everyday, at Winchester Galleries in Victoria, BC.

The artist receives a UBC Okanagan Internal Research Grant in support of research for Pearson's international exhibition, Point of Origin, organized for Artspace Centre for Contemporary Art, in Sydney, Australia.

The Vancouver Art Gallery acquires his large painting *Hotel Room*, 2002, and the Two Rivers Art Gallery in Prince George, BC, acquires his *Diana Krall* series paintings *I'm Only Happy When I'm With You*, and *The Silence That Punctuates the Melancholy Sound*, both 2000.

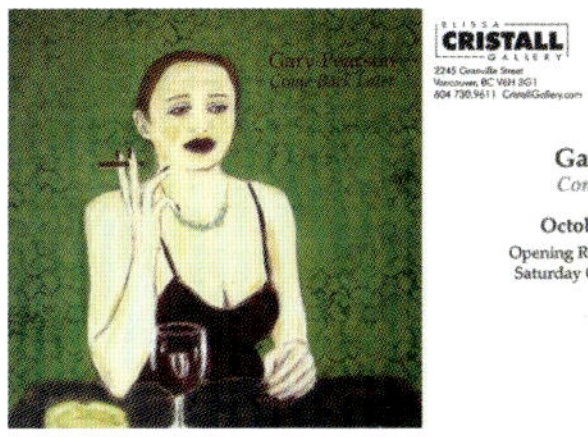


Exhibition announcement for Come Back Later at the Elissa Cristall Gallery, Vancouver, BC, 2006.

**2007**

As part of his curatorial research for the Point of Origin exhibition the artist travels to visit selected artists Ceal Floyer in Berlin and Dora Economou in Athens. The exhibition also includes Huseyin Sami, Rolande Souliere, Jack Jeffrey, Taras Polataiko and Kelly Wood.

In October Pearson has a solo exhibition titled Come Back Later at the Elissa Cristall Gallery in Vancouver, BC.

He co-founds the arts and literary journal *Lake: A Journal of Arts and Environment* at UBCO with Sharon Thesen, Nancy Holmes and Briar Craig. Pearson serves as co-editor of visual arts for the journal along with Craig. In the first issue Pearson publishes an interview with artist Kristi Malakoff, titled "The Undigested World Itself".

The Kamloops Art Gallery purchases his paintings *When I Get to Baton Rouge* and *I'm Going Back to Greenville*, both 2005.

**2008**

Pearson has a solo exhibition curated by Jen Budney for the Kamloops Art Gallery titled The End is My Beginning. The accompanying catalogue has an essay by David Bateman, and an artist's interview with Jen Budney. The exhibition is reviewed by Liz Wylie for *Border Crossings* magazine and by Portia Priegert for *Galleries West*, and is covered in regional newspapers. Pearson gives a poetry reading titled *Jazz and Poetry* at the Commodore Lounge in Kamloops.

Pearson joins the Winsor Gallery in Vancouver.

His Point of Origin exhibition, curated for Artspace Centre for Contemporary Art, Sydney, Australia opens in September and Pearson travels to install the show and attend this event.

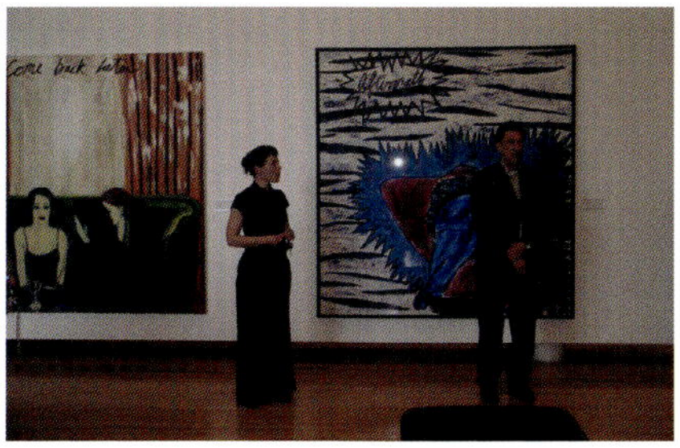

Curator Jen Budney and Gary Pearson at the opening reception for Pearson's solo show at the Kamloops Art Gallery, Kamloops, BC, Gary Pearson: New Paintings and Video, 30 March 2008. From left to right: *Come Back Later*, 2007; *Aftermath*, 2007.

**2009**

Pearson has a solo exhibition in May titled Somewhere at the Winsor Gallery in Vancouver, and is in a group exhibition titled Take Your Time, curated by Bill Jeffries for the Simon Fraser University Gallery in Burnaby, BC. The catalogue has essays by Bill Jeffries and Vanessa Sorensen.

Pearson publishes a book chapter titled "The Outskirts of Town: A Peripheral Centre for Art, Agency, and Academia", in *Rethinking the Contemporary Art School: The Artist, the PhD, and the Academy*, Brad Buckley and John Conomos eds, Halifax: The Press of the Nova Scotia College of Art and Design, 2009.

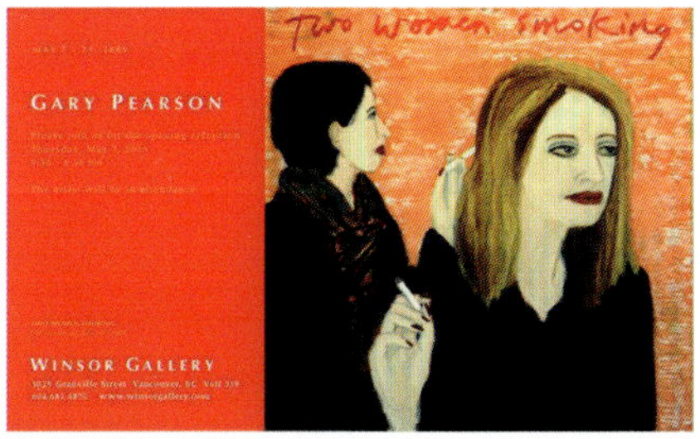


Exhibition announcement for Somewhere, Winsor Gallery, Vancouver, BC, 2009.

**2010**

Pearson has work in the group exhibition Constructions of Identity: Recent Acquisitions, curated by Liz Wylie for the Kelowna Art Gallery. Pearson's work in the exhibition features a selection of seven of recently purchased works on paper dating from 1987 to 1999.

In November Pearson travels for a month-long artist's residency at the *Bus from Guadalajara Artist's Residence Project* in Ajijic, Jalisco, Mexico. He films the Spanish-language episode of his video titled

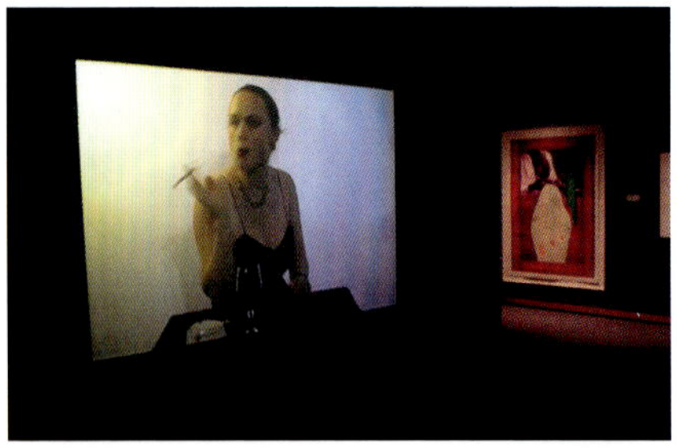

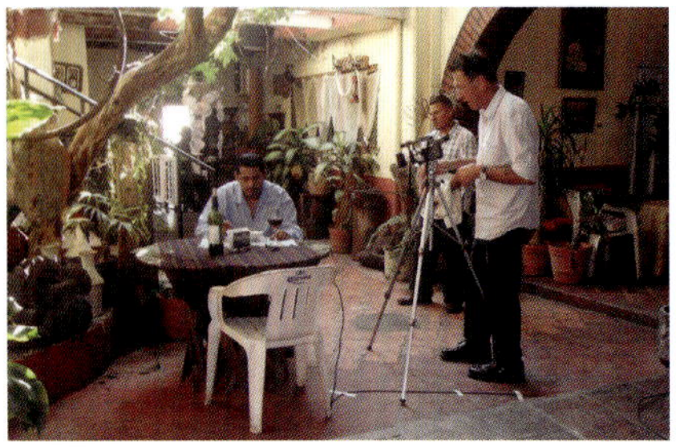

Installation view: 1 2 3 Soliloquy, 2011 McMaster Museum of Art, McMaster University, Hamilton, ON.

Gary Pearson as seen directing his video, *The Waiter Joke*, at Bar El Camaleón, Ajijic, Mexico, November, 2010.

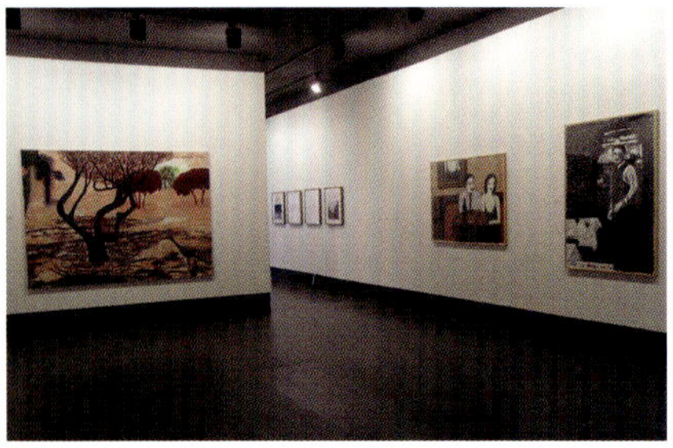

Installation view: Scenes for a 'Smoker's Theatre', 2012, Winsor Gallery, Vancouver, BC.

*The Waiter Joke*, and shoots the experimental narrative video *Miracruz*, as well as producing many works on paper. These paper studies lead to numerous large canvasses later, including *The Incident at the Guadalupe Bar*, *Una Cansión Triste*, *The Loggia*, *The Garden Hose*, and the large drawing *Springtime Started out Brand New*, which are all exhibited at the Winsor Gallery in Vancouver in 2012.

**2011**

Pearson is invited by Ihor Holubizky, Senior Curator at the McMaster Museum of Art in Hamilton, ON, to exhibit his two *Soliloquy* videos and recent photo-prints, along with a curatorial engagement with the Museum's permanent collection.

For this co-curatorial project Pearson focuses on the Museum's extensive collection of expressionist art and, working with Holubizky, selects a range of work by artists such as Edvard Munch, Max Beckmann, Otto Dix and Lutz Dille to show alongside with and bring context to Pearson's own work. The exhibition, titled 1 2 3 Soliloquy, opens 20 January, and is accompanied by an illustrated catalogue with essays by Ihor Holubizky and Gary Pearson. The McMaster Museum of Art later acquires Pearson's videos *Soliloquy* and *Soliloquy2* for their permanent collection.

The premiere of Pearson's video *The Waiter Joke* is held at Sturgeon Hall in Kelowna on 18 October. *The Waiter Joke* is a 7:24 minute, five-language video enactment of the classic line: "Waiter, there's a fly in my soup!" Two characters, the waiter and the cafe patron, perform in every version.

**2012**

In February Pearson has a solo exhibition titled Scenes for a 'Smoker's Theatre' at the Winsor Gallery in Vancouver.

He travels to visit dOCUMENTA (13) in Kassel, Germany, and also goes to Hamburg and Berlin.

The Kamloops Art Gallery purchases his painting *Under the Blue Palms*, 2005.

**2013**

Pearson has work included in a group exhibition titled Nous reviendrons, vous reviendrez, curated by Jack Jeffrey and Bernard Plasse, the latter being the owner of Galerie du Tableau. The show is held in the salon d'honneur de la Préfecture in Marseille, France. The other artists included are Rodney Graham, Jack Jeffrey, Jayce Salloum and Ian Wallace, all based in Vancouver, BC.

Pearson's work is featured in book titled *Okanagan Artists in their Studios*, by Patricia Ainslie (published by Frontenac House, Calgary).

He is interviewed by Gail Mowatt for the radio program *The Muse*, CKVS 93.7 FM – Voice of the Shuswap, Salmon Arm, BC. The broadcast length is 1 hour and 17 minutes.

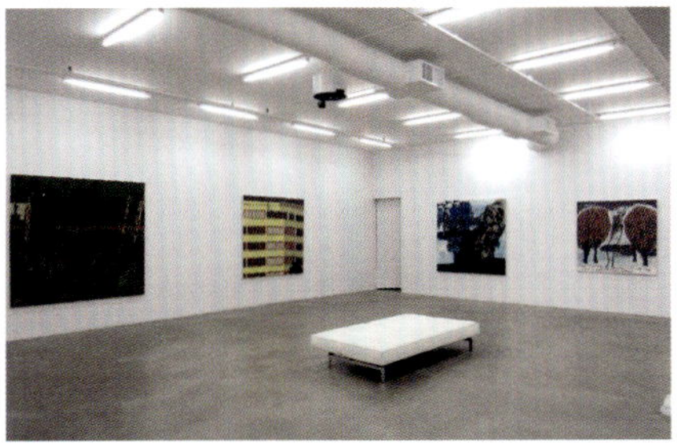
Installation view: Turn Back, Detour, Go On, 2014, Winsor Gallery, Vancouver, BC.

The artist travels to Barcelona where he presents a paper at a conference titled 1st Conference on Arts-Based and Artistic Research, held at the University of Barcelona.

**2014**

Pearson has a solo exhibition titled Turn Back, Detour, Go On at the Winsor Gallery in Vancouver, BC.

He travels to Granada, Spain, where he presents a paper at a conference titled 2nd Conference on Arts-Based and Artistic Research, held at the University of Granada. He visits the Alhambra and the Sacromonte district of Granada, experiences that later lead to several paintings, including *The Flamenco Dancer*, *The Conversation*, and *The Green Coat*.

Pearson is a conference presenter at the Project Anywhere Conference 2014, held in New York. The title of the event is Art and Research at the Outermost Limits of Location-Specificity, and is held at the School of Art, Media, and Technology at Parsons School of Design, a division of The New School in New York. The title of Pearson's paper is "Reflections on Critique and Critical Judgment in Art".

**2015**

Pearson is included in group exhibition Living, Building, Thinking: Art and Expressionism, curated by Ihor Holubizky, from the McMaster Museum of Art's permanent collection, and held at the Art Gallery of Alberta in Edmonton.

He travels to Porto, Portugal, to present a paper at the 3rd Conference on Arts-Based and Artistic Research, held at the University of Porto. Pearson's conference paper is titled "On the Question of Quality in the Absence of Connoisseurship".

He spends the month of June at the Bus from Guadalajara, Artist's Residence Project in Ajijic, Jalisco, Mexico, where he produces large works on paper using ink and watercolour. These works lead to his oil-on-canvas *Fountain* series.

**2016**

The artist is included in a group exhibition titled Drawing from Life, curated by Liz Wylie, at the Kelowna Art Gallery. For this exhibition Pearson creates a large multi-part ink on paper drawing titled *Trees on Knox Mountain*.

He is also included in an expanded iteration of the exhibition Living, Building, Thinking: Art and Expressionism, curated by Ihor Holubizky, held at the McMaster Museum of Art, in Hamilton.

Pearson travels to Helsinki to present a paper at the 4th Conference on Arts-Based and Artistic Research, held at the Aalto University. The title of his conference paper is "A Brief Sketch of Cross-Cultural Codes and Artistic Models in the Formation of Modern and Contemporary Sculpture".

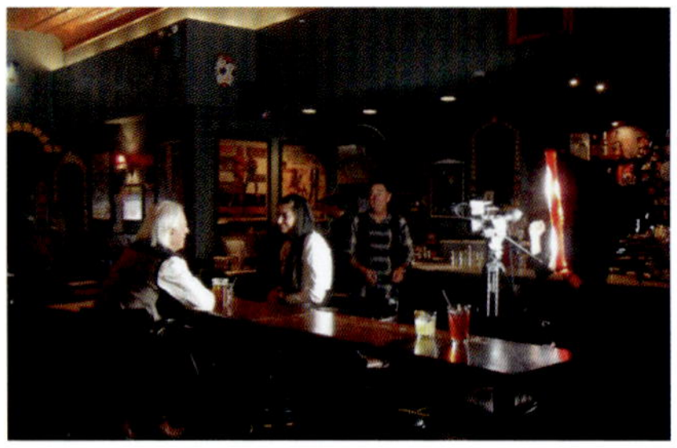

Pearson, *The Cocktail Bar (4 Vignettes)*, production still, 2017.

Accompanied by his wife, Dagmar, he also travels to Tallinn, Estonia, and Riga, Latvia.

Pearson makes a donation of his four-part oil-on-paper work *After Hours*, 2000, to the UBC Okanagan permanent collection.

**2017**

The artist premieres his video, *The Cocktail Bar (4 Vignettes)*, 2016, at Fernando's Pub, Kelowna, BC, on 22 February.

He retires from his position as Associate Professor in Visual Arts at the University of British Columbia, Okanagan, and receives the title of Professor Emeritus.

Pearson is elected as a member of the Royal Canadian Academy of Arts (RCA).

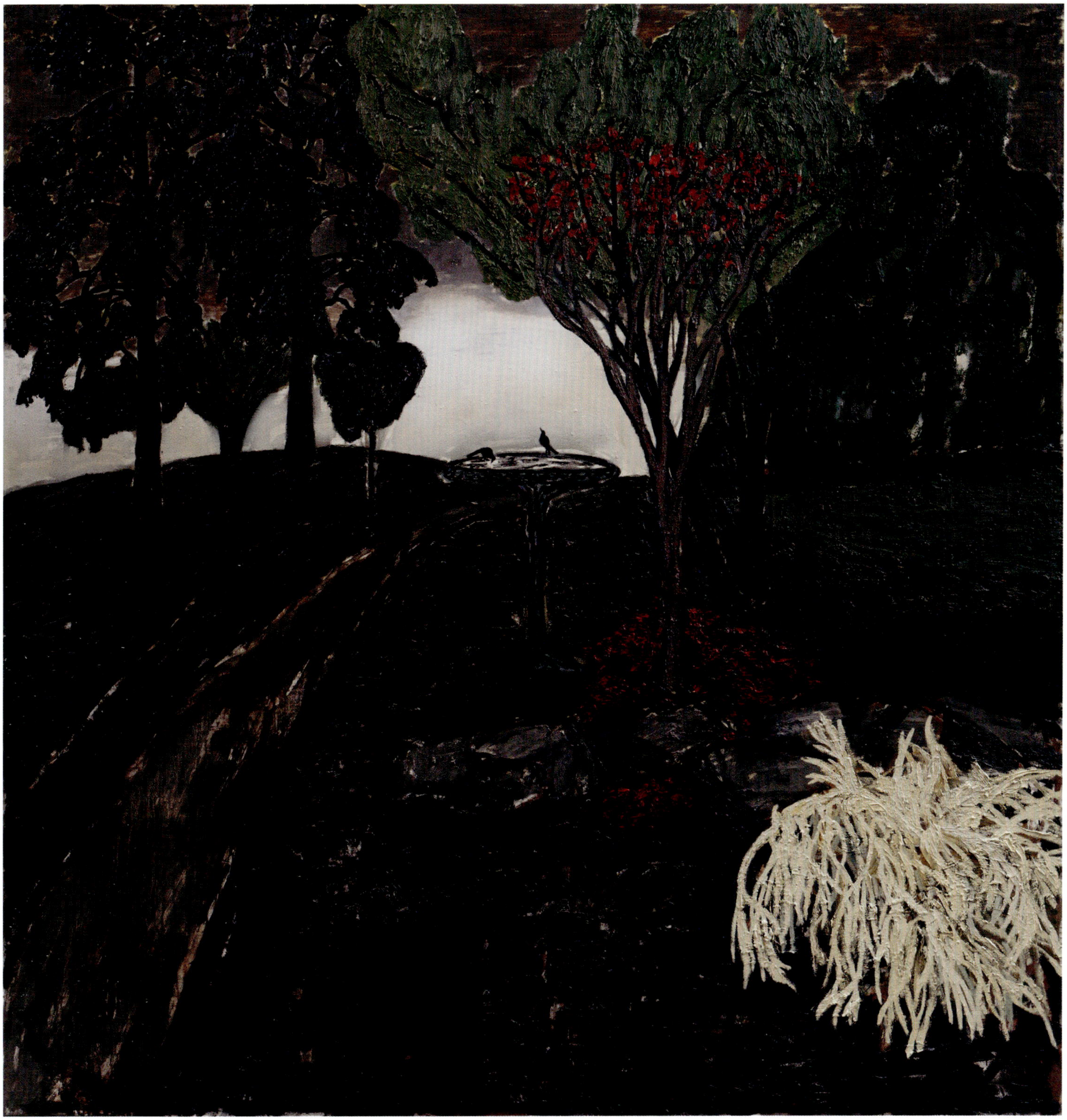

*The Bird Bath*, 2016

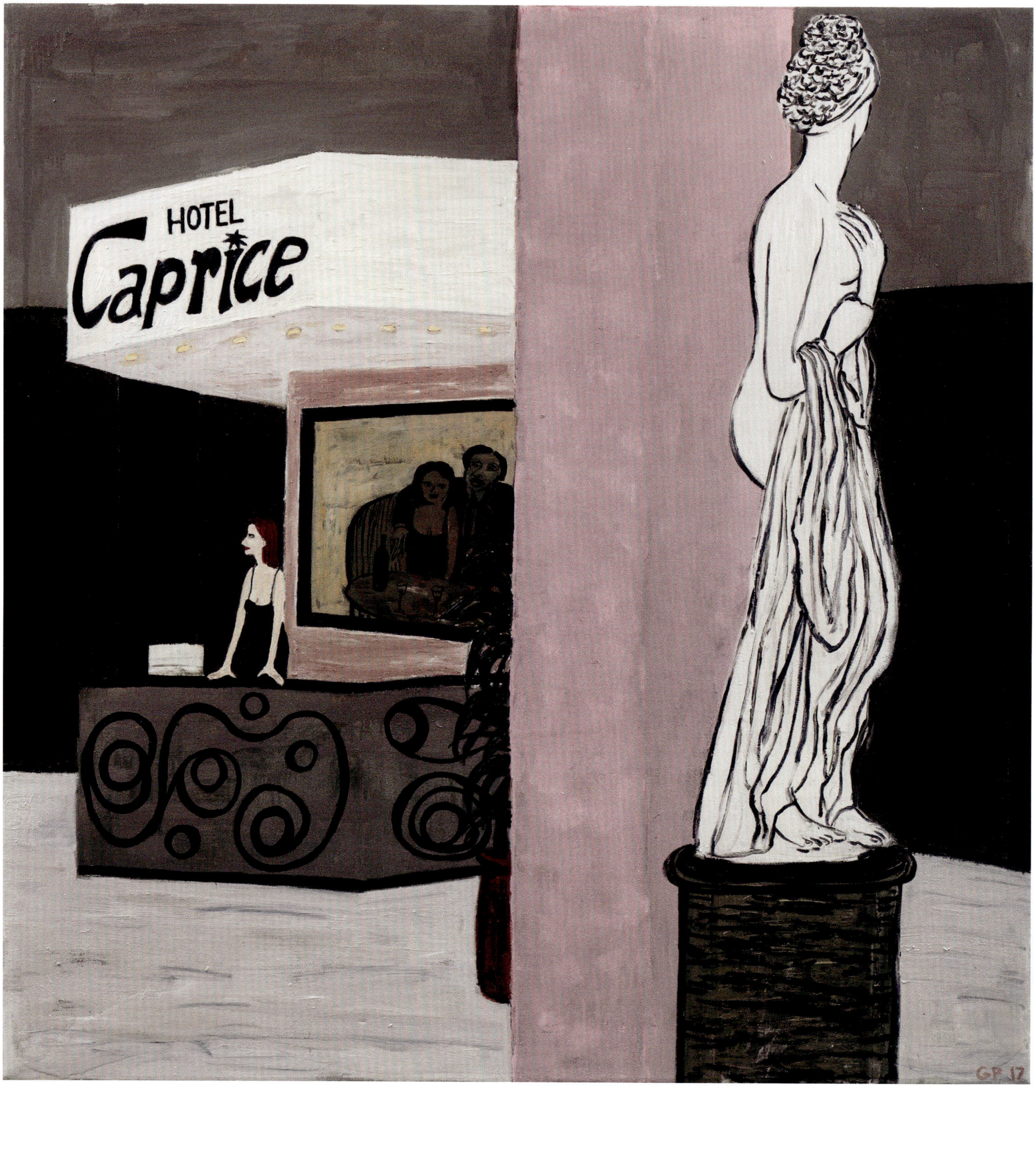




*Hotel Caprice*, 2017

## Selected Bibliography

### Publications by the Artist


"Valerie Blass: To Only Ever Say One Thing Forever the Same Thing", *Sculpture Magazine*, vol 35, no 4, May 2016, pp 77–78.

"Landon Mackenzie Parallel Journey: Works on Paper (1975–2015)", in *Border Crossings*, vol 35, no 1, March–May 2016, pp 108–109.

"Reflections on Critique and Critical Judgment in Art", in *Anywhere*, vol 1, Simone Douglas and Sean Lowry eds, New York, NY: Project Anywhere and Parsons The New School; Australia: University of Newcastle, School of Creative Arts, 2015, pp 88–91.

"On the Question of Quality in the Absence of Connoisseurship", conference paper for The 3rd Conference on Arts-Based Research and Artistic Research, Portugal: University of Porto, January 2015, pp 28–30. http://3c.nea.fba.up.pt/sites/3c.nea.fba.up.pt/files/FINAL_PEARSON,%20Porto%20Art%20%26%20Resarch%20Conference%20Paper.pdf

"Erwin Wurm: One Minute Sculpture", *Sculpture Magazine*, vol 33, no 9, November 2014, p 79.

"Christos Dikeakos: Nature Morte at the Kelowna Art Gallery, Kelowna BC, June 21–October 5, 2014", in *Border Crossings*, vol 33, no 4, December–February, 2014–2015, pp 88–89.

"Two Short Case Studies & a Memoir: Good Art and/or Good Research?", *Fundamentals, criteria and contexts based arts and artistic research investigation,* Marin Viadel, R Roldan and J Molinet Medina, eds. Spain: University of Granada, 2014, pp 121–123. http://digibug.ugr.es/handle/10481/34212

"Erin Shirreff: Pictures, at The Contemporary Art Gallery, Vancouver, April 19-June 16, 2013," in *Border Crossings*, vol 32, no 3, September–November 2013, pp 89–90.

"Academia and Art First Research", conference paper for The 1st Annual Conference on Arts-Based and Artistic Research, F Hernández-Hernández, F and R Fendler eds, Spain: University of Barcelona, 2013, pp 35–38. http://diposit.ub.edu/dspace/.../Proceedings_ABR-ArtisticResearch_2013UnivBarcelona.pdf

"Ian Wallace: At the Intersection of Painting and Photography, Vancouver Art Gallery, October 27, 2012-February 24, 2013", *Border Crossings*, vol 32, no 1, March–May, 2013, pp 83–85.

"Ken Lum: It takes me back somewhere, I'm not sure where...", *Sculpture Magazine*, vol 31, no 9, November 2012, pp 42–45.

"David Alexander, The Shape of Place, Kelowna Art Gallery, Jan. 14-March 25, 2012", *Border Crossings*, vol 31, no 2, June–August 2012, pp 85–87.

"On the Nature of Things, the Kamloops Art Gallery, Kamloops, BC, Oct. 15 – Dec. 31, 2011", *Border Crossings*, vol 31, no 1, March–May 2012.

"The Point Is, Kelowna Art Gallery, Kelowna BC, August 20-October 30, 2011", *Border Crossings*, vol 30, no 4, December–February 2011–2012, pp 119–121.

"1 2 3 Soliloquy: An Essay on the Exhibition", *1 2 3 Soliloquy*, Hamilton, ON: McMaster University Museum of Art, 2011.

"On the Go, A Short Narrative Reading: Nhan Duc Nguyen", *Nhan Duc Nguyen: A Shrine to Literature*, Vernon, BC: Gallery Vertigo, 2011.

"Alan Wood: in conversation with Gary Pearson", *Lake, A Journal of Arts and Environment*, issue 5, Kelowna, BC: University of British Columbia Okanagan, 2010, pp 5–13.

"Fear and Desire in the Art of Roja Aslani", *Roja Aslani: Nostalgia Isn't What it Used to Be,* Calgary, AB: Stride Gallery, 2010.

"The Outskirts of Town: A Peripheral Centre for Art, Agency, and Academia", *Rethinking the Contemporary Art School: The Artist, the PhD, and the Academy*, Brad Buckley and John Conomos, eds. Halifax, NS: Press of the Nova Scotia College of Art and Design, 2009, pp 164–181.

"Susan Rothenberg, Sperone Westwater Gallery, New York, Feb. 9-April 11, 2009", *Border Crossings*, vol 28, no 3, August 2009, pp 124–126.

"Joseph Plaskett, Paris's Moveable Feast," *Border Crossings*, vol 28, no 3, August 2009, pp 100–105.

"Point of Origin: A Curatorial Essay in Seven Parts", *Column 3*, summer 2009, pp 15–24; 160–166.

"Rebecca Belmore, Vancouver Art Gallery, Summer 2008", *Sculpture Magazine*, vol 28, no 4, pp 77–78.

"Alan Wood, Winsor Gallery, Vancouver, November 13-December 7, 2008", *Border Crossings*, vol 28, no 1, February 2009, pp 99–100.

"Location and Actuality: Gary Pearson interviews Christos Dikeakos, Jeff Wall, and Ian Wallace", *Lake: A Journal of Arts and Environment*, no 2, Kelowna, BC: University of British Columbia Okanagan, 2008, pp 40–58.

"Nexus: Histories and Communities at the Kelowna Art Gallery, Kelowna, BC, Nov. 24, 2007-March 2, 2008", *Museums Roundup*, spring 2008, no 240, pp 14–15.

"Ian Wallace", *Border Crossings*, vol 27, no 1, February 2008, pp 108–109.

"An Hour Before the Wind Blows the Colour Away", exh cat for David T Alexander, Vancouver, BC: Bau-Xi Gallery, 2008.

"The Undigested World Itself, Gary Pearson interviews Kristi Malakoff", *Lake: a journal of arts and environment*, Kelowna, BC: University of British Columbia Okanagan, no 1, 2007, pp 16–26.

"Alan Wood", *Nexus, Histories and Communities*, British Columbia: Kelowna Art Gallery, 2007, p 40.

"Kristi Malakoff", *Canadian Art*, spring 2007, vol 24, no 1, p 103.

"Notes on Notes for an Art School", *Beauty and the Beast*, Vancouver, BC: University of British Columbia, 2006.

*Beauty and the Beast*, Kelowna, BC: Alternator Gallery of Contemporary Art, 2006.

"Andrea Zittel: Critical Space", *Border Crossings*, vol 25, no 3, August 2006, pp 108–109.

"Ceal Floyer: Draft, Contemporary Art Gallery, Vancouver," *Sculpture Magazine*, vol 25, no 3, April 2006, pp 76–77.

"Untitled", *Lubos Culen: Victory Elementals*, Kelowna, BC: University of British Columbia Okanagan, Fina Gallery, 2006.

"Oblique Stories and Oblique Angled Sydney: Video Script", *Oblique Stories*, Australia: Sydney College of the Arts, University of Sydney, 2005.

"Rodney Graham 'a little thought'", *Sculpture*, vol 24, no 6, July–August 2005, pp 75–76.

"Looking at John Macdonald's Paintings", *John Macdonald*, Montreal, QC: Galerie de Bellefeuille, 2005, p 3.

"Youth Matters: A Profile of Randy Grskovic", *The Phoenix*, April 13 2005, p 6.

"Tony Scherman: pensées impensables (unthinkable thoughts)", *Museums Roundup*, fall 2004, no 228, pp 12–13.

"Tony Scherman: pensées impensables (unthinkable thoughts)", *Border Crossings*, vol 23, no 4, November 2004, pp 111–112.

"Ian Wallace: The Barcelona Series, at American Fine Arts", *Border Crossings*, vol 23, no 1, May 2004, pp 90–92.

"Jack Jeffrey: Recent Work, at Artspeak Gallery, Vancouver", *Sculpture Magazine*, vol 22, no 7, September 2003, pp 76–77.

"Dangerous Games", *Shauna Oddleifson: Dangerous Games*, Kelowna: Okanagan University College, Fina Gallery, 2003.

"Lyndal Osborne: Geographies and Objects of Enticement, at the Kelowna Art Gallery", *Sculpture Magazine*, vol 21, no 8, October 2002, p 87.

"Lyndal Osborne: Geographies and Objects of Enticement, at the Kelowna Art Gallery", *Border Crossings,* no 82, May 2002, pp 72–73.

"The Art of Geert Maas", *Passion and Vision: The Work of Geert Maas*, Kelowna, BC: Kelowna Art Gallery, 1999, pp 10–11.

*The Creative Voice: Life and Art in the Okanagan*, Prince George, BC: Caitlin Press, 1998.

"Hotel on Fire", *Hotel on Fire*, Kelowna, BC: Kelowna Art Gallery, 1997.

"Curatorial Statement and Artist Interviews", *Posit Poznan: Lee Goreas, Jack Jeffrey, Gary Pearson*, Poznan: International Artists Centre, 1995.

"By Train: Berlin-Łódź" *New Observations*, September–October 1993.

"Claim, by Jack Jeffrey, at Okanagan Artists Alternative", *Boomtown* [Kelowna, BC], April 1993, p 5.

"Formation Schema: first order, second order, third order, fourth order", *Second Order: Paradise*, Vancouver, BC: Patrick Doheny Fine Art, 1992.

"40 Years of British Sculpture at the Kelowna Art Gallery", *Boomtown* [Kelowna, BC], October–November 1992, p 4.

"Drawing and Abstraction", *Abstraction/Drawing*, Vancouver, BC: Or Gallery, 1987, pp 4–12.

Additionally, the artist wrote monthly art reviews and pieces on cultural topics for *Off-Centre Magazine*, Kelowna, BC, September 2004–November 2006.

**Publications on the Artist**

**Articles and Reviews**

Albers, Sandra, "Symbolism or Metaphor", *The Kamloops News*, 27 June 1984.

Allen, George, "Artistic Community Welcomes New Member", *The Kamloops News*, 29 September 1983.

Bakke, Monika, "Taksowka z Kanady," *Gazeta Wyborcza,* 8 July 1995, p 3.

Barton, Adriana, "Alone in a Crowd", *Western Living*, vol 35, no 8, October 2005, p 10.

"BC painter explores today's urban woes", *The Daily News* [Kamloops, BC], 28 March 2008, p B2.

Belton, Robert, *Sights of Resistance: Approaches to Canadian Visual Culture*, Calgary, AB: University of Calgary Press, 2001.

Brennan, Maev, "Artist's Foreboding Imagery", *Capital News* [Kelowna, BC], 8 March 1991, p 14.

_____, "Performance Art Comes To Alternator", *The Daily Courier* [Kelowna, BC], 28 September 1995.

_____, "Spectacle Did Not Threaten", *The Daily Courier* [Kelowna, BC], 5 October 1995, p C1.

Christiansen, Atle, "Drift – 92," *Dag Og Tid* [Farsund, Norway], 17 September 1992.

"Des artistes de Vancouver se dévoilent", *Galerie du Tableau* [Marseilles], 24 October 2013.

Failing, Patricia, "The Pacific Northwest: Sex, Landscape and Videotapes", *ArtNews*, vol 90, no 10, December 1991, pp 88–91.

Farr, Sheila, "North of the Border", *Reflex,* vol 4, no 3 May–June 1990, p 24.

_____, "Maps to Nowhere", *Reflex*, vol 6, no 5, September–October 1992, p 23.

Gilroyed, Anne, "Vivid thoughts from the Okanagan", *Nanaimo Daily News*, 30 March 1995, p B1.

Gordon, Jean, "The Eye of the Beholder", *West*, vol 2, no 9, October 1990, pp 30–41.

Hammerstadt, Josh, "Artist didn't have a One Way Ticket", *Prince George This Week*, 6 March 2005, p 11.

Hanon, Andrew, "Pearson Writes Valuable Reference Book", *Capital News* [Kelowna, BC], 13 November 1998, p 8.

Johnson, Mia, "Gary Pearson: Scenes from a 'Smoker's Theatre'", *Preview*, February–March 2012.

"KAG combines jazz, poetry", *The Daily News* [Kamloops, BC], 2 May 2008, p B4.

"Kelowna's Gary Pearson has Major Show in Kamloops", *Off-Centre Magazine* [Kelowna, BC], May 2008.

Kroeger, Monique, "Somewhere: A Solo exhibition by Gary Pearson", *The Source* [Vancouver, BC], 4 May 2009.

Laurence, Robin, "Human Geometry", *Vanguard*, vol 17, no 6, December–January 1988–1989, p 43.

_____, "Odd Geometrics Transcend Their Awkwardness", *The Georgia Straight*, vol 24, no 1159, 9 March 1990, p 23.

Lightfoot, Mark, "First Show for New Talent", *The Citizen* [Prince George, BC], 7 January 1981.

MacClement, Hazel, "An Artist Turns Author", *The Daily Courier* [Kelowna, BC] 1 November 1998, p C3.

"Nous reviendrons, vous reviendrez," *Eye and Mind* online, 21 December 2013. *http://eyeandmind.wordpress.com/2013/12/21/des-canadiens-a-marseille-nous-reviendrons-vous-reviendrez/*

Oakes, Julie, "Depths of the Ersatz", *Vie Des Arts* [Montreal, BC], no 237, winter 2014, pp 80–81.

Opstad, Gunvald, "Haerverk pa Bragdoya", *Faedrelandsvennen* [Kristinansand, Norway], 18 July 1992.

_____, "Drift", *Hrymfaxe Kunsttidsskrift* [Aarhus, Denmark], no 3, September 1992, pp 3–8.

Pederson, Bernt Erik, "Drift Tar Form", *Farsunds Avis*, 16 June 1992, p 7.

Priegert, Portia, "Social Grit", *Event* [Kelowna, BC], 9 November 2000, p 12.

_____, "Gary Pearson: The End is My Beginning", *Galleries West*, 31 August 2008.

_____, "Scenes from a 'Smoker's Theatre'", exh cat *Scenes from a "Smoker's Theatre"*, Vancouver: Winsor Gallery, 2012.

Rosenberg, Ann, "Man's Triumphs of Technology Critiqued as False Gods", *Vancouver Sun*, 3 November 1990, p D10.

_____, "Art in the Okanagan", *Vancouver Sun*, 30 March 1991, p D7.

_____, "Drawing Out City's Finest", *Vancouver Sun*, 30 May, 1991, p. F4.

_____, "Nature Becomes the Canvas", *Vancouver Sun*, 22 August 1992, p D9.

Sabat, Christina, "Saskatchewan Art: Tradition and Diversity", *Arts Atlantic*, issue 31, vol 8, no 3, 1988, pp 11–12.

Sabatino, Greg, "A Picture's Worth a Thousand Words", *Kamloops This Week*, 9 May 2008, p C2.

Truscott, Eileen, "Studio Watch: Gary Pearson", *Extension Magazine* [Toronto, ON], vol 1, no 3, winter 1992, pp 14–15.

Turnbull, Glenna, "Dark Musings", *Capital News* [Kelowna, BC], 19 June 2003, p 3.

Vegh, Stephanie, "1 2 3 Soliloquy", *Akimbo – Akimblog*, online blog, 15 February 2011.

Wylie, Liz, "The End is My Beginning", *Border Crossings*, vol 27, no 3, August 2008, pp 185–186.

_____, "Rare chance to see professors' own art work up close", *Capital News* [Kelowna, BC], 10 December 2008, p B13.

_____, "Constructions of Identity", *Capital News* [Kelowna, BC], 29 September 2010, p B11.

Youds, Mike, "Windows on Everyday Lives", *The Daily News* [Kamloops, BC], 28 March 2008, p B2.

**Books and Catalogues**

Ainslie, Patricia, *Okanagan Artists in Their Studios*, Calgary, BC: Frontenac House, 2013.

Bateman, David, "From 'a ray of sunlight' to 'le soleil': forsaking meaning in Gary Pearson's painting and poetry", *Gary Pearson: The End is My Beginning*, Kamloops, BC: Kamloops Art Gallery, 2008.

Belton, Robert J, "Case Study 5.3.100", *Sights of Resistance: Approaches to Canadian Visual Culture*, Calgary, BC: University of Calgary Press, 2001.

Budney, Jen, "Gary Pearson in Conversation with Jen Budney", *Gary Pearson: The End is My Beginning*, Kamloops, BC: Kamloops Art Gallery, 2008.

Holubizky, Ihor, "Epilogue", *1 2 3 Soliloquy*, Hamilton, ON: McMaster University Museum of Art, 2011.

_____, "Encounters of Self and Memory", *Living, Building, Thinking: Art & Expressionism*, Edmonton, AB: Art Gallery of Alberta, 2016.

Jeffries, Bill, "Slow Paint," *Take Your Time*, Burnaby, BC: Simon Fraser University Gallery, 2010.

Laurence, Robin, "Drawing +", *Drawing Plus*, Victoria, BC: Open Space, 1994.

McWilliam, David. "Disjuncture: As a Syntax", *Jennifer Gordon, Kathleen McFall, Gary Pearson: Disjuncture: As a Syntax*, Vancouver, BC: Charles H Scott Gallery, 1990.

Richmond, Cindy, "Saskatchewan Art: Tradition and Diversity", *Saskatchewan Art: Tradition and Diversity*, Fredericton, NB: University of New Brunswick Art Centre, 1987.

Sawchyn, Linda, "One Way Ticket for a Lonely Planet", *Gary Pearson: One Way Ticket*, Kelowna, BC: Kelowna Art Gallery, 2003.

Sorenson, Vanessa, "Immediacy and the Noughties", *Take Your Time*, Burnaby, BC: Simon Fraser University Gallery, 2010.

Truscott, Eileen, "Fourth Order: Interview with the Artist", *Second Order: Paradise*, Vancouver, BC: Patrick Doheny Fine Art, 1992.

Turner, Michael, "Trains and Stations", *Gary Pearson: One Way Ticket*, Kelowna, BC: Kelowna Art Gallery, 2003.

Wilkin, Karen, "Introduction", *Second Order: Paradise*, Vancouver, BC: Patrick Doheny Fine Art, 1992.

_____, "About Gary Pearson: Continuum and Interruption", *Gary Pearson: One Way Ticket*, Kelowna, BC: Kelowna Art Gallery, 2003.

Wylie, Liz, "Private Worlds", *Nexus: Histories and Communities*, Kelowna, BC: Kelowna Art Gallery, 2007, pp 115–124.

_____, "Extending our Boundaries", *Boundaries*, Kelowna, BC: Kelowna Art Gallery, 2008.

_____, "Piecing it Together", *Constructions of Identity*, Kelowna, BC: Kelowna Art Gallery, 2010.

_____, "Drawing Conclusions", *Drawing from Life*, Kelowna, BC: Kelowna Art Gallery, 2016.

_____, "Writ Large", *The Big Picture*, Kelowna, BC: Kelowna Art Gallery, 2017.

**List of Reproductions**

Facing T of Cs: *Happy New Year*, 2016, oil, oil enamel, enamel spray paint and polyurethane on canvas, 193 × 203 cm. Collection of the artist. Photo: Yuri Akuney, Digital Perfections

p 4: *The Incident at the Guadalupe Bar*, 2011, oil, oil enamel, polyurethane, enamel spray paint on canvas, 204 × 193 cm. Winsor Private Collection. Photo: Yuri Akuney, Digital Perfections

p 6: *I'm Only Happy When I'm with You*, 2000, oil and etching ink on canvas, 137 × 137 cm. Collection of Two Rivers Art Gallery, Prince George, BC. Photo: Kim Clarke

p 9: *The Scream*, 1990, powdered pigment and acrylic gel medium on canvas, 172 × 172 cm. Collection of the Kelowna Art Gallery. Photo: Yuri Akuney, Digital Perfections

p 11: *Everything Comes and Goes*, 2011, oil, ink on paper, 132 × 144 cm. Private collection. Photo: Yuri Akuney, Digital Perfections

p 13: *Please Don't Smoke During the Concert*, 2000, oil and etching ink on canvas, 137 × 137 cm. Collection of the artist. Photo: Yuri Akuney, Digital Perfections

p 14: *Hotel Room*, 2002, oil on canvas, 226 × 253 cm. Collection of the Vancouver Art Gallery. Photo: Kim Clarke

p 15: *One Way Ticket*, 2002, oil on canvas and collaged canvas, 226 × 228 cm. Collection of the Kelowna Art Gallery. Photo: Yuri Akuney, Digital Perfections

p 16: *Come Back Later*, 2007, oil on canvas, 204 × 193 cm. Collection of the artist. Photo: Yuri Akuney, Digital Perfections

p 18: *Please Don't Smoke During the Concert*, 1999, ink, collage and rubber stamp on paper, 56 × 76 cm. Collection of the artist. Photo: Yuri Akuney, Digital Perfections

*I'll Take a New York Club Any Day!*, 1999, oil, etching ink and graphite on paper, 56 × 76 cm. Collection of the artist. Photo: Dagmar Pearson

*She Pushed the Limits on the Piano Solos*, 2000, ink and oil on paper, 56 × 76 cm. Collection of the artist. Photo: Yuri Akuney, Digital Perfections

*I Was Behaving Myself*, 2001, oil and pencil crayon on paper, 56 × 76 cm. Collection of the artist. Photo: Yuri Akuney, Digital Perfections p 19: *Die Verbindung*, 1990, powder pigment, powder graphite, sand and gel medium on canvas, 173 × 173 cm. Collection of the artist. Photo: Yuri Akuney, Digital Perfections

*Rainbow Effect*, 1990, powder pigment, powder graphite, sand and gel medium on canvas, 173 × 173 cm. Collection of the artist. Photo: Yuri Akuney, Digital Perfections

p 21: *Arthur Rimbaud in New York*, 1991, powdered pigment, powdered graphite, coffee grounds and gel medium on canvas, 268 × 228 cm. Collection of the artist. Photo: Kim Clarke

p 22: *The Gates of Paradise (Large Drawing)*, 1990, oil on paper mounted on canvas, diptych, overall size 152.4 × 304.8 cm. Collection of the artist. Photo: Yuri Akuney, Digital Perfections

p 23: *The Gates of Paradise*, 1990, powdered pigment, acrylic gel medium, gold paint and canvas collage on canvas, 231 × 170 cm. Collection of the artist. Photo: Yuri Akuney, Digital Perfections

p 24: *Untitled*, 1996, powdered pigment and acrylic gel medium on canvas, 112 × 96 cm. Collection of the artist. Photo: Yuri Akuney, Digital Perfections

p 25: *Spectacle*, 1996, powdered graphite and ink on paper, 76 × 56 cm. Collection of the Kelowna Art Gallery. Photo: Yuri Akuney, Digital Perfections

pp 26–27: *Ashtray*, 1996. A suite of twenty-seven oil on paper monoprints, each 36 × 31 cm. Collection of the Kelowna Art Gallery. Photo: Yuri Akuney, Digital Perfections

p 29: *Café Blues*, 1979, graphite, masking tape and collage on paper, 56 × 76 cm. Private collection. Photo: Dagmar Pearson

p 30: *Please Don't Smoke During the Concert*, 1999, first in series of ten, The Night of the Diana Krall Concert, ink and oil on paper, 35 × 25 cm. Collection of the artist.

*Everyone Was Just Hanging On*, 1999, second in series of ten, The Night of the Diana Krall Concert, ink and oil on paper, 35 × 25 cm. Collection of the artist.

*I'm Only Happy When I'm With You*, 1999, third in series of ten, The Night of the Diana Krall Concert, ink and oil on paper, 35 × 25 cm. Collection of the artist.

*The Second Number Was All or Nothing at All*, 1999, fourth in series of ten, The Night of the Diana Krall Concert, ink and oil on paper, 35 × 25 cm. Collection of the artist.

*I Was Behaving Myself*, 1999, fifth in series of ten, The Night of the Diana Krall Concert, ink and oil on paper, 35 × 25 cm. Collection of the artist.

*She Pushed the Limits on the Piano Solos*, 1999, sixth in series of ten, The Night of the Diana Krall Concert, ink and oil on paper, 35 × 25 cm. Collection of the artist.

*I Fell under Her Spell Too*, 1999, seventh in series of ten, The Night of the Diana Krall Concert, ink and oil on paper, 35 × 25 cm. Collection of the artist.

*I Stayed for One More Song and Then Left*, 1999, eighth in series of ten, The Night of the Diana Krall Concert, ink and oil on paper, 35 × 25 cm. Collection of the artist.

*I'll Take a New York Club Any Day!*, 1999, ninth in series of ten, The Night of the Diana Krall Concert, ink and oil on paper, 35 × 25 cm. Collection of the artist.

*It Was Our First Time in Berlin*, 1999, tenth in series of ten, The Night of the Diana Krall Concert, ink and oil on paper, 35 × 25 cm. Collection of the artist.

All photos on p 30: Dagmar Pearson

p 31: *The Cocktail Bar*, 2007, oil on paper, 130 × 150 cm. Collection of Kelowna Art Gallery. Photo: Yuri Akuney, Digital Perfections

p 32: *The Toast*, 2001–2, oil on paper attached to canvas, 226 × 228 cm. Collection of the Kelowna Art Gallery. Photo: Yuri Akuney, Digital Perfections

p 34: *Self Portrait, New Orleans*, 2004, oil on paper, 107 × 107 cm. Collection of the artist. Photo: Dagmar Pearson

p 35: *The Bay Leaf Tree*, 2007, oil, oil enamel on canvas, 204 × 193 cm. Collection of the artist. Photo: Yuri Akuney, Digital Perfections

p 36: *Knox Mountain*, 2013, oil and oil enamel on canvas, 168 × 168 cm. Private collection. Photo: Yuri Akuney, Digital Perfections

p 37: *The Garden Hose*, 2011, oil on canvas, 204 × 193 cm. Collection of the artist. Photo: Yuri Akuney, Digital Perfections

p 40: *I Stayed for One More Song and Then Left*, 2000, oil and etching ink on canvas, 137 × 137 cm. Collection of the artist. Photo: Kim Clarke

p 41: *It Was Our First Time in Berlin*, 1999, oil, ink, paper collage on paper, 56 × 76 cm. Collection of the Kelowna Art Gallery. Photo: Yuri Akuney, Digital Perfections

p 42: *I Fell Under Her Spell Too*, 2000, oil on paper, 56 × 76 cm. Private collection. Photo: Yuri Akuney, Digital Perfections

p 43: *Lori and Joshua*, 2004, oil on paper, 56 × 76 cm. Collection of the Kelowna Art Gallery. Photo: Yuri Akuney, Digital Perfections

p 45: *Aftermath*, 2007, oil on paper, 204 × 193 cm. Collection of the artist. Photo: Yuri Akuney, Digital Perfections

p 47: *02911*, 1991, powdered pigment and acrylic gel medium on canvas, 203 × 168 cm. Collection of the artist. Photo: Yuri Akuney, Digital Perfections

p 48: *This One is Dedicated to You*, 1990, powdered pigment, powdered graphite, graphite, gel medium, sand, metallic paint and collage on canvas, 168 × 129 cm. Collection of the artist. Photo: Yuri Akuney, Digital Perfections

p 49: *Forty-Eight Blue Flames*, 1991, powdered pigment, metallic paint, and acrylic gel medium on canvas, 229 × 168 cm. Collection of the artist. Photo: Yuri Akuney, Digital Perfections

p 50: *Untitled*, 1992, powdered pigment and acrylic gel medium on canvas, 221 × 233.5 cm. Photo: Yuri Akuney, Digital Perfections

p 51: *Untitled*, 1992-93, powdered pigment and acrylic gel medium on canvas, 198 × 165 cm. Collection of the artist. Photo: Yuri Akuney, Digital Perfections

p 52: *Zündergeben*, 1994, powdered pigment and powdered graphite on paper attached to canvas, 203 × 160 cm. Collection of the artist. Photo: Jim Jardine

p 53: *Landscape Between Poznan and Kutno*, 1993, powdered pigment and powdered graphite on canvas, 203 × 193 cm. Collection of the artist. Photo: Yuri Akuney, Digital Perfections

*Night Sky over Poznan*, 1993, powdered pigment and acrylic gel medium on paper, 203 × 193 cm. Collection of the artist. Photo: Jim Jardine

*Ashes*, 1994–95, powdered pigment and powdered graphite on canvas, 203 × 193 cm. Collection of the artist. Photo: Jim Jardine

*Hamburg*, 1994–95, powdered pigment and powdered graphite on canvas, 203 × 193 cm. Collection of the artist. Photo: Jim Jardine

p 54: *Conversation*, 1994–95, powdered pigment and powdered graphite on canvas, 203 × 193 cm. Collection of the artist. Photo: Jim Jardine

*Untitled*, 1994–95, powdered pigment and acrylic gel medium on canvas, 203 × 193 cm. Collection of the artist. Photo: Yuri Akuney, Digital Perfections

*Victim of Anonymity*, 1994–95, powdered pigment and powdered graphite on canvas, 203 × 193 cm. Collection of the artist. Photo: Jim Jardine

*Untitled*, 1995, powdered pigment and acrylic gel medium on canvas, 203 × 193 cm. Collection of the artist. Photo: Yuri Akuney, Digital Perfections

p 55: *Heinrichplatz in Berlin Kreuzberg April 17, 1998*, 1998, oil on paper, triptych, overall dimensions: 420 × 100 cm. Collection of the artist. Photo: Kim Clarke

p 56: *Two of Everything*, 1998, oil on paper, three sheets, each 172 × 122 cm, overall size 172 × 366 cm. Collection of the artist. Photo: Yuri Akuney, Digital Perfections

p 57: *After Hours*, 2000, oil on paper, four parts, each 122 × 122 cm. Collection of the University of British Columbia Okanagan, Kelowna, BC. Photo: Kim Clarke

p 59: *Under the Blue Palms*, 2005, oil, oil enamel and enamel spray paint on canvas, 193 × 204 cm. Collection of the Kamloops Art Gallery. Photo: Yuri Akuney, Digital Perfections

p 60: *When I Get to Baton Rouge*, 2005, oil and oil enamel on canvas, 200 × 168 cm. Collection of the Kamloops Art Gallery. Photo: Yuri Akuney, Digital Perfections

p 61: *Texas Tattoo*, 2004, oil on paper, 106.5 × 106.5 cm. Collection of the artist. Photo: Yuri Akuney, Digital Perfections

*Here Sit (study)*, 2004, oil on paper, 106 × 106 cm. Collection of the artist. Photo: Dagmar Pearson

*Bad Rhythm Here*, 2004, oil on paper, 106 × 107 cm. Collection of the artist. Photo: Dagmar Pearson

*Yuma, AR*, 2004, oil on paper, 106.5 × 106.5 cm. Collection of the artist.

p 62: *Savannah, GA*, 200, oil and enamel on canvas, 137 × 137 cm. Collection of the artist.

*San Clemente, CA*, 2004, oil and enamel on canvas, 137 × 137 cm. Private collection. Photo: Dagmar Pearson

*Near Lake Charles, LA*, 2004, oil and enamel on canvas, 137 × 137 cm. Collection of the artist. Photo: Yuri Akuney, Digital Perfections

*Eucalyptus Trees*, CA, 2004, oil and enamel on canvas, 137 × 137 cm. Collection of the artist. Photo: Yuri Akuney, Digital Perfections

p 63: *I'm Going Back to Greenville*, 2005, oil on mat board, 132 × 101 cm. Collection of the artist. Photo: Yuri Akuney, Digital Perfections

*Voodoo Authentica*, 2005, oil and ink on paper, 76 × 56 cm. Collection of the artist. Photo: Dagmar Pearson

*I'm Going Back to Greenville*, 2005, oil, pencil crayon, chalk pastel and collaged paper on paper, 76 × 56 cm. Collection of the artist. Photo: Dagmar Pearson

*I'm Going Back to Greenville*, 2005, oil on canvas, 160 × 140 cm. Collection of the Kamloops Art Gallery. Photo: Yuri Akuney, Digital Perfections

p 67: *The Green Bar*, 2007, oil on canvas, 200 × 240 cm. Collection of the artist. Photo: Yuri Akuney, Digital Perfections

p 74: *Girl and Dog*, 2014, oil on canvas, 204 × 193 cm. Collection of the artist. Photo: Yuri Akuney, Digital Perfections

pp 78–81: *Face of the Earth, the Surface of Mars*, 2015, ink, watercolour and oil on paper, each 28 × 38 cm. Collection of the artist. 40 works: 20 Earth and 20 Mars, not individually titled. Photo: Dagmar Pearson

pp 84–85: *Rise and Fall*, 2014, ink, oil and rubber stamp on paper, each 40.64 × 40.64 cm. 20 works, all collection of the artist except the first, which is held in a private collection. Photo: Winsor Gallery, Vancouver

p 86: *Fountain at Lake Chapala Waterfront*, 2015, ink and watercolour on paper, 35 × 27 cm. Collection of the artist. Photo: Dagmar Pearson

p 88: *Fernandina Palms*, 2004, oil on paper, 107 × 107 cm. Private collection. Photo: Dagmar Pearson

*Somewhere*, 2008, oil on canvas, 76 × 76 cm. Private collection.

*Two Women Smoking*, 2008, oil on canvas, 76 × 76 cm. Private collection. Photo: Dagmar Pearson

*Shepherd Street (at night)*, 2009, oil on paper, 142 × 150 cm. Private collection. Photo: Dagmar Pearson

p 89: *The Healing Center (monochrome version)*, 2009, oil on paper, 130 × 142 cm. Collection of the artist.

*The Wine Bar*, 2007, oil on paper, 76 × 76 cm. Collection of the artist. Photo: Dagmar Pearson

p 90: *Portrait of a Red-Haired Woman (back view)*, 2007, oil and oil enamel on canvas, 77 × 77 cm. Private collection. Photo: Dagmar Pearson

*Palm Tree*, 2008, oil on canvas, 76 × 76 cm. Private collection. Photo: Yuri Akuney, Digital Perfections

*The Secret*, 2011, oil and oil enamel on canvas, 76 × 76 cm. Private collection. Photo: Yuri Akuney, Digital Perfections

*The Green Coat*, 2014, oil on canvas, 66 × 66 cm. Private collection. Photo: Yuri Akuney, Digital Perfections

p 91: *Speak Low*, 2013, oil and oil enamel on canvas, 168 × 168 cm. Collection of the artist. Photo: Yuri Akuney, Digital Perfections

p 92: *Volcanic Ash Grounds Air Traffic in Northern Europe (Air)*, 2010, oil, oil enamel, spray enamel and cold wax medium on canvas, 122 × 122 cm. Collection of the artist. Photo: Winsor Gallery, Vancouver

*Crippled by Drought, Russia Places Ban on Grain Exports (Fire)*, 2010, oil, oil enamel, spray enamel and cold wax medium on canvas, 122 × 122 cm. Collection of the artist. Photo: Winsor Gallery, Vancouver

*With Little Fanfare, Well is Plugged with Cement (Water)*, 2010, oil, oil enamel, spray enamel and cold wax medium on canvas, 122 × 122 cm. Collection of the artist. Photo: Winsor Gallery, Vancouver

*Earth*, 2010, oil, oil enamel, spray enamel, and cold wax medium on canvas, 122 × 122 cm. Private collection. Photo: Winsor Gallery, Vancouver

p 94: *Anna's Piano Bar and Smoking Room*, 2011, oil on canvas, 204 × 193 cm. Collection of the artist. Photo: Yuri Akuney, Digital Perfections

p 95: *Untitled (Portrait Sketch)*, 2009, coloured pencil on paper, 35 × 25 cm. Collection of the artist. Photo: Dagmar Pearson

*Man Covering His Face*, 2009, charcoal on paper, 35 × 25 cm. Collection of the artist.

*Aftermath (the Sleep of Reason)*, 2009, ink and watercolour on paper, 35 x 27 cm. Collection of the artist. Photo: Dagmar Pearson.

*One More Time around Might Do It*, 2009, ink on paper, 35 x 27 cm. Collection of the artist. Photo: Dagmar Pearson

p 96: *Day of the Dead*, 2010, ink and watercolour on paper, 27 × 35 cm. Collection of the artist.

*In the Restaurant*, 2010, ink and watercolour on paper, 27 × 35 cm. Collection of the artist.

*Plant Studies*, 2010, ink and watercolour on paper, 27 × 35 cm. Collection of the artist.

*Soundtrack from the Sergio Leone Spaghetti Western*, 2010, ink and watercolour on paper, 27 × 35 cm. Collection of the artist.

*Study for Incident at the Guadalupe Bar*, 2010, ink on paper, 27 × 35 cm. Collection of the artist.

*Ajijic, Jal., Mexico*, 2010, ink and watercolour on paper, 27 × 35 cm. Collection of the artist.

*Study of Potted Plant*, 2015, ink on paper, 27 × 35 cm. Collection of the artist.

*The Sea Serpent*, 2015, ink on paper, 27 × 35 cm. Collection of the artist.

All photos on p 96: Dagmar Pearson

p 97: *Akkrum, Holland*, 2014, ink on paper, 27 × 35 cm. Collection of the artist.

*Near the Canal*, 2014, ink and watercolour on paper, 27 × 35 cm. Collection of the artist.

*Sneek, Holland*, ink and watercolour on paper, 27 × 35 cm. Collection of the artist.

*Windmill, Holland*, 2014, ink and watercolour on paper, 27 × 35 cm. Collection of the

*Landscape Between Weisel and Bornich*, 2014, ink and watercolour on paper, 27 × 37 cm. Collection of the artist.

*Rhine River from Lookout*, 2014, ink and watercolour on paper, 27 × 35 cm. Collection of the artist.

*National Park, Kettle Falls, WA*, 2014, ink and watercolour on paper, 27 × 35 cm. Collection of the artist.

*June 2015 (Mexico)*, 2015, ink on paper, 27 × 35 cm. Collection of the artist.

All photos on p 97: Dagmar Pearson

p 98: *Fatigue*, 2010, ink and watercolour on paper, 76 × 56 cm. Collection of the artist.

*In the Restaurant, Ajijic*, 2010, ink and watercolour on paper, 90 × 68 cm. Collection of the artist.

*Untitled (tree drawing)*, 2011, watercolour and ink on paper, 46 × 32 cm. Collection of the artist.

*Untitled (tree drawing)*, 2011, ink and oil on paper, 46 × 29 cm. Collection of the artist.

*Palm*, 2015, ink and watercolour on paper, 76 × 56 cm. Collection of the artist.

*Palm Tree*, 2015, ink on paper, 35 × 27 cm. Collection of the artist.

All photos on p 98: Dagmar Pearson

p 99: *Una Cansión Triste (A Sad Song)*, 2011, oil, oil enamel and enamel spray paint on canvas, 168 × 229 cm. Private collection. Photo: Yuri Akuney, Digital Perfections

p 101: *Trees on Knox Mountain*, 2016, ink and paper collage on paper (twelve sheets), overall size 365.7 × 640 cm. Collection of the artist. Photo: Kyle L Poirier

p 103: *It's Burning!*, 2013, oil, oil enamel and enamel spray paint on canvas, 168 × 168 cm. Collection of the artist. Photo: Yuri Akuney, Digital Perfections

p 104: *Condominium*, 2013, oil on canvas, 168 × 168 cm. Collection of the artist. Photo: Yuri Akuney, Digital Perfections

p 106: *Girl and Dog*, 2014, oil on canvas, 204 × 193 cm. Collection of the artist. Photo: Yuri Akuney, Digital Perfections

p 109: *No. 28 Carrer de Ferran*, 2013, oil on paper, over-painted monoprint, 119.5 × 71 cm. Private collection. Photo: Winsor Gallery, Vancouver

p 111: *The Flamenco Dancer,* 2014, oil and oil enamel on canvas, 204 × 193 cm. Collection of the artist. Photo: Yuri Akuney, Digital Perfections

p 112: *Springtime Started Out Brand New*, 2010, ink and watercolour on paper, 132 × 104 cm. Private collection. Photo: Yuri Akuney, Digital Perfections

*Study for Una Cansión Triste*, 2010, ink on paper (two sheets), overall size 36 × 53 cm. Collection of the artist. Photo: Dagmar Pearson

*The Conversation*, 2015, oil on canvas, 66 × 66 cm. Private collection. Photo: Winsor Gallery, Vancouver

p 113: *Mother and Child*, 2014, oil, oil enamel and enamel spray paint on canvas, 193 × 203 cm. Collection of the artist. Photo: Yuri Akuney, Digital Perfections

p 114: *Untitled (Dogs)*, 2015, ink and watercolour on paper, 152.x 106.5 cm. Collection of the artist. Photo: Yuri Akuney, Digital Perfections

*Untitled*, 2015, ink and watercolour on paper, 152 x 106.5 cm. Collection of the artist. Photo: Yuri Akuney, Digital Perfections

p 115: *Fountain and Potted Plant*, 2015, ink and watercolour on paper, 106.5 × 152.5 cm. Collection of the artist. Photo: Yuri Akuney, Digital Perfections

*The Bird Fountain*, 2015, ink and watercolour on paper, 106.5 × 152.5 cm. Collection of the artist. Photo: Yuri Akuney, Digital Perfections

*The Blue Fountain*, 2015, ink and watercolour on paper, 106.5 × 152.5 cm. Collection of the artist. Photo: Yuri Akuney, Digital Perfections

p 116: *The Bird Fountain*, 2015, oil, oil enamel and enamel spray paint on canvas, 193 × 259 cm. Collection of the artist. Photo: Yuri Akuney, Digital Perfections

*The Romance*, 2015, oil, oil enamel and enamel spray paint on canvas, 193 × 259 cm. Collection of the artist. Photo: Yuri Akuney, Digital Perfections

p 118: *The Large Fountain*, 2015, oil and oil enamel on canvas, 193 × 259 cm. Collection of the artist. Photo: Yuri Akuney, Digital Perfections

*The Fountain of Good and Evil*, 2015, oil, oil enamel and enamel spray paint on canvas, 193 × 259 cm. Collection of the artist. Photo: Yuri Akuney, Digital Perfections

p 119: *Honky Tonk*, 2017, oil, oil enamel and enamel spray paint on canvas, 193 × 203 cm. Collection of the artist. Photo: Yuri Akuney, Digital Perfections

p 133: The Bird Bath, 2016, oil, oil enamel and enamel spray paint on canvas, 203 × 193 cm. Collection of the artist. Photo: Yuri Akuney, Digital Perfections

p 134: Hotel Caprice, 2017, oil, oil enamel and enamel spray paint on canvas, 203 × 193 cm. Collection of the artist. Photo: Yuri Akuney, Digital Perfections

p 142: *The Queue (dripping milk)*, 2017, oil and oil enamel on canvas attached to canvas, 190 × 114 cm. Collection of the artist. Photo: Yuri Akuney, Digital Perfections

# Authors' Biographies

**Ihor Holubizky** is Senior Curator at the McMaster Museum of Art, McMaster University, Hamilton, and Adjunct Assistant Professor at McMaster University. He has held curatorial positions across Canada and in Australia, and has his PhD in Art History from the University of Queensland, Brisbane, Australia. Holubizky has contributed to numerous publications in Canada, the United States, Europe and Australia on a wide range of topics in visual and performative culture, and cultural and social history. His most recent publications are *Predisposed to Thinking Through the Eye of Mutual Convenience*, 2015, and *Living Building Thinking, Art and Expressionism*, 2017, both McMaster Museum of Art, Hamilton, ON, Canada.

**Aaron Peck** is the author of a novel, *The Bewilderments of Bernard Willis*, 2008, and a monograph, *Jeff Wall: North & West*, 2016. His art writing regularly appears in *Artforum*. He currently splits his time between Vancouver, BC, and Brussels, Belgium, where he teaches at Emily Carr University of Art + Design and l'Ecole nationale supérieure des arts visuels de la Cambre, respectively.

**Michael Turner's** fictions include *Hard Core Logo*, 1993, *The Pornographer's Poem*, 1999, and *8 × 10*, 2009. A frequent collaborator, he has written scripts with Stan Douglas, poems with Geoffrey Farmer and songs with cub, Dream Warriors, Fishbone and Kinnie Starr.

**Liz Wylie** was curator of the Kelowna Art Gallery from 2007 to 2017. Previously she held the position of University of Toronto Art Curator for 11 years. As well as her work as a curator, she has been writing reviews and articles on contemporary and historical Canadian art since 1977. Her recent publications include monographs on the Canadian artists Keith Langergraber, Keith Harder, John Hartman, Bill Rodgers, Christos Dikeakos, John Hall, Landon Mackenzie and Deborah Koenker. Wylie holds an MFA in Art History from Concordia University in Montreal. She is a past president of the Ontario Association of Art Galleries.

# Artist's Acknowledgements

I would first like to thank curator Liz Wylie for her continued support during her tenure at the Kelowna Art Gallery and for initiating this exhibition and accompanying publication. Liz's diligent work in seeing this process through to its organizational conclusion is deeply appreciated. I am extremely indebted to my wife Dagmar for her ongoing support of my art practice: her tireless work on preparation for this exhibition, including archival searches and data organization, scanning and photography; and for countless other projects and professional assistance. I also want to acknowledge the friendship and support of colleagues over the years, and to name but a few: Christos Dikeakos, Jack Jeffrey, Mary and Jack McCulloch, Ian Wallace, Meeka Walsh, the late Alan Wood, the late Annette Hurtig, Brad Buckley, Karen Wilkin, Jen Budney, David Alexander, Ihor Holubizky, Glenn Harper, among many others. I would also like to extend my most sincere gratitude to the writers who contributed to the publication: Liz Wylie, Aaron Peck, Michael Turner, and Ihor Holubizky. Thank you. It's an honour to have your thoughtful, engaging and often entertaining ideas, observations, reflections and questions accompany the images that populate the exhibition publication. Thanks to Yuri Akuney for his excellent photographic documentation and to Joseph Atkinson at Black Dog Publishing. And, thank you to the Executive Director of the Kelowna Art Gallery, Nataley Nagy, the Board of Directors and staff for all their support and contributions to the exhibition. Finally, art needs an audience, so thanks very much to all the visitors to this and other art exhibitions.

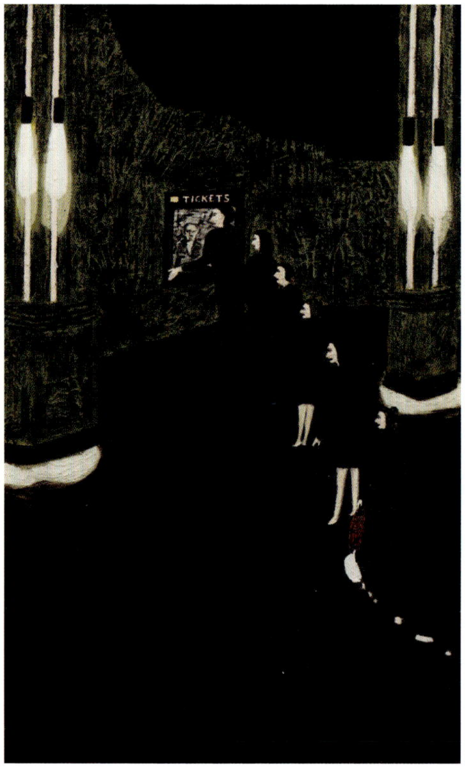


*The Queue (dripping milk)*, 2017

Black Dog Publishing Limited
308 Essex Road, London, N1 3AX
United Kingdom

+44 (0)20 7713 5097
info@blackdogonline.com
www.blackdogonline.com

This publication originates from Gary Pearson: Short Fictions, an exhibition curated by Liz Wylie presented at the Kelowna Art Gallery from 13 January–18 March 2018.

Designed by Joseph Atkinson at Black Dog Publishing
Cover image: Gary Pearson, *Anna's Piano Bar and Smoking Room*, 2011

All opinions expressed within this publication are those of the authors and not necessarily of the publisher.

British Library in Cataloguing Data
A CIP record for this book is available from the British Library

ISBN 978 1 911164 50 0



Black Dog Publishing Limited, London, UK, is an environmentally responsible company. *Gary Pearson: Short Fictions* is printed on sustainably sourced paper.

KELOWNA Art GALLERY

OPUS
Opus Art Supplies
Resources for the Creative Individual

reuse recycle reduce

art design fashion
history photography
theory and things

black dog publishing london uk

www.blackdogonline.com

## List of Works in the Exhibition

### Paintings

*Under the Blue Palms*, 2005, oil, oil enamel and enamel spray paint on canvas, 193 × 204 cm. Collection of the Kamloops Art Gallery.

*When I Get to Baton Rouge*, 2005, oil and oil enamel on canvas, 198.5 × 167.5 cm. Collection of the Kamloops Art Gallery.

*Anna's Piano Bar and Smoking Room*, 2011, oil and oil enamel on canvas, 203 × 193 cm. Collection of the artist.

*The Incident at the Guadalupe Bar*, 2011, oil, oil enamel, polyurethane and enamel spray paint on canvas, 203 × 193 cm. Winsor Private Collection.

*Speak Low*, 2013, oil and oil enamel on canvas, 168 × 168 cm. Collection of the artist.

*The Flamenco Dancer*, 2014, oil and oil enamel on canvas, 203 × 193 cm. Collection of the artist.

*Girl and Dog*, 2014, oil on canvas, 203 × 193 cm. Collection of the artist.

*Mother and Child*, 2014, oil, oil enamel and enamel spray paint on canvas, 193 × 203 cm. Collection of the artist.

*The Bird Fountain*, 2015, oil, oil enamel and enamel spray paint on canvas, 193 × 259 cm. Collection of the artist.

*The Large Fountain*, 2015, oil and oil enamel on canvas, 193 × 259 cm. Collection of the artist.

*The Romance*, 2015, oil, oil enamel and enamel spray paint on canvas, 193 × 259 cm. Collection of the artist.

*The Fountain of Good and Evil*, 2015, oil, oil enamel and enamel spray paint on canvas, 193 × 259 cm. Collection of the artist.

*The Bird Bath*, 2016, oil, oil enamel and enamel spray paint on canvas, 203 × 193 cm. Collection of the artist.

*Hotel Caprice*, 2017, oil, oil enamel and polyurethane on canvas, 203 × 193 cm. Collection of the artist.

*Honky Tonk*, 2017, oil, oil enamel and enamel spray paint on canvas, 193 × 203 cm. Collection of the artist.

*Happy New Year*, 2016, oil, oil enamel, enamel spray paint and polyurethane on canvas, 193 × 203 cm. Collection of the artist.

*The Queue (dripping milk)*, 2017, oil and oil enamel on canvas attached to canvas, 190 × 114 cm. Collection of the artist.

### Works on Paper

*It Was Our First Time in Berlin*, 1999, oil, ink and paper collage on paper, 56 × 76 cm. Collection of the Kelowna Art Gallery.

*What Keeps Mankind Alive?*, 2000, oil on paper, 56 × 76 cm. Collection of the Kelowna Art Gallery.

*I'll Take a New York Club Any Day*, 2000, oil, etching ink, graphite, and paper collage on paper, 56 × 76 cm. Collection of the artist.

*I Was Behaving Myself*, 2001, oil, pencil crayon, and rubber stamp on paper, 56 × 76 cm. Collection of the artist.

*The Cocktail Bar*, 2006, oil on paper, 130 × 150 cm. Collection of the Kelowna Art Gallery.

*The Healing Center (Monochrome Version)*, 2009, oil on multi-part paper, 140 × 150 cm. Collection of the artist.

*Fountain and Potted Plant*, 2015, ink and watercolour on paper, 106.5 × 152.2 cm. Collection of the artist.

*The Bird Fountain*, 2015, ink and watercolour on paper, 106.5 × 152.2 cm. Collection of the artist.

*The Blue Fountain*, 2015, ink and watercolour on paper, 106.5 × 152.2 cm. Collection of the artist.

*Untitled*, 2015, ink and watercolour on paper, 152.5 × 106.5 cm. Collection of the artist.

*Untitled* [dogs], 2015, ink and watercolour on paper, 152.5 × 106.5 cm. Collection of the artist.

*No. 28 Carrer de Ferran*, 2013, oil over monoprint, 119.5 × 71 cm. Collection of the artist.

*Untitled (Mexican Shrub)*, 2010, ink and watercolour on paper, 35 × 27 cm. Collection of the artist.

*Study for The Incident at the Guadalupe Bar*, 2010, ink on paper, 27 × 35 cm. Collection of the artist.

*Study for Una Cansión Triste*, 2010, ink on paper, 35 × 24 cm. Collection of the artist.

*The Hapless Waiter*, 2011, oil and ink on paper, 144 × 104 cm. Collection of the artist.

*Gyro Beach*, 2011, oi’ nd ink on paper, 104 × 144 cm. Collection of the artist.

*The Flamenco Dancer (sketch)*, 2014, ink and watercolour on paper, 34 × 24 cm. Collection of the artist.

*Girl and Dog (sketch)*, 2014, ink and watercolour on paper, 34 × 24 cm. Collection of the artist.

*Fountain (study)*, 2015, ink and oil on paper, 34 × 24 cm. Collection of the artist.

*Fatigue*, 2010, ink and watercolour on paper, 76 × 56 cm. Collection of the artist.

*Café Blues*, 1979, graphite, masking and collage paper on paper, 56 × 76 cm. Private collection. Collection of the artist.

*The Wine Bar*, 2007, oil on paper, 76 × 76 cm. Collection of the artist.

*Man Covering His Face*, 2009, charcoal on paper, 35 × 25 m. Collection of the artist.

*Untitled (Portrait Sketch)*, 2009, coloured pencil on paper, 35 × 25 cm. Collection of the artist.

*Fountain, Ajijic waterfront, Lake Chapala*, 2015, ink and watercolour on paper, 35 × 27 cm. Collection of the artist.

*Ajijic, palm tree at waterfront*, 2015, ink on paper, 35 × 27 cm. Collection of the artist.

*Short Fictions*, undated, untitled, digital photo-prints, ten works each 40.5 × 30.5 cm. Collection of the artist.

### Videos

*Berlin Jazz Story*, 2000, video, colour, audio, 20:30 min.

*Soliloquy*, 2006, video, colour, no audio, 12:47 min.

*Soliloquy2*, 2008, video, colour, no audio, 12:47 min.

*The Waiter Joke*, 2011, video, colour, audio, 07:24 min.

*The Cocktail Bar (4 Vignettes)*, 2016, video, colour, audio, 6:00 min.